FINISH
BIG

FINISH
BIG

How Great Entrepreneurs
Exit Their Companies on Top

BO BURLINGHAM

PORTFOLIO / PENGUIN

PORTFOLIO / PENGUIN
Published by the Penguin Group
Penguin Group (USA) LLC
375 Hudson Street
New York, New York 10014

USA | Canada | UK | Ireland | Australia | New Zealand | India | South Africa | China
penguin.com
A Penguin Random House Company

First published by Portfolio / Penguin, a member of Penguin Group (USA) LLC, 2014

LIBRARY OF CONGRESS CATALOGING-IN-PUBLICATION DATA
Burlingham, Bo.
Finish big : how great entrepreneurs exit their companies on top / Bo Burlingham.
pages cm
Includes index.
ISBN 978-1-59184-497-6 (hardback)
1. Executives—Retirement. 2. Executives—Resignation. 3. Sale of business enterprises.
4. Small business—Planning. 5. Entrepreneurship. I. Title.
HD38.2.B867 2014
658.4'07132—dc23
2014022255

Printed in the United States of America
1 3 5 7 9 10 8 6 4 2

Set in Goudy OldStyle Std
Designed by Alissa Rose Theodor

For Lisa, the love of my life; for Jake and Maria, Kate and Matt;
and for Owen, Kiki, Fiona, and Jack,
because family is everything.

CONTENTS

FINISH
BIG

INTRODUCTION

Are We There Yet?

Every entrepreneur exits. It's one of the few absolute certainties in business. Assuming you've built a viable company, you can choose when and how you exit, but you can't choose whether. It's going to happen. You can count on it.

That this simple fact of business life comes as a shock to many owners of private companies is in itself a testament to how little attention the final phase of the journey receives compared to other aspects of business. Do an online search for business marketing, finance, customer service, managing, or culture, and you'll find oceans of information. What's available on exits is a mere trickle by comparison, and almost all of it has to do with maximizing the amount of money you can get from a sale of your business. But there are many other aspects to the process and they play a larger role than the size of the deal in determining whether the exit has a happy ending—that is, whether you "finish big."

Or so I have learned. When I set out to write this book, I didn't know much about exiting a business. *Inc.* magazine, where I've worked for more than three decades, had paid scant attention to the subject over the years. My introduction to it—and, I suspect, that of many *Inc.* readers as well—had come from a series of columns I had written with veteran entrepreneur Norm Brodsky about an offer he'd received for his records-storage business, CitiStorage. Norm and I have been doing a monthly column in *Inc.* called "Street Smarts" since 1995. (We've also written a book of the same name.) While he'd said on numerous occasions that he intended to sell CitiStorage someday, he enjoyed what he was doing so much that I imagined he was talking about the distant future. So I was taken aback when, in the summer of 2006, he told me he was in serious discussions with a potential acquirer.

He had recently attended an industry conference where he had met a partner in a private equity firm that had a significant stake in a competitor. The partner had asked Norm what it would take to get him to sell CitiStorage. Norm had named a price he thought was higher than anyone would pay. The partner didn't bat an eye. Norm had then said that, in addition to CitiStorage, an acquirer would have to buy two adjunct businesses—a trucking company and a document-destruction company. That apparently was not a problem either. There had been a series of follow-up discussions. Norm told me he was waiting for the would-be buyer to send over a so-called "letter of intent" (LOI) outlining the preliminary understanding they had reached. He expected the LOI to be followed soon after by "due diligence"—the in-depth investigation that a buyer does prior to the negotiation of the purchase and sale agreement.

Norm wasn't sure where the discussions might lead, but he said this could be the opportunity of a lifetime. The money being discussed would be enough, not only to satisfy him and his two minority partners, but to share the wealth with his managers and employees. He also felt that the timing was right given his age, sixty-three, and the unusually high premiums being paid for companies like his in 2006. I told our editor at *Inc.*, Loren Feldman, what Norm had said and he suggested we write about the offer in our column. When I relayed the suggestion to Norm, he said, "Okay. Why not?"

At the time, neither one of us had any idea what we'd just signed up for. It turned out not to be a column but a series of columns. For the next nine months, we chronicled the unfolding drama in as close to real time as you can get in a monthly publication. Nothing similar had ever been done before or is likely to be done again. Even Norm admitted after the series ended that, when we started, he didn't really think the sale would happen. He said he wouldn't have agreed to do it if he'd known in advance that we'd wind up giving a blow-by-blow account of the negotiations to the entire world.

But once we'd started, it was hard to stop, especially after it became clear that we were attracting a growing number of followers who eagerly awaited each new installment. At one point, Norm invited readers to send him advice about whether he should go through with the sale. Hundreds of e-mails poured in. People would stop him on the street or at conferences and ask him to share the latest developments that hadn't yet been published.

The saga took many unexpected twists and turns, the most surprising of which was the last one. After much thought and discussion, Norm had made up his mind to sell. The series had become so popular by then that *Inc.*'s editor in chief, Jane Berentson, decided to announce his decision on the cover of the magazine. But just a few days before the contract was to be signed, he learned that the ultimate decision maker among the buyers was the person he trusted least—a crucial piece of information that the other side had failed to mention. That fact and its cover-up made him question whether he could depend on the acquirer to keep its promises about the treatment of his employees after the sale. To the astonishment of everyone, including Norm, he decided to walk away.

So ended the real-time magazine series—but not the story. Norm and his partners subsequently sold a majority stake in the business to a so-called business development company right as the economy was sliding into the Great Recession. Although many more twists and turns followed, they occurred out of the public eye. Meanwhile, the response to the series had made me realize there was an enormous gap in the business literature and it had to do with the experience of selling a business. That experience was clearly a huge unknown to many business owners.

It was new territory for me as well. Up to that point, I'd had only a vague understanding of the exit process. I'd never given much thought to the details of when, how, why, or what it felt like. In my mind, the exit was simply an event that marked the end of a journey. I had always been more interested in what happened during the journey—the experiences people had, the discoveries they made, the obstacles they encountered, the joys and sorrows along the way. I'd also tended to regard exiting as a choice, not a necessity. I associated it with cashing out, and I associated cashing out with giving up. I had written many articles and three books about entrepreneurs who didn't have the slightest interest in exiting their businesses, focused as they were on creating great, enduring companies. Some of these owners had walked away from nine-figure paydays rather than risk having their companies wind up in the wrong hands.

But, as time passed and we all grew older, it began to dawn on me—and on many business owners as well—that sooner or later they would have no choice but to take such a risk. We really weren't going to live forever after all. The best the owners could do would be to orchestrate transitions of ownership and leadership that would improve the odds of their companies surviving and thriving after they were gone.

But how? Where do you even begin? For that matter, when should you begin? What are your options? How much money should you be looking for? What role models are there, if any? What pitfalls should you be aware of? How do you identify and qualify potential successors, if that's the route you choose to take? Alternatively, how do you find potential acquirers? What sort of outside help do you need? How much should you tell other people in the company? What will you do after you leave? And on and on and on.

Once I took a closer look at exiting, I realized that it is a far more complex subject than I'd realized. It isn't an event. It is a phase of business, just as the start-up period is a phase. As in a start-up, there are many factors that affect how successful the exit will be. For that matter, there are different ways to define what a successful exit looks like.

That was my hunch, at any rate. Granted, the books and articles I read on the subject all shared an assumption that an exit was successful if the owners didn't "leave anything on the table"—that is, if they got the best possible price from the buyer. But none of these books and articles had been written by owners who'd actually gone through the process of selling their companies. Norm's experience had shown that there was much more to it than getting a good price. I couldn't help wondering about the experiences of other exiting business owners. And so I decided to find out.

Over the next three years or so, I had conversations with scores of entrepreneurs who had exited, were in the process of exiting, or were getting ready to exit their companies. More than a hundred of those conversations were in-depth interviews that I conducted either in person or by telephone. While it soon became clear that no two exit experiences were exactly alike, it was equally obvious that some were a lot better than others. By that, I mean that some people wound up happy with the process and satisfied with the way it turned out, while others looked back on it as a nightmare and came away with deep regrets about the outcome. My question was, why. What did the people with "good exits" do differently from those who'd had "bad exits"?

I had to begin by clarifying in my own mind what a good exit consisted of. For most people, I'd found, there were four elements:

1)   Owners felt that they'd been treated fairly during the exit process and appropriately compensated for the work they'd put in and the risks they'd taken to build their businesses.

2)   They had a sense of accomplishment. They could look back and know that through their businesses they'd contributed something of value to the world and had fun doing it.

3)   They were at peace with what had happened to other people who'd helped build their businesses—how those people had been treated, how they'd been rewarded, and what they'd taken away from the experience.

4)   They had discovered a new sense of purpose outside of their businesses. They had new lives that they were fully engaged in and excited about.

For some people, there was a fifth element:

5)   The companies they'd created were going on without them and doing better than ever, and they could take pride in the way they'd handled one of the most difficult tasks faced by any CEO: succession.

It was harder to generalize about bad exits, if only because what might be terrible for one person was sometimes unimportant for another. But I figured almost all owners would think they'd had a bad exit if they walked away feeling that the process had been unfair; that they hadn't received the reward they deserved; that what they'd built was being destroyed; that their people were being screwed; or that they felt completely lost and had no idea what to do next.

So how had the owners who'd had good exits gone about preparing for the day they would leave? What were the patterns? Looking at them as a group, I could identify eight common characteristics, and I've organized this book around them.

The first was the same one I'd noticed in entrepreneurs who'd built great businesses, including those I'd written about in my book *Small Giants*: These were all people with a crystal clear understanding of who they were, what they wanted out of business, and why.

Second, the owners who'd exited well had realized early on that it was not enough just to have a viable business. Most viable businesses are, in fact, unsellable. To create market value, these owners had learned to look at their businesses through the eyes of a potential buyer or investor.

Third, they had given themselves plenty of time—measured in years, not months—to prepare for their eventual departure and had developed options, so that they, or their heirs, would never find themselves in a situation where they would be forced to sell under disadvantageous circumstances.

The fourth characteristic didn't apply to all owners, but it was vitally important to a significant percentage of them, including those with the highest aspirations for their companies. I'm referring here to succession—specifically, the importance of leaving the company in good hands.

Fifth, happy former owners had had the right kind of help, which had come not just from professionals who specialize in the buying and selling of businesses but also from former business owners, who had learned how to do it by making mistakes in exiting their own companies.

Sixth, the owners had thought about and come to terms with their responsibilities to employees and investors. While every owner did not reach the same conclusion, those who had had good exits had all given the matter serious thought and were at peace with whatever decisions they had made.

Seventh, these owners had also understood in advance whom they were selling their companies to and what was motivating the buyers. Owners who didn't often had nasty surprises later when it became clear what the new owners actually planned to do.

Eighth, the owners who did best had a vision of what they would do after the sale and thus were better able to handle their metamorphosis from top banana one day to ordinary piece of fruit the next.

These eight factors, I found, went a long way toward explaining the vast differences in the experiences of the entrepreneurs I interviewed, and I couldn't help but think that current and future business owners would benefit by knowing about them. That said, my purpose in writing this book is not to provide a how-to guide, but rather to illuminate the exit process by telling the stories of entrepreneurs who've gone through it. Many of those people have had good exits, as defined above. Other stories are cautionary, in recognition that we often learn what works by observing what hasn't worked. In most cases, I have been able to use the real names of the people and companies involved. For several, however, I've used pseudonyms, in some instances because of my source's legal commitments, in others to avoid gratuitous harm to the people mentioned. When I have disguised an individual, I have so indicated. Other than changing names and, in two instances, some telltale details about the company, I have reported what actually happened.

As in *Small Giants*, the companies I write about are all privately owned and closely held, with one exception: Cadence Inc. in chapter 5, which I would describe as quasi-public. Three of the companies, in fact, were in *Small Giants*: Zingerman's, CitiStorage, and ECCO. There are some issues I've deliberately avoided—for example, the unique succession challenges faced by family businesses when ownership and leadership are passed from one generation to the next. There is plenty of information elsewhere on that topic. Nor do I address the unique challenges of very small businesses whose primary purpose is to provide the owner with an income. If they're sellable at all—and the great majority aren't—what's being sold is a job, not a company. Nevertheless, I think that both family business owners and solo entrepreneurs will find much to identify with in the stories I tell.

In listening to the entrepreneurs I interviewed, I was constantly reminded of an old saying: You should build a business today as if you will own it forever but could sell it tomorrow. Most of the great entrepreneurs I've been privileged to know have followed that dictum. My friend and sometime coauthor Jack Stack of SRC Holdings (which was sold to its employees) makes the comparison to keeping up the market value of your home—fixing the roof, adding rooms, painting regularly—even if you have no intention of moving anytime soon. The same logic applies to businesses. Oddly enough, you're far more likely to have a company that's built to last if you simultaneously build it to sell. You're also far more likely to have a happy exit.

Of course, if you're like most entrepreneurs, you'd probably prefer not to think about your exit just yet. Fortunately, the window for crafting a good one can stay open for a fairly long time. When you finally climb through it, you're liable to make a surprising discovery, namely, that the process has helped you to build a better company. That's what Ray Pagano found in 2004 when he began preparing to get his company, Videolarm, ready for sale: The company improved so much and so fast that he regretted he hadn't started sooner.

1

Every Journey Ends

> **Now is the time to start thinking about your exit.**

The day was beginning to sizzle at the Regatta Point Marina in Delta-ville, Virginia, but the air was cool inside the *Bella Vita*, which was resting quietly in its slip after completing its three-week maiden voyage around Chesapeake Bay. While an electronics specialist performed tests on the control panel, Ray Pagano, dressed in a T-shirt, shorts, and slippers, showed a guest around. "We have all the amenities," he said. "More than we need, probably." Tanned and trim at sixty-eight, he wore a vaguely sheepish smile as he conducted his tour of the vessel, a brand-new sixty-foot Selene Ocean Trawler that had been custom-made for him at a shipyard in China. It had been his gift to himself after com-pleting the sale of Videolarm, the company he'd founded thirty-five years earlier, and a fine gift it was, with its beautiful cherrywood panel-ing, granite bathroom counters, and queen beds in the cabins fore and aft.

Pagano is clearly enjoying the *bella vita* for which his boat is named. He has none of the second thoughts or regrets that plague so many owners after the sale of their companies. Indeed, his exit has been as happy as anyone could hope for—in part because of his former employees, most of whom were still working for the company that bought Videolarm. "Every time I stop by, they welcome me with open arms," he said. "That's amazing to me. It's more than I could have expected. I guess I must have done something right. I ask myself, what really made the difference?"

To answer that question, you have to go back to 2004, when Pagano began thinking seriously about having a life after business. Videolarm was twenty-eight years old and well established as a leader in its field, the manufacturing of housings for security cameras. Pagano had revolutionized that field in 1976 when, at thirty-three, he developed a housing that resembled a streetlight and used a much smaller motor than other outdoor security cameras. It took him the next eight years, however, to persuade the major camera manufacturers to try the apparatus. He scraped by, supporting himself doing installation and security consulting until he finally landed an account with RCA, which at the time was a big name in the field. That was all he needed. Pagano's products performed as promised, and he was able to leverage his success with RCA to sign up other large customers, including Sony, Panasonic, and Toshiba.

Over the next two decades, Videolarm's patented designs became the industry standard. By 2004, they were ubiquitous. The company, meanwhile, was doing $10.4 million in sales, with forty-two employees, and Pagano, who had just turned sixty-one, was ready to move on. He had other interests and passions that he wanted to pursue, and a limited number of years to pursue them. The time had come, he decided, to think about leaving.

But how? He'd long had the notion in the back of his mind that one of his three children might someday take over the company. It had become clear, however, that such a solution was not in the cards. Selling the business was a possibility. So was a merger, or finding someone else to run it, although he was wary of doing any deal that would require him to stick around. "I don't want an earnout," he told one of his advisers, Gary Anderson, who chaired Pagano's chapter of TEC (The Executive Committee, now called Vistage International), a membership organization for owners and executives of small to midsized businesses. "I want to sell it and leave. I have other things I want to do in my life besides this." That same year, 2004, a competitor approached Pagano about selling Videolarm and named a price. Pagano took it to Anderson, who thought he could garner a much better offer if he made some changes in the business.

At the time, Videolarm was fairly typical of companies run by the entrepreneurs who started them. It was essentially a benevolent dictatorship. The entire business revolved around Pagano, who put his nose in every part of it and kept his managers on a short leash. Communication was decidedly top-down, and financial information closely guarded. CFO Janet Spaulding was forbidden to share it with other employees. Pagano himself made every important decision and quite a few not so important ones. Managers, for their part, were aware that he could "pull the rug out" from under them at any moment, as one of them said. "People respected Ray and feared him," said Spaulding, "and I think the fear was sometimes greater than the respect."

Other employees shared those feelings toward Pagano. They knew he cared about them. They believed he at least intended to treat them fairly. They could also see that he held himself to the same standards he demanded of them. If there were any doubts on that score, they were erased when he fired his own son over an infraction of a company rule—a gut-wrenching decision that still brings tears to his eyes.

But autocratic management, benevolent or otherwise, can undermine the value of a company. Anderson noted as much in advising Pagano on how to prepare for an eventual sale. "You're going to have to extract yourself from the business," he said. "You're going to have to bring up your management team, give them more responsibility, coach them more, and let them run the operation." Pagano didn't argue. He knew Anderson was right. Sale price aside, the number of potential acquirers, and thus Pagano's own exit options, would be severely limited as long as he was essential to the company's operation. He had to remake the business so that it could run without him if he wanted to improve his chances of getting a deal he'd be happy with.

Pagano decided, based on some research he'd done, that he needed to begin by giving everyone in the company a tangible reason to take on more responsibility. He believed he could accomplish that with phantom stock, which would allow people to benefit from any increase in Videolarm's equity value without being given—or having to acquire—real stock. All employees, including assembly workers and office staff, would receive "shares" that Pagano would divide up based on salary and his assessment of how important each person was to the company's long-term success. He told the members of his TEC group about his plan. Most of them thought he was out of his mind. But he was convinced it was the right way to go. So he rolled out the program, explaining to the employees that the phantom shares would entitle them to a portion of the sale proceeds should Videolarm ever be sold.

They weren't sure what to make of the gesture. Pagano was notoriously tightfisted with money. Many of them thought the phantom stock program was some kind of trick to get them to work harder. They either ignored it or treated it as a joke. "To us, it was just pretend money," said Spaulding.

But Pagano was serious—so serious that he proceeded to introduce his own, truncated version of open-book management, which involves teaching employees to understand and use financial information in their work. He'd read books on it, and while he couldn't bring himself to go as far as some other practitioners, he was convinced that people needed a basic knowledge of the numbers if they were going to be able to figure out how they could improve a business's performance and thereby increase its value. So he organized meetings to talk about financials. He began by asking employees to give their own estimates of sales and profits—and was stunned when they speculated that Video-larm's sales were in the hundreds of millions of dollars (they were less than $11 million at the time) and that he was taking home millions of dollars each month. Pagano responded by walking them through an income statement and a balance sheet, noting the capital investments a manufacturer like Videolarm had to make, the taxes it paid, the government oversight it was subject to, the cost of the benefits it provided, and so on. Employees had many questions and comments. Pagano put out a suggestion box to capture them and took care to respond to each one. He also began writing monthly letters to employees' families, which he sent to their homes, and invited family members to come in to view new products. "We truly wanted to involve everyone in the business," he said.

Realizing it was crucial to strengthen the management team, he made a conscious effort to increase the autonomy and authority of his three senior managers—in finance, operations, and marketing. He also sought out one of his former TEC chairs, Rick Houcek, who had formed a business called Soar with Eagles, which worked with companies to plan annual strategic meetings and develop implementation systems. Houcek urged Pagano to bring not just the senior people but all the managers together at an off-site meeting and let them develop an annual plan. The results, Houcek said, would go a long way toward achieving what he wanted to do.

Pagano announced a three-day off-site for everyone from frontline supervisors on up, about fifteen people. Houcek would facilitate. He told Pagano to just sit and listen while people aired their views on what the company needed. Pagano admitted it was hard not to feel defensive when his managers shared their grievances, but Houcek persuaded him to hold his tongue and let the managers come up with the plan. If he tried to force his plan on them, they would not take responsibility for executing it. In the end, the managers settled on about thirty ways to improve Videolarm's management and performance, with specific assignments for each one. Thereafter, they began to meet as a group every month to review how they were doing on their commitments.

Meanwhile, there were other changes going on. Pagano set up an incentive program for the entire workforce, based on achieving certain profit targets for the company and specific goals for each department. The targets were ambitious, higher than what the company had done in the past, and Pagano indicated that he intended to keep raising the bar as time went along. Not surprisingly, the program was again met with distrust, especially on the shop floor, but Pagano promised that he would reorganize the factory to make their jobs easier. He did, and productivity began to rise.

At the same time, the company made some critical strategic moves that allowed it to increase sales to the big camera manufacturers—the most profitable part of the business. The impact of those moves, as well as the management changes, soon showed up on the bottom line. Pagano had set the initial goal for company pretax profit at 8 percent. From there, it increased annually, first to 12 percent, then 15 percent, then 18 percent. Although the annual goal remained 18 percent thereafter, performance continued to improve, eventually hitting a remarkable 21 percent on sales of about $19.5 million.

Pagano couldn't help being delighted, not only with the results, but with the way they were being achieved. "The system completely changed my job," he said. "It let me take a step back from the company, and that was good for everyone. It allowed the stars in the company to show they were stars."

Gary Anderson, for one, was impressed. "It was unbelievable," he said. "Ray became my poster child for how to do it right, and it made a big impression on other members of the TEC group. You could see the impact of what he'd done as soon as you set foot inside the company."

By early 2008, Pagano felt it was time to start looking for a buyer. How someone goes about that is a subject for a later chapter. Suffice it to say that he wound up selling Videolarm to a large company, Moog Inc., at what was arguably the worst moment to do a deal in recent memory: Friday, February 13, 2009, five months after the collapse of Lehman Brothers triggered the most severe economic downturn since the Great Depression. Despite the timing, the selling price—$45 million—was four times the offer Pagano had received before making the management changes.

As for the employees, most had completely forgotten about the phantom stock program Pagano had installed four years earlier. On the eve of the sale, Pagano showed up with papers they had to sign before receiving their payouts from the deal. They were shocked and delighted to learn just how large the payouts were. Assembly workers received as much as $40,000 each, enough for one of them to build a home for his parents in Mexico.

And how did Pagano feel? "Liberated," he said.

He eased into semiretirement after the sale, keeping busy with his boat and a boutique business he started with his wife, selling yachting ornaments and gifts. He fished, played some golf, and did a little traveling. "That's as much as I can handle," he said. While he didn't miss being CEO of Videolarm, he still felt a strong connection to the company, including the people and the culture, which had scarcely changed following the sale. "It's uncanny how Moog's culture and our culture matched up. It exceeded my expectations. And it's allowed me to feel very much at peace and sort of proud." He was proud of how things had turned out and also of what he'd accomplished along the way. "I see our products everywhere I go. It's a constant reminder of how we changed the industry. That is as much of an ego inflator as seeing the company develop over the years. I just feel very lucky. Lucky in all that has taken place and lucky that I still have the contacts I do with the company and a great deal of pride in the product."

Luck may have played a role. It usually does. But you can't discount the importance of the decisions Pagano made back in 2004, when he first got serious about planning his exit from Videolarm. "There's no question that the company's performance got better," he said. "It was just amazing to see the transition once we got the people involved. If I did anything right, that was it. I really just wish I'd done it sooner."

In other words, Pagano's company actually improved because of the way he went about preparing to leave it. Therein lies a lesson for other business owners.

It's a Journey

I have some advice for anyone who owns a business or is planning to launch one: If you haven't already begun thinking about your eventual exit, now is the time to start. You should do so even if you currently believe that you'll never want to sell the business, that you'll just keep it forever, or leave it to your children, or give it to your employees, or close it down. It doesn't matter. For your sake and your company's sake, you should begin to think now about the circumstances under which you might leave and do all you can to ensure that the company could be sold at some point for as much money as possible. Of course, someday you will have to leave, and either the ownership will change hands or the business will be liquidated. You may leave feet first, but leave you will, one way or the other. The more prepared you are when that day comes, the more likely it is that the parting will be a happy one—or at least not a burden on those you leave behind. That's not the only reason, however, for beginning to think about an exit plan. There are at least two others.

First, the process will lead you to look for and adopt better business practices, as Ray Pagano did. It will also force you to ask questions about your business that otherwise might not occur to you. Who, for example, are the potential buyers or investors? What qualities do they value in a business? What would cause them to pay more for it? Why might they pay less? What do they view as your business's vulnerabilities? Once you identify the weaknesses, you can work on eliminating them and start doing the things that will keep them from coming back. In other words, you'll begin to view your company as a product, and you'll learn how to make it a top-of-the-line product. You'll have a better, stronger company as a result.

Just as important, thinking about an exit plan will force you to ask important, difficult questions about yourself. In particular, you'll find it necessary to clarify in your own mind who you are, what you want out of business, and why. People who know the answers to those questions almost always have happier exits. They're also able to make better decisions for themselves and their businesses while they're still in the owner's seat.

Granted, you may believe you already know why you're in business. If you're like most entrepreneurs, you're doing it to earn a living and be your own boss. Perhaps you also have a dream of some sort—to build a great company, transform an industry, serve mankind, create a terrific place to work, leave a mark in the world, help your community, or simply become financially independent. It takes a lot of hard work, discipline, persistence, and resourcefulness to achieve any of those dreams. For that matter, it takes hard work to create a viable business. Kudos to you if you can do it. But you need to recognize that doing it is not the end of the journey.

And that's the point: Building a business is a journey. It may be a lifelong journey, or it may last just a few years. It may be the only journey of its type that you'll ever experience, or it may be one of many. You may see it as your life's calling, or it may turn out to be a side trip or a detour on the way to something else. The one thing we can say for sure about your journey is that it will end. The open questions are when, how, and why. You have considerable influence over the answers to all three, provided you begin thinking about them early enough and bear in mind that the end is not the creation of a successful business. That's the middle. The end is the successful completion of the journey. As serious mountaineers say, the primary goal when you climb Mount Everest is not to reach the summit. It's to come back alive and enjoy the experience of having done it.

The End Is the Beginning

Now, I'm hardly the first to suggest that you should have some idea of your preferred destination as you proceed along your journey. Stephen R. Covey made a similar argument in *The Seven Habits of Highly Effective People,* one of which was "begin with the end in mind." That was a fundamental rule of business for Harold Geneen, the man often credited with inventing the modern international conglomerate while serving as CEO of the ITT Corporation from 1959 to 1977. The book he wrote with Alvin Moscow, called *Managing,* is a classic in the business genre, and it opens with the following observation: "You read a book from beginning to end. You run a business the opposite way. You start with the end, and then you do everything you must to reach it."

That said, it's easy to misinterpret what exactly is involved in "beginning with the end in mind," at least as far as business exits are concerned. It doesn't necessarily mean that you have the final stages of your journey all mapped out in advance. Nor does it mean that you're locked into a plan and can't change it later. Rather, "beginning with the end in mind" asks you to recognize, from the start, that your involvement with the business will end at some point, and to allow this simple truth to guide you as you go along. While many of the decisions you make won't have much influence, if any, on the endgame, others will, and some could have major consequences that you may miss if you haven't developed the habit of keeping in mind the goal of a happy exit.

That's not a habit that most founders and owners cultivate. In the early days, they focus on survival. Some never leave the survival stage. The more fortunate ones move on to the growth stage. Either way, they run the risk of getting caught in what Covey calls "the activity trap," the tendency "in the busy-ness of life to work harder and harder at climbing the ladder of success only to discover it's leaning against the wrong wall."

Busyness is certainly one of the reasons that owners don't think about whether or not their journey is taking them to a place they really want to wind up. They're constantly preoccupied—it goes with the territory—and figuring out the ultimate destination doesn't seem particularly urgent alongside, say, meeting the next payroll or landing the next big customer or dealing with a pressing cash flow problem. Thinking concretely about the exit can also be difficult to do, which provides additional incentive to procrastinate. So the vast majority of business owners don't give their exit much thought until, for one reason or another, they have to—at which point their options are often starkly limited.

The mistake they make grows partly out of their tendency to regard the exit as simply an event, and a relatively distant one at that. But the exit is actually a critical phase of a business owner's journey and an integral part of the entrepreneurial experience. "It's like passing the 26.2-mile mark of a marathon, or crossing home plate after a home run," said Canadian entrepreneur John Warrillow, who has started five businesses and sold four of them. "I don't believe you are really an entrepreneur until you've exited, because you haven't completed the cycle. You're still standing on third base. It is not about starting. Anyone can start a business. Until you've actually sold one, you haven't touched all the bases."

Whether or not you buy Warrillow's whole argument, he's correct that the exit phase of a business owner's journey is as important as, if not more important than, any other phase, although you'd never know it from perusing the literature on entrepreneurship. Information about start-ups dwarfs what's available on end-ups, and yet the end-up is invariably a much bigger deal. Indeed, it's the biggest deal that most entrepreneurs will ever do, with far-reaching consequences for them, their families, their employees, and almost everyone else they care about. It can fundamentally alter their circumstances and color how they look back on the main work of their lives.

Warrillow is one example of someone whose exit changed his life. He grew up and built his first four businesses in Toronto. The largest of the four, Warrillow & Co., provided big companies with in-depth research and analysis on marketing to small and midsized businesses. Its sale in 2008 allowed him to embark on a new career as an author and speaker. It also freed him, his wife, and their two young children to move to the south of France for three years—an adventure they could scarcely have contemplated while he was still immersed in his company.

Or take Michael LeMonier, who has built three companies and sold two in his twenty-five years as an entrepreneur in the staffing industry. The first was a clerical staffing firm in downtown Chicago. The founder of the firm, which was struggling, had reached out to LeMonier for advice and assistance. LeMonier, who'd worked for years in large staffing companies before becoming a consultant, agreed to buy 49 percent of the stock and help turn the business around. Eighteen months later, with the turnaround complete, he walked away with an amount equal to fourteen times his investment. He then did a similar deal with the owner of another run-down Chicagoland staffing company, acquiring 50 percent of the stock for $2,500. Over the next six years, he grew the agency from five to six hundred employees and from about $125,000 to $11 million in sales. After buying out the original owner, he wound up selling the business to a large, publicly owned employment services company for $5 million—a return of almost 200,000 percent on his original investment.

That deal changed everything. "The first closing was the end of a partnership," LeMonier said. "It was great, but that's all it was. The second closing was a huge celebration because, for me, it was crossing the goal line to financial freedom. It meant that I'd have the privilege of choice moving forward. From then on, I could choose the amount of time I spent working on my next business—the one I have now. I get to decide how intense, how long, how hard. That's freedom."

Or consider Barry Carlson's exit. He had been a part owner of three businesses when, in 1996, he cofounded Parasun Technologies Inc., an Internet service provider for remote areas of western Canada. Two of those businesses had been sold without much impact on his life. Parasun, which he sold eleven years later for almost $15 million, was another story. "The sale of a company as an abstract concept is fine, but having somebody pile real money onto the table is a whole different thing," he said. "It changes the game. I don't care who you are, it's nice to see a big pile of money on the table with your name on it. It's not so much that the money changes your life. For some people it does; for some it doesn't. But it's the way you look at it that's important." At the time of the sale, he thought he'd retire. He and his wife moved from downtown Vancouver, British Columbia, to Vancouver Island, across the Strait of Georgia. They traveled a bit. They worked on their garden. He puttered around and played some golf. But after a year and a half Carlson got an itch to return to business and joined a couple of boards. Within five years, he'd completed the circle and was back working full-time as the chairman of two start-ups and CEO of a third.

And yet the end result is not always a happy one, even for those who wind up with a pile of money on the table. Despite having absolute financial security, often for the first time in their lives, many owners find themselves dealing with unanticipated regrets, fighting against depression, and desperately in need of a new identity and sense of purpose. For them, life after the exit is a bleak period, and it can last for years.

The Four Stages of an Exit

I can't say definitively why such melancholy afflicts some former owners and not others. Circumstances vary from case to case, after all, as do the personalities, predilections, and psychologies of the individuals involved. What I can say is that the longer people have spent preparing for their exits, the less likely they are to experience these problems. It's not just a matter of putting in the time. It's also about successfully navigating the four stages of the exit process:

- Stage one is exploratory. It involves investigating the many possibilities, doing the necessary introspective work, and deciding what you do and don't care about in an exit. It may also include coming up with a number—that is, the amount of money you'd be happy to walk away with when the time comes—and a time frame.
- Stage two is strategic. It requires learning to view your company as a product itself, not just as a deliverer of products or services, and then building into it the qualities and characteristics that will maximize its value and allow you to have the kind of exit you want.
- Stage three is about execution. It's the process you go through to get a deal done, whatever type of exit you may be looking for, be it a sale to a third party, a management buyout, a gift to your children, a liquidation of assets, or any of the other possible outcomes.
- Stage four is the transition. It begins with the completion of the deal and ends when you're fully engaged in whatever comes next.

Until you've moved on—not just physically but psychologically—to a new venture, a new career, a redefined role, or even retirement, your exit isn't complete.

Of course, every company, every owner, and every exit is unique, and these stages unfold differently for different people. For some former owners I know, the transition phase has been excruciating; for others, it has been quick and painless. One owner described the deal stage as "a nine-month dental extraction"; another recalled it as "fun, exciting, educational, exhilarating." Some entrepreneurs spend years figuring out how they want to leave; others seem to know the answer intuitively. Still others simply skip that stage—and later pay the consequences.

There can also be overlap between the stages, especially the first three. Smart entrepreneurs, for example, always build a business today so that it could be sold tomorrow (stage two) whether or not they've decided exactly how they'd like to exit (stage one). Nor is it uncommon for owners to go through the process of negotiating the sale of the business (stage three), only to back off at the last minute, take what they've learned, and revise their strategic plans (stage two) accordingly—perhaps with a different view of where they'd like to end up (stage one). The only stage that very rarely allows for reprises is the fourth one, the transition phase. Hence the importance of getting the first three right.

That begins with understanding what the possibilities are. There are more than most people imagine. Let's assume your preference is to sell the business rather than liquidate it. A key question is, whom would you sell it to? A family member? A third party? Employees or managers? The public? With each type of buyer, moreover, there are dozens of potential variations. Take the third-party option. Would you prefer to sell to a private equity firm, an individual looking for a promising business opportunity, a competitor, or a large company seeking to expand its market or its capabilities? Would you want to remain with the company afterward or get out? How important is it that a buyer be committed to preserving your company's culture? What long-term aspirations, if any, do you have for the business? How concerned are you about the effect of the sale on your employees? Are you looking to leave a legacy, and if so, what kind? Would you accept an earnout, with a portion of the sales price being determined by the company's performance after the sale? And on and on.*

Sooner or later, all such questions will have to be answered. How you answer them will shape the type of exit you have. The more you've pondered them, and the more you've found out about other owners' experiences and weighed them against your own inclinations, the clearer you will be about what you want and the likelier it is that you'll be happy with the result.

To be sure, you may already have the answers. Some owners, after all, have an exit plan in place before they even get started. Others take on investors whose need for a so-called liquidity event (usually a sale to a third party; sometimes an initial public offering) puts the matter squarely on the table. Still others view themselves as investors and the businesses they buy or start as investments, pure and simple. For them, the whole idea is to maximize a company's value and then sell it. But such people are a distinct minority. In my experience, they are far outnumbered by founders and owners so busy coping with the current challenges of running their companies, or working to reach the next level, or simply hanging on from day to day, month to month, and year to year that they don't take the time to think about, let alone prepare themselves and their companies for, their inevitable departure.

If you're lucky, you can get away with it. Like Ray Pagano, you may be able to go for years, even decades, without giving much thought to the issue and still have the opportunity at the end to make the adjustments needed to orchestrate a graceful exit. But you'll be taking a risk. The journey doesn't always end when you want or expect it to. I'm not

---

* You can find a complete list of the exit options, as well as a list of the key questions to ask yourself, at www.finishbigbook.com.

referring here to the proverbial danger of being run over by a bus. That risk always exists, and prudent companies have contingency plans in place to deal with it. Contingency plans are different from exit plans, however. The former are needed to protect the people left behind. The latter protect the owners, whose life doesn't end, after all, with the sale of the company. Indeed, the hardest part of the exit is seldom the sale itself. It's usually what comes afterward, in the transition stage, when you enter the next phase of your life and have to live with the consequences of the decisions you've made.

For Ray Pagano, those consequences were mostly good, in part because he'd been so clear from the start about his goals. By the time he began preparing for his eventual departure, he knew exactly what he wanted: a life after Videolarm in which he could do everything he'd been putting off while he built the company. He had a mental vision of that life, and aside from the boat and more time with his family, it included peace of mind about the manner of his leaving. "I always felt that, if it was possible to walk away and feel good, that's what I wanted," he said.

Everything he subsequently did flowed from that vision. It dictated not only the changes he made internally but the kind of deal he was willing to do, the terms of the sale, and the type of buyer he was willing to sell to. "More than once, I heard him say, 'I will not sell if my employees are not going to be treated as well as they are now,'" said Janet Spaulding, the controller. "I saw it. He put it in writing. 'This is my family. I want them treated well.'"

The clarity of Pagano's vision did not save him from feelings of loss, as well as liberation, in the months after the sale. Those feelings are, if not inevitable, then extremely common, particularly if someone has been deeply involved in running the business for a long time. They were far outweighed, however, by the sense of accomplishment Pagano felt after a lifetime of entrepreneurship and his gratitude that his former employees were thriving under their new owners.

As a result, he was spared the kind of regret that can cloud any exit and make any transition extremely painful. Others are not so fortunate. But if you've prepared yourself emotionally—if you've figured out who you are, what you want, and why, and if you've made your decisions accordingly—your transition can be as smooth as Ray Pagano's.

2

•●●•

Who Am I If Not My Business?

> **It begins with knowing who you are,
> what you want, and why.**

At 2 a.m. on the night before selling a majority stake in his company, CrossCom National, Bruce Leech sat in his office, staring at the documents he was supposed to sign in advance of the closing. Within a matter of hours, he would become independently wealthy—a multi-millionaire at the age of forty-eight, with a clean slate, a solid balance sheet, and the likelihood of another big payday in a few years, when the company, including his remaining stock, would be sold again. You'd think he'd be getting ready to pop the champagne corks and celebrate the culmination of a long journey, capped off by a handsome reward. And yet something nagged at him as he sat there, surrounded by stacks of papers representing the past twenty-three years of his life.

He'd been barely that old when he'd launched CrossCom in 1981 with two partners, hoping, like hundreds if not thousands of others, to capitalize on the breakup of Ma Bell by selling telecommunications equipment to businesses. It had been a rough start-up. His partners had bailed out within three years. Leech himself had decided to wind down the business and was training for a new job when he got a message on his answering machine from Walgreens. The pharmacy giant wanted him to install phone systems in all twelve hundred of its stores—in three months. Although he didn't have a clue about how he could do it in such a short period of time, Leech said, "No problem," quit his new job, and didn't look back.

Over the next two decades, CrossCom grew into one of the leading installation and service companies for internal telecommunications systems, with three hundred employees, $70 million in sales, and a blue-chip roster of giant retailers as customers. Leech couldn't have been happier in the early years. "It was thrilling," he recalled. "I jumped out of bed in the morning. I worked till late at night. I loved every minute of it." But as time went by, his enthusiasm began to wane. He was able to revive it temporarily when CrossCom expanded into the United Kingdom in 1995. Having never been outside the United States before, he was excited about the prospect of opening a new branch in Europe. He even moved to London for a year to get it up and running.

It wasn't just the business opportunity that appealed to him. "Looking back, I can see it might have been an escape from the U.S. business," he said. "I guess maybe I was getting a little bored, and the U.K. was neat. So I did that for a few years, and then it was time for Bruce to pack up his toys and come back home and face the reality of what I was probably avoiding, and that was the fact I was burned out."

He had more to deal with than burnout, however. Due in part to his long absences abroad, his marriage was a shambles, and his company was in disarray. The marriage didn't survive; he and his wife were divorced in 2000. He attempted to address the organizational problems in the company by turning over the role of CEO to an ambitious young protégé, Greg Miller, who had demonstrated a gift for managing operations, something that didn't much interest Leech. Although he remained active in the business thereafter—mainly doing sales and marketing—his heart wasn't in it. "I wasn't getting any meaningfulness out of it," he said. "I was looking for something bigger. And I had lost a lot. I had a sense of loss in my marriage, a sense of loss in not being connected with the kids, and a sense of loss in CrossCom, now that Greg was running it. So it was a lot of loss without anything really to replace it. Financially, I was also a mess. My bank account was running low. I owed money to my ex-wife. I had a son going off to college. My houses were pledged to the bank. It was scary."

But he was not without resources. There was always his equity in the business. He figured he could sell 40 percent of the stock and still control the company. He hired a broker, who put him in touch with Goense Bounds & Partners, a private equity firm, and helped him work out the broad terms of the deal. Leech then met with his lawyer, who asked why he wanted to bring a large outside investor into his life. He said he thought it would give him more freedom by easing his financial concerns. The lawyer laughed. "Freedom?" she said. "That's the last thing you'll have. You won't be able to make any big decision about the company without clearing it with your new partners." Leech was shocked and called off the deal.

His indecision wound up costing CrossCom several hundred thousand dollars in walk-away fees, not to mention a morale problem with his managers, who had worked hard preparing for the sale, were due to receive a portion of the proceeds, and looked forward to having the outside capital needed to grow the business aggressively. Meanwhile, the financial pressures remained. Leech's fears intensified when word came that CrossCom was losing one of its major customers, the Eckerd Pharmacy chain, representing $9 million of its $70 million in sales. "I remember waking up at three in the morning in a cold sweat and going into the office. I talked to Greg about my worries, and he said, 'Yeah, you're in a tough spot. If we hit a real bad hiccup here, I'll be out of a job, but Bruce, you could lose everything. Does that bother you at all?' I don't think I slept for another month after that conversation."

The prospect of financial ruin convinced Leech he had to sell after all, even if it meant giving up control of the business. He went back to Goense Bounds, which was willing to do a deal at the same valuation it had offered before—but with a catch. Now the firm insisted on getting 60 percent of the equity, rather than the 40 percent they'd settled on the first time. Leech, who had given 20 percent to his management team, would thus be left with a 20 percent share. He agreed, whereupon the dealmakers sprang into action. A date was set. The lawyers finished their work. The documents were sent over to be signed.

And so Leech found himself sitting there at 2 a.m., reflecting on his journey and wondering if he was making the right decision. Greg Miller had stopped by earlier that evening. "Well, Bruce," he'd said, "you've gotten all the input you need for this. Everybody thinks it's the right thing, but I guess that's up to you to decide. Good luck. I'll see you in the morning."

Miller was right: Everyone was encouraging Leech to do the deal—his board, his managers, his lawyers and accountants, his friends, and his family. But he couldn't shake the feeling that he was missing something. "I never felt more alone in my life," he recalled years later. "It was terrible. Then a flash of the obvious hit me: All these people who were saying this was best for me were getting a piece of the deal. While I consider many of them friends, there was a little voice inside of me asking whether anyone was looking out for my best interests. There was no answer to that."

But what could he do at that point? "I was a little bit terrified. I felt I couldn't call off the sale again. Everybody was counting on me to pull the trigger. So I signed all the papers."

The Curse of the Poorly Planned Exit

There are any number of ways that a business owner's journey can end, and many of them, like Leech's, leave little, if any, time for preparation. Some owners get tired. Some get bored. Some are hit by personal tragedy. Some receive an unexpected offer they feel they can't refuse. Some are blindsided by changes in their industry or the economy. Some become victims of their customers' troubles. Some simply run out of cash. The list is almost endless.

Hastily planned exits seldom turn out to be happy ones. They are particularly difficult for owners who haven't given much thought to what comes next. Instead, they're guided by what other people want. They react to events and circumstances according to what other people think they should do or what other people have conditioned them to do. In the process, they lose the opportunity to shape their future, which is arguably the greatest potential reward that ownership offers. It's why most people start or buy businesses in the first place.

At the beginning of the journey, you really do have an opportunity to influence where it will lead and how it will end. The range of options open to you is as wide as it will ever be. But as time goes along, your options narrow. Intentionally or not, the decisions you make and the actions you take begin to affect your exit possibilities, including what you have to sell, how much you can sell it for, who the potential buyers are, and what is required to get the company ready.

It's obviously in your interest to keep open the options that will allow you to reach your preferred destination—assuming you know what it is. That means, first, clarifying in your mind who you are, what you want out of your business, and why. Otherwise you won't be able to choose among the possibilities. You may not even recognize the possibilities. And when you finally do exit, you'll have no idea what to do next.

"I really hadn't thought about my life after the sale," Leech said. "A friend of mine who'd sold his business had told me, 'Don't sell until you know what you're going to do next.' I remember his voice like it was yesterday, but I didn't pay attention, and it was a huge void for me, not having the answer to that question."

It took a couple of months for Leech to realize the hole he was in. The sale had closed in early November 2004, and the holidays kept him busy through the end of the year. In January, he decided it was time to get back to work. He didn't know what he'd do. Although he remained on CrossCom's board, he didn't have any day-to-day responsibilities there. No matter. He figured that if he just made himself available, something would turn up. With that in mind, he rented an office in downtown Chicago and ordered business cards. Then he waited . . . and waited . . . and waited. "I began to feel real alone. I thought I'd be able to network with the other businesspeople in the building, but they pretty much kept their doors closed. And all my friends were still working. There was nobody to hang out with, not even my kids, who were in school. I didn't know what to do. I started to feel insignificant. At CrossCom, I'd had three hundred employees looking up at me as Uncle Bruce. Then all of a sudden I was irrelevant. Nobody needed me anymore. Nobody really cared. People did the obligatory, 'How you doing? Must be nice to be retired.' I hate that word. I was in my mid-forties. It wasn't time to hang things up."

Leech began to search for something to replace what he'd lost. He thought maybe he could find it in the not-for-profit world and got involved with a couple of organizations dedicated to relieving poverty around the globe. He traveled to Africa for one of them and joined the other's medical teams on annual trips to Bolivia. He also discovered a passion for education, specifically the education of young people entering the business world, and began working with students at Michigan State University, his alma mater, and DePaul University, where he'd earned his MBA. But while he considered his Third World trips "life-changing" and his teaching experiences "fantastic," they didn't fill the void. "I've learned that once you're an entrepreneur, you're an entrepreneur forever," he said. "I still had a yearning to do business. Not that I needed the money. What I needed was to do something meaningful, and to do it for compensation. Giving your time away for free is extremely significant, but I think former business owners also need to feel validated by remaining engaged in the game of business."

As Leech struggled to find his way, he increasingly questioned his decision to sell a controlling stake in CrossCom National. The new majority owners had effectively shut him out of the company. Despite his position as board member and major shareholder, he was treated like an outsider who had little, if anything, to contribute. Strategic discussions happened without him. No one sought his opinion. He was completely marginalized, which led to frustration, and the frustration led to second-guessing. He began to feel as though he'd been railroaded into doing the deal. Yes, he'd been tired, burned out, a little depressed perhaps, but weren't there other possibilities?

His thoughts crystallized during a visit to a Chicago company called Tasty Catering, which had been repeatedly honored as one of the best places to work in Illinois. "I saw the culture they had, and it hit me," he said. "That was what we'd had at CrossCom. We'd built something special, and we lost it. But until then I don't think I realized how special it was. At the time, everyone was saying, 'Think of what you can do with $20 million. You can pay off your ex-wife, buy a new airplane.' Then I sold, and there was nothing. So I spent the next three years lamenting over what I'd left, not looking at what I was going to."

He did eventually find a new calling. In 2008, he and his friend Dave Jackson, who'd also had a rough exit experience, founded a service and networking organization, Evolve USA, for people who have sold, are selling, or are thinking about selling their businesses. (More about that in chapter 6.) "I wasn't at all prepared when I sold," Leech said. "I didn't know what it meant to be prepared. That's what I want others to think about. When people talk about moving on, the focus is almost always on the transaction, but that's only 20 to 30 percent of it. The other 70 to 80 percent is the emotional part. You have to think about that in advance, because once the deal guys get involved, you get marched down that road and the next thing you know, you're sitting on the outside."

Why Ask Why?

It's more or less a given that in business, knowledge is power. No one has to tell you how crucial it is to know what trends are shaping your market; what concerns your customers have; how technology is affecting your industry; what new sources of competition you may be facing; how committed and energized your employees are; and so on. Yet, oddly enough, owners often overlook the most important subject of analysis from a business perspective, namely themselves.

Nothing will have a greater impact on your business than having a deep knowledge of yourself. I'm talking here about understanding what you want and don't want, what you care most about, what makes you tick, what your true passion is, what your weaknesses are, what energizes you and what leaves you cold. Owners who know themselves tend to make better decisions, build better companies, become better leaders, and have more rewarding business careers than those who don't. They are also far more likely to have happy exits. That's because they're able to develop a good sense of where they want to wind up, which is impossible if you don't have a high degree of self-awareness. Granted, knowing your ultimate goal does not guarantee that you'll reach it. But not knowing it is a fairly good guarantee that you won't.

Now, some people will note, quite rightly, that achieving self-awareness is a lifelong occupation. It's not as if you can set aside a weekend to figure out who you really are. We're talking here about a long-term process. One entrepreneur I know sits down at the beginning of every year to write a detailed vision of his life ten to fifteen years in the future. His business partner does it as well.

Without some such process, you run the risk of being unprepared, not just for the end of your journey, but for whatever follows. When you finally do transition out of your company, you'll run smack into the question of who you are, what you want, and why. There won't be any escaping it. You'll have enormous trouble figuring out what the next thing should be until you answer those questions or happen to stumble across an opportunity that answers them for you. Like Leech, you'll wander around, searching for a purpose. How long that period lasts and how painful it is will depend partly on you and partly on luck. But this much is certain: by the time you come up with answers, you will no longer have all the options you would have had if you had started asking—and answering—the questions while you still had a business. Hence the importance of beginning your search in stage one of the exit process, if not sooner.

I should emphasize here the importance of asking not just who and what, but why. It's all too easy to settle for superficial answers to the first two questions. Answering the why forces you to dig deeper and to think about how confident you are about the who and the what.

Norm Brodsky, my sometime coauthor, learned the hard way about the importance of asking why. As he was building his first business, CitiPostal, a messenger delivery service, in the 1980s, he knew exactly what he wanted: a company with at least $100 million in sales. He said that he never asked himself why. If you'd pressed him for an answer, he would probably have admitted that he has a big ego in need of regular feeding and seizes every opportunity to prove he is the best at whatever he does. There's a lot more to him than that, though, and he might well have reconsidered his goal if he'd taken a close look at the rationale behind it.

But he didn't, and his determination to reach the $100 million mark eventually led him to make a very bad acquisition. While the deal boosted CitiPostal's sales overnight from $45 million to $120 million, it turned the company's $1.1 million annual profit into a loss of $10 million and set in motion a chain of events that landed Brodsky in bankruptcy court the following year. He spent the next three years working his way through Chapter 11, which gave him plenty of time to think about who he was, what he wanted, and why.

His first step was to come to terms with what had just happened. He initially shied away from accepting responsibility for the debacle, which could easily be blamed on external factors. No one, after all, could have predicted the stock market crash of October 1987, which had wiped out a substantial portion of his business. And who knew that at about the same time, the number of fax machines would suddenly reach the critical mass required to make them a viable alternative to deliveries by messenger? Yes, the acquisition had been a mistake, but everyone makes mistakes, Brodsky told himself. The problem lay in the timing of external events he couldn't have foreseen.

In the end, it was a magazine quote from an investment banker that broke through his wall of denial. The banker, who had once tried to invest in CitiPostal, said that when he finally got hold of the financials, he was shocked to see the company was "a basket case." He said, "I took one look . . . and thought, 'This is embarrassing. No company can exist with this capital structure.'"

Brodsky immediately grasped the implications of that statement. The banker was saying, in effect, that the bankruptcy had been foreseeable and avoidable. If that was true, the obvious question was, why hadn't Brodsky foreseen and avoided it? In his heart, he knew the answer, as difficult as it was to accept: He hadn't been paying attention.

He'd been so focused on his $100 million goal and so confident of his ability to make the merger work that he'd been blind to the danger. In fact, he'd enjoyed the danger. The risk energized him. That was a basic character trait. "I like going up to the edge of the cliff and looking down," he said.

So CitiPostal hadn't been done in by the stock market crash or the rise of fax machines after all. It had been done in by Brodsky's gambler instincts. By succumbing to them, he had put the company in a position that made it vulnerable to unexpected events, while exposing his three thousand employees to a level of risk they should never have faced. More than 98 percent of them had lost their jobs as a result—through no fault of their own.

Whatever else he might be, Brodsky is a man with a conscience. It crushed him to realize he was directly and personally responsible for the calamity that had befallen more than twenty-nine hundred of his employees—people he had hired and who had done everything he'd asked of them. He resolved never again to make a decision that would put employees' livelihoods in jeopardy.

And that was just the beginning of Brodsky's conversion to another way of doing business. He knew he couldn't change who he was. But he was honest enough with himself to accept the by now obvious fact that some aspects of his personality could be a threat to him and others if he didn't control them. Noting this, he took a number of steps designed to offset his weaknesses, reinforce his strengths, and keep himself from committing the same mistakes in the future. For openers, he began surrounding himself with people who were steady-going, analytical, and detail-oriented. He admitted to himself that he was an awful manager, didn't enjoy managing, and should henceforward leave it to people who did. He taught himself to listen carefully to arguments and opinions he would previously have run right past. He instituted a new protocol for dealing with problems that involved figuring out what role, if any, he had played in creating them. And he came up with a rule that he would make big decisions only after taking a shower. Because he showered in the morning, the rule forced him to put off big decisions for at least a day, ensuring he had time to think.

Equally important, he changed his business goals. The bankruptcy had cured him of his excessive focus on sales and his eagerness to own a big company. Having $100 million in sales was meaningless in itself, he realized, especially if you had a low-margin business like messenger delivery. He'd be much better off owning a $20 million company with high margins—and plenty of cash flow.

Right about then, a delivery customer happened to call in with an unusual request. She had twenty-seven boxes she needed to store somewhere and was wondering if CitiPostal offered that service. Brodsky, who had never heard of such a service, did some quick research and concluded that records storage was just the type of business he was looking for. And so was born his second company, CitiStorage. Over the next seventeen years, he and his employees built it into one of the largest and most respected independent records-storage companies in the country. In 2007, Brodsky sold a majority stake in CitiStorage and two affiliated companies, plus an interest in the prime real estate on which they were located, to a business development firm, Allied Capital, for about $110 million. Looking back, he said that the sale would never have happened if he hadn't made the changes he'd realized were necessary once he had a clear idea of who he was, what he wanted, and why.

The Investor Mind-set

Fortunately, you don't have to go through Chapter 11 to acquire that level of clarity about who you are and what you want. But a crisis can be an opportunity to learn, and many owners who've had happy exits can trace the path they've followed back to a troubling event that seems to have set them on a particular course.

For Michael LeMonier, the staffing industry entrepreneur I mentioned in chapter 1, the event was his abrupt dismissal from a job at a large staffing company he'd served for nine years, rising to the position of division vice president. He was fired—or "liberated," as he put it—after clashing with a new boss. "I told him he was an ass," LeMonier said. Whatever prompted his termination, he took a lesson out of the experience: "It showed me how wrong I was having all of my ego tied up in my work."

That proved to be a guiding principle as he embarked on his entrepreneurial career. He regarded the businesses he owned as investments, not as his life's work. "Each one is just a chapter in the book," he said. "It's not who I am. Sure, I'm passionate about it. You're always passionate about a winning investment. But I look at it differently from other business owners I know, probably because of the way I approach it to begin with." He meant that for him, starting and exiting are two sides of the same coin. "I see my role as an owner as growing the business and preparing an exit. Whenever I think about going into a business, I look at not only where does this begin but also where it ends."

His companies play no role in his sense of who he is, what he wants, and why. "The business is not my purpose," he said. "Rather, it gives me the opportunity to discover my purpose more deeply and more personally. And when I ask myself, 'Who am I, if not my business?,' I have an answer. It is that I'm a child of God, a husband, a father."

A skeptic might note that LeMonier doesn't actually start businesses. He buys them, builds them, and sells them. Although he is an operator rather than purely an investor, it's easy to understand how he would come to view his businesses as investments and why he might choose not to be defined by them.

The same cannot be said of John Warrillow, who has been starting businesses since he was a third grader in Toronto. Like LeMonier, he begins with the end in mind, partly, he said, because he grew up around successful businesspeople. His father, James Warrillow, launched the magazine now known as *PROFIT*, the Canadian counterpart to *Inc.* in the United States. "Intentionally or otherwise, he exposed me to entrepreneurs who had exited and who had thought about the end before the beginning," said Warrillow. And yet, predisposed as he is to selling any company he starts, he would have had a much harder time parting with his largest and best-known business, Warrillow & Co., if he, too, had not gone through an experience that clarified in his own mind who he was, what he wanted, and why.

The idea for the business had come from a radio show Warrillow had been producing and hosting that featured interviews with successful entrepreneurs. One of the sponsors, RBC Royal Bank, was having trouble getting small businesses to respond to its direct mail and engage with its salespeople, and the bank's marketers asked Warrillow for help. At first he advised them for free, as a favor to an advertiser, but he soon began charging for his services. It didn't take long for him to figure out that other companies might also be willing to pay for such advice, and so in 1997 Warrillow & Co. was born.

He was twenty-six years old at the time and most of the people he hired were about the same age. Looking back, he describes the culture of the company as "high school." They worked and played together, and over the next seven years grew revenues to about $4 million. Warrillow himself was focused on improving his leadership skills and building a great business. He attended seminars, lectures, and conferences and devoured management books that preached the importance of having a great work environment. "I was getting really far down the path of creating the kind of culture where, you know, people bring their dogs to work, you have a lot of fun retreats, and everybody loves each other," he said. What's more, he believed in it—which only increased his shock and disappointment when key people began to leave.

The first to go was one of the most senior account executives, who took a job with a customer. A couple of months later, the head of research went to work for another customer. Those two were then followed by other employees. In the space of about six months, 40 percent of Warrillow's staff left, generating turmoil in the company and threatening relationships with customers.

It was no mystery why the employees were leaving. "They had better opportunities," he said. "They went to work in big companies, and we were small. We were pulling ourselves up by our bootstraps. Everybody did three jobs. There wasn't a lot of structure. And keep in mind that our business involved working with very large organizations. So our people were constantly exposed to the benefits and perks these companies could offer."

Nevertheless, he felt betrayed. "It was like when your girlfriend breaks up with you as a teenager," he said. "I can't think of any other way to describe the feeling." Employees, he concluded, weren't nearly as invested in having a great workplace as he was and didn't appreciate everything he'd been doing to create one. "It was a very tough period," he said.

He soldiered on, hiring new people to replace those who'd left. Together they put the company back on track. But the episode forever changed the way he viewed the business. "I promised myself I would never be so emotionally invested in it again. I would never let it be a replacement for my social life or my family life. It helped that, right about then, my wife and I had our first child. Becoming a father was a game changer. I realized there were many more important things than the company, which accelerated the process of separating myself from it. As far as business was concerned, I became pretty hardened. It became quite clinical to me."

In effect, Warrillow removed himself emotionally from his business. Whereas once he had been passionate about creating a great workplace and a great company, he now had a more hardheaded view of what he was doing. The business, he felt, was first and foremost a tool for making money. As such, it could enable an owner to create a great life outside of work, but the business was a means to that end, not an end in itself. The result was that when he sold it four years later, he had a much easier time leaving than many other entrepreneurs who cash out. "I had heard that selling a business can be like losing a child or getting divorced. I never had any of those emotions. Maybe it's because I had gone through this period. If I hadn't, I might have felt a greater sense of remorse about leaving."

A Calling or a Job?

There are, of course, some business owners who've delved as deeply as LeMonier and Warrillow into the question of who they are, what they want, and why—and come to the opposite conclusion. They readily acknowledge their emotional attachment to their businesses. Their identities, they admit, are completely intertwined with the companies they own. Some of these people have devoted a substantial portion of their lives to building enterprises that aim to be the best at what they do, offering great service to customers, building great relationships with suppliers, and creating great work environments for employees. Day in, day out, they see examples of the ways in which their companies are improving the lives of the people they touch.

But those owners will eventually have to exit as well, and doing it happily and gracefully is a bigger challenge for them than for people like LeMonier and Warrillow. To begin with, they have additional factors to consider in choosing a new owner because of their concern about the fate of the company after they leave. They also have to deal with their "remorse about leaving," as Warrillow put it. They'll have less remorse, however, if they've found a new calling they feel even more passionate about. That can happen. People change, and as long as they're sufficiently self-aware to notice, so will their plans.

Chip Conley discovered he was changing sometime in 2007, after spending most of his adult life building one of the leading boutique hotel chains in the country. He'd been just twenty-six years old in 1987 when he launched his first hotel, the Phoenix, in San Francisco's Tenderloin district. Twenty years later, his Joie de Vivre Hospitality chain had grown to include more than thirty properties in California and earned a national reputation for its creative hotel concepts, exemplary customer service, and perennial designation as one of the San Francisco Bay Area's best places to work. Conley himself had been honored as the most innovative CEO in the Bay Area—a region famous for its multitude of innovative CEOs. He'd also written two books and was about to publish his third and most influential one, titled *Peak: How Great Companies Get Their Mojo from Maslow,* which described the ideas, principles, and techniques he'd used to survive the depression that had hit the California hotel industry following the dot-com bust and the terrorist attacks of 9/11.

Up until then, he'd never given much thought to leaving the company. Although he'd received numerous feelers from potential acquirers over the years, nothing had come of them, mainly because Conley wasn't ready to step down as CEO. "I had no interest in relinquishing that role," he said. "I saw Joie de Vivre as my calling and assumed I'd be doing it till I was seventy-five or eighty years old."

But something changed as he was writing and giving talks about *Peak* and his previous book, *Marketing That Matters.* He found he really enjoyed the solitary, introspective, reflective aspect of the writing process and the gregarious, explicative, teaching, and sharing aspect of public speaking. It dawned on him that he might actually like writing and speaking more than running Joie de Vivre. "If a calling energizes you and a job depletes you, I began to see that being the CEO of this hotel company was starting to feel more like a job," he said. "I mean, I could give four or five speeches a week and not get tired because it was so energizing. But my main career was still being CEO. I realized, 'Omigod, I've got a problem.' What had been consuming me for twenty years was not what I wanted to consume me in the future."

Nevertheless, when he was again approached about selling, in early 2008, his initial reaction was, "Of course not. I'm not ready." Then he had second thoughts. "There was a voice in my head saying, 'Come on. You can't keep doing both of these simultaneously.'" He agreed to explore the possibility of a sale. Telling nobody but his assistant and his father, who is also his closest adviser, he began negotiating to sell Joie de Vivre, meeting secretly with the would-be acquirer, the investment bankers, and others involved in the due diligence process. It went on for almost six months. "It was very awkward for me, having the company evaluated and getting used to the idea that I might actually sell it," he said. "But eventually we got to a place where, over dinner one night in June, we came to an agreement on the value. And I said, 'Sure, let's do it.'"

There was a glitch, however. The buyer's plan was to merge Joie de Vivre with two other hotel companies that he hadn't yet completed deals with. Conley heard nothing for the next two weeks. He finally called the buyer, who told him that they were having trouble coming to terms with the other companies. By then the economy was already in recession, and real estate prices were beginning to drop as the air came out of the housing bubble. A week or so later, the buyer informed him that the deal was off.

Conley said he felt like a groom left standing alone at the altar. "I had mentally, emotionally, psychologically gotten myself to the place of being open to actually selling and moving on," he said. "So I was like, 'Okay, so now what do I do?'"

This was the second piece of bad news he'd received that day. Earlier, a controller at one of his hotels had admitted that he had embezzled more than a million dollars over the previous four years. That evening, Conley broke his ankle during a baseball game and was in the hospital for the next ten days.

Things didn't get any better thereafter, as he was beset by medical complications related to the ankle fracture. In mid-August, he collapsed while signing books after a speech in St. Louis, and his heart actually stopped beating for several seconds. Paramedics were able to revive him, and after a couple of days in the hospital he continued on his way. He was still recovering on September 15 when Lehman Brothers filed for Chapter 11 and the economy went into free fall. Hotel companies that had taken on too much debt during the bubble years, including Joie de Vivre, were especially hard hit. With annual revenues dropping 20 percent to 25 percent, Conley suddenly found himself fighting to stave off bankruptcy for the second time in seven years. "The first time, I felt like a gladiator," he said. "The second time, I felt like a prisoner." The stress was even greater because Joie de Vivre had been in the process of launching fifteen new hotels in twenty-one months. As the crisis deepened, he began getting late-night phone calls from the intoxicated spouses of his hotel partners, distraught that they were facing bankruptcy and might not be able to send their children to college.

As if he needed further reminders of how grim things could get, Conley also began hearing about friends who'd committed suicide—seven of them, all men about his age, over a two-year period. One was his insurance broker, a key adviser who had always seemed as solid as a rock and who also happened to be named Chip. Conley went to the memorial service, where he listened to a stream of speakers share their remembrances of the other Chip.

The cumulative effect of the unremitting bad news was to reinforce

Conley's conviction to find a way out of Joie de Vivre and move on to his new calling. The stakes came into even sharper focus at the end of the year, when he took a week off over the New Year holiday and spent it in Big Sur, on the California coast. "I had one of the best weeks I've had in the last five or ten years," he said. "I just did things I really wanted to do, including three days writing. I realized that my whole life could be like this."

The experience removed whatever lingering uncertainty he may have had about the path he was on, and he immediately felt better as a result. What had been an existential question suddenly became a practical question: not whether to leave but how. The memory of that week kept him going in the months ahead. "When I've been in that difficult place as the entrepreneur, feeling like the walls are closing in, I've been able to go back there in my mind and say, 'This is where I'm going to be someday, and I really like it a lot.' I can touch it and taste it and feel it. Because of that week, the future isn't so abstract. Some people imagine their life after the sale—playing golf, living in Ireland or Italy—and it's so far removed from where they are that it's not tangible. You can't feed on it. It doesn't sustain you."

It took another year and a half for Conley to do a deal, during which time he spoke with more than twenty-five potential acquirers, ultimately settling on Geolo Capital, a private equity firm led by John A. Pritzker, one of the heirs to the Pritzker family fortune. In June 2010, Conley sold Geolo a majority stake in Joie de Vivre. Sixteen months later, Geolo merged it with another boutique hotel chain, Thompson Hotels. The merger gave Conley the opportunity to distance himself further from operations, which he welcomed. He relinquished his title as executive chairman of the business but stayed on as a "strategic adviser," as well as minority shareholder.

Although he was fully engaged in his new career by then, he had not completely severed his emotional ties to Joie de Vivre or given up hope that it would remain a great company. It had been one by almost any definition during his tenure as CEO. But it was now part of a new entity, Commune Hotels & Resorts, and the latter's fate was largely out of his hands.

Conley had accepted that reality. Indeed, he had accepted the possibility that Joie de Vivre might disappear altogether, especially after Thompson's chief executive—an industry veteran—became CEO of the merged company. "I wasn't at all sure what would happen to Joie de Vivre," said Conley. "So I had to get comfortable with the idea that my legacy in life was not just this company I'd put twenty-four years into building. There had been years and years I'd gone without pay. Why? Because I'd been trying to build something memorable and lasting, a prize that other people could actually model or emulate. But I'd reached a point where I could no longer influence that, and I realized I'd only make myself anxious if I focused on things I had no control over. I also had other things in my life that I wanted to pour my heart into."

He was already working on a new book, *Emotional Equations*, and keeping up a busy schedule of speaking engagements. In January 2013, he started his next business, Fest300, an online guide to the 300 festivals that he and his fellow festival enthusiasts judged to be the best in the world. Then in March, he was approached by Brian Chesky, the cofounder and CEO of Airbnb, the immensely popular Web site for people looking to rent or rent out lodging. Chesky said he wanted Airbnb to become the world's most admired hospitality company and asked Conley for his help. Conley agreed to work part-time as Chesky's hospitality adviser. Within a month, he was working full-time as the company's head of global hospitality and strategy. Joie de Vivre was well behind him by that point, and in early 2014 he cashed out his remaining stock in Commune Hotels & Resorts.

Looking back, Conley had no regrets about selling the company that had dominated his life for almost a quarter century. To the contrary, he believed he'd stayed at Joie de Vivre five to ten years longer than he should have. "If you're a curious person who likes to be constantly learning, you reach a point of diminishing returns," he said. "The time and energy you're putting in is not giving you back as much learning as it used to or as much as you feel you need."

He said he is having as much fun these days as he had during his best years at Joie de Vivre, but it's different. "The fun then was having my fingerprints all over a business that I was completely immersed in. The fun now is about not having it be only my fingerprints. It's about serving and being part of something bigger than me."

The Wake-up Call

Conley would be the first to admit that he was fortunate to find a new passion in life just as his old passion was beginning to cool. He is not necessarily typical, however. Many people whose aim is "to build something memorable and lasting" don't lose their passion for it. They want to keep working in and on their businesses as long as they can.

But they, too, will exit someday, even if it means getting carried out on a stretcher. And unless they've made adequate preparations by then, there's little chance that their businesses will last much longer than they do. More to the point, they will leave in their wake a huge mess for someone else to clean up. It requires a higher level of self-awareness to anticipate the danger and take the steps necessary to make sure that such a disaster is not what you will be remembered for.

No one could fairly accuse Paul Saginaw and Ari Weinzweig, the cofounders of Zingerman's Delicatessen in Ann Arbor, Michigan, of lacking in self-knowledge. They'd launched their business in 1982. By 1992, it was world-famous, written up in various national magazines and newspapers as one of the best delis anywhere. Having accomplished their original goals, the partners confronted the question of what to do next. After two years of intense discussion and soul-searching, they came up with a vision to create Zingerman's Community of Businesses (ZCoB), a collection of food-related companies in the Ann Arbor area. In addition to the deli, it could—and eventually did—include a bakery, a restaurant, a creamery, a coffee roastery, a candymaker, a mail-order business, a caterer, a training company, and more. Each business would be owned jointly by a managing partner who worked there and the parent company, owned by Saginaw and Weinzweig, Dancing Sandwich Enterprises (DSE). It was a bold vision, and they could never have come up with it if they hadn't known who they were, what they wanted, and why.

And yet they had a blind spot. When asked about his exit plan, Weinzweig would respond in a tone of exasperation. "Why would I want to exit? I've created a job that lets me do everything I love. I travel all over the world. I work with really great people. I never eat bad food. I study all day and teach a lot and help people have a good life. There's nothing I want to do that I can't do here. So why would I leave?"

Saginaw at least acknowledged the inevitable. "I don't feel the need to get out, but I can't work forever, so I guess I'd better think about it," he said. "Currently our exit strategy is death."

They did take some precautions against the possibility of unexpected endings to their respective journeys. They were aware, for example, of the financial problems that could arise when one of them died. The surviving partner would have to deal with the Internal Revenue Service, which would insist on collecting estate taxes, as well as any heirs who might look to get their inheritance in cash. (They'd agreed that no heirs would enter the business.) Accordingly, Saginaw and Weinzweig took out life insurance policies on each other, which—in theory at least—would provide the survivor with enough money to cover any such needs.

But Saginaw, who had a family, knew they should do more. "What happens when the second one dies?" he would ask his partner from time to time. "Who gets the shares?"

Weinzweig, who was single, would just shrug. "Why should we worry about that?" he said. "We'll be dead. Whoever is still here can work it out any way they like."

Fortunately, they remained very much alive for the next few years, which allowed everyone to put exit and succession planning on a back burner. Saginaw still brought it up occasionally, and his concern was shared by Ron Maurer, the administrative vice president and chief financial officer who had joined Zingerman's Service Network, the administrative arm of ZCoB, in 2000. In 2008, Maurer introduced Saginaw to a financial planner he'd met. Their discussions highlighted the need to get a realistic assessment of the company's fair market value. Without it, they couldn't know whether Saginaw and Weinzweig were carrying enough insurance. So they hired a Chicago-based firm to do a valuation, which revealed that the insurance was in fact woefully inadequate. In order to purchase new policies, both Weinzweig and Saginaw would have to get physical examinations. Saginaw, who'd been feeling out of sorts, kept putting his off, hoping that whatever was bothering him would go away.

Then came the event that changed everything: While playing tennis one day in July 2009, Saginaw suffered what he later learned was a heart attack. Somehow he finished the game and went about his business for a day and a half, until he finally told his wife, who was in California, and she forced him to go to a hospital emergency room. The diagnosis came as a shock. "Until you have what they call 'an episode' and a doctor tells you that you have coronary heart disease, you don't really think about your mortality," he said. "Most people will do some self-examination at that point."

With his mortality fresh in mind, the persistent concern he'd had about ZCoB's future became a matter of utmost urgency. What really would happen to ZCoB, he wondered, if he and Ari died? What needed to be done to protect the other members of the community? Didn't the managing partners of the individual businesses face the same financial risks in the event of a death—and thus have the same need for life insurance—as the two founding partners? And how would ZCoB be governed when the founding partners were no longer around?

In January 2010, Saginaw brought his concerns to an off-site meeting in San Francisco of all sixteen partners. He argued that the group needed to form a special committee on governance to consider a whole range of questions about how ZCoB would operate in the future. "I said, 'We really need to think about how we pass on ownership and control, which are two different things. When both Ari and I are gone, the problem won't be the loss of our expertise or spiritual leadership or whatever. It will be that we haven't figured out how to hold the center together. And we also have to think about how this thing is going to scale up. I mean, our governance model works pretty well now, but will it work for thirty partners? For sixty? For a hundred? If not, what changes will have to be made?'"

The group agreed on the need for such a committee, and Saginaw made sure the biggest critics, including Weinzweig, were on it. "Then my work was basically done," he said. "I could go on autopilot. I got what I needed, which was to have everybody thinking about this stuff, especially those people on the committee. They were so critical, I knew they were going to be very good at ferreting out what we needed to know."

A Plan to Keep Calm and Carry On

Four years later, the process was still unfolding. One subject would lead to another, and then another, and then another. Step by step, the group began to completely reimagine how the business would operate when neither of the founding partners were around anymore. If one died, for example, how would a new co-CEO be selected? What would happen when the second founding partner died? Who would inherit Dancing Sandwich Enterprises, or would it disappear? If so, what would happen to the intellectual property it owned? And where would its revenue stream from the operating businesses go? Would a new entity be created? Who would own it? What would happen to the stake that DSE owned in each of the businesses? And on and on.

Along the way, new issues emerged, notably the question of employee ownership. Saginaw and Weinzweig had long wanted to create a means for employees to have some ownership, but that was difficult because ZCoB wasn't a business entity in which they—either individually or through an employee stock ownership plan (ESOP)—could own shares.* DSE was a business entity, of course, but opening it to partial employee ownership would have ramifications for the constituent businesses, raising a host of complicated issues that Saginaw and Weinzweig weren't ready to deal with at the time. They'd also wanted employee advocates in the partnership group—one to advocate for staff, one for customers, one for suppliers, and one for the community, but that idea had proven tricky as well. "So we just put the idea in our backpacks and left it there for several years," said Saginaw.

With or without employee ownership, the company needed a method for valuing the stock on a regular basis. Private companies with ESOPs are required to have an annual valuation done by a specialist firm, which uses a set of complex formulas to arrive at a version of fair market value acceptable to the IRS. Weinzweig didn't like that approach. "You wind up with a number that comes out of a black box no one understands," he said. "We practice open-book finance here. I want people to be able to calculate

---

* There are several forms of employee ownership, of which an ESOP is but one. It is actually a kind of retirement plan created and governed by federal law. Among the others are stock option plans, employee stock purchase plans, restricted stock plans, and worker cooperatives. More about all this in chapters 5 and 7.

what the value is going to be." As a member of the governance committee, he'd begun researching unconventional ways of handling the various issues it was dealing with. At a business conference, he met a Dutch attendee who suggested some different rules of thumb for valuation. Weinzweig and his colleagues took those ideas and devised their own formula for what they called "business value," which served as their approximation of "fair market value," as recognized by the IRS and the courts. When they did the calculation using the formula, it yielded a result close to the figure offered by the valuation firm ZCoB had hired. The partners decided they would adopt it but also keep doing regular "black box" valuations as a check on the formula's continued reliability.

Reflecting on the process four years into it, Saginaw acknowledged the challenge of doing exit planning the way he and Weinzweig had gone about it—"because you don't have a road map, but that can make it more fun too." What the process isn't going to do is make either one of them independently wealthy. Not that they have to struggle to make ends meet, but it's reasonable to ask whether or not they're forgoing a reward that many people would say they've earned. After all, they've devoted their lives to building this company. They took all the financial risk in the beginning and most of the responsibility as time went along. Don't they deserve to get paid for the value they've created?

Saginaw, too, has thought about that. "This whole process has been easier for us because, as different as Ari and I are, neither of us has ever been driven by the money. Sure, we all would like the financial noose to be a little looser around our necks, but it gives you an enormous amount of freedom to play with your business, to experiment with it, if you can get your head around the idea that you don't need a lot of money. You just need enough. Then you can focus on leveraging the business to provide the most joy, to create the most empowerment for the most people. You can be extraordinary. You can do just wonderful things that you could never do if you were going for a lot of money. Because when you want a lot, there's never enough."

We won't know how it all turns out until the founding partners have shuffled off this mortal coil. Neither Saginaw nor Weinzweig has any intention of leaving before then. From that perspective, I suppose you could say that death is still their exit plan. It's hard to believe that the company won't change thereafter without the presence of two outsized personalities like theirs. But at least they will have given their successors a fair shot at continuing the record of remarkable accomplishments that ZCoB has compiled during their lifetimes. They've been able to make this choice for one reason, and one alone: They are crystal clear about who they are, what they want, and why.

3

Deal or No Deal

> **Build a business that can be sold when and to whom you want to sell it.**

It was late on a November afternoon in bucolic Bolinas, California, and although Bill Niman had indicated that, yes, he was willing to talk to me about his unhappy exit from the company he'd founded, he had other matters to attend to first. For openers, there were the seventy-eight heritage turkeys that were cackling, clucking, gobbling, and squawking as they flew into trees, jumped up on fences, and generally resisted the efforts of Bill and his wife, Nicolette, to herd them into their coop for the night. Meanwhile, over at the cattle barn, a grieving cow was waiting for them. The cow had recently lost her calf in childbirth, and Bill and Nicolette had a plan to unite her with another calf that had been rejected by his mother. The rest of the herd was spread out across Niman's thousand-acre ranch on the shores of the Pacific Ocean.

These days, Niman's ranch is called BN Ranch, for legal reasons. Under the contract he signed before leaving Niman Ranch Inc. in 2007, he is not allowed to attach his family name to any meat-selling venture, and he fully intends to sell as much meat from the ranch as he can. In addition to heritage turkey and grass-fed beef, he's thinking about partnering with farmers who raise all-natural, free-range, pasture-bred sheep and hogs. This time around, however, he's not looking to build a national meat company like Niman Ranch. Rather, he sees BN Ranch as a demonstration farm that will prove you really can make money and get the best-tasting meat by raising animals humanely, forswearing the use of hormones and antibiotics, and following the most environmentally sound farming practices.

Of course, many would say he has already proved that once, or at least the part about the best-tasting meat. Beginning in the mid-1970s, Niman Ranch built a reputation for producing the highest-quality, most flavorful beef, pork, and lamb in the world. It was one of the first meat producers whose offerings were featured by name on the menus of the finest restaurants and in the meat cases of high-end supermarkets. Today its brand is among the most recognizable in gourmet food. Along the way, it has helped inspire movements around sustainable farming, humane animal treatment, and other causes that Niman has championed.

But Niman himself no longer has anything to do with the company that bears his name. In August 2006, a majority stake in the business was sold to Natural Food Holdings, a subsidiary of Hilco Equity Partners, based in Northbrook, Illinois. Niman soon decided he couldn't live with the changes that the new management team was making, and so he left, taking with him a cow, a steer, and his remaining stock in the company, which turned out to be worthless. In 2009, a special meeting of the stockholders voted to accept an offer from Natural Food Holdings to buy the whole company. By the time the most recent investors were paid off, there was nothing left for the early ones and the holders of common stock, including Niman.

And so it was that after spending his entire adult life building his business, revolutionizing the industry, setting a new standard for meat quality, creating a famous brand, and racking up a couple hundred million dollars in sales, Niman wound up with nothing. Indeed, you might say less than nothing: His name is now attached to products that he doesn't believe in and won't buy. "I'm not willing to eat Niman Ranch beef myself," he said, "and so I don't recommend it to others."

How could this have happened? Niman has pondered the question in the years since he left the company. Sitting in the living room of the modest four-room house that he and Nicolette now share with their young sons, Miles and Nicholas, and their Great Dane, Claire, he explained why he'd felt he couldn't stay. As he laid out his case, there was passion in his voice, but also a faint smile on his face. Although he clearly cared about the issues involved, he seemed somewhat removed from them, as well he might be. Niman Ranch is not part of his life anymore, and on the surface he appeared content with his current lot.

"And why shouldn't he be?" I thought. After all, he lives on a pristine stretch of Pacific coastline, is engaged in work that he loves, and has a happy home life with Nicolette, an environmental activist and author. The birth of their sons has brought new joy into his life. "Do I want to miss this?" he asked at one point. "Hell, no. It's the only thing I haven't done. I want to savor it." He paused. "But knowing what's going on in the industry, how animals are being tortured daily, and having had the platform . . . it's hard not to have some feelings . . ." His voice trailed off. Though the word "regret" was not spoken, it hung in the air.

No, I realized, he hadn't yet put Niman Ranch behind him. On the contrary, Niman bristled when I suggested that he seemed at peace with his decision to walk away. "Do I?" he said. "What I feel is bitter disappointment. And I have to take responsibility."

The Misery of a Forced Sale

Exiting, as I've noted, is not so much an event as a phase of business. It's arguably the most important phase, in that it determines whether or not you get what you want out of your journey of building a company. The climax to that phase is the deal. We tend to view the success of a deal by the amount of money that changes hands, but a good deal is about more than money. It's also about having as much control as possible over the timing of the deal and the choice of whom to do the deal with. No amount of money is enough if you're forced to sell to a buyer you don't like or trust and to do it when you don't want to—because you've run out of other options.

Such outcomes are known as forced sales. They are extremely common and can happen at any time and for any number of reasons. Maybe the owner dies unexpectedly, leading to an estate tax liability that can be covered only by selling the business. Maybe you're a supplier to large manufacturers who issue new qualifications for vendors that your company can't meet. Maybe you lose a critical supplier, or get hit with a devastating lawsuit, or make an ill-advised acquisition, or are diagnosed with brain cancer, or wind up in a messy divorce. The possibilities are endless, and the devil is always in the details.

Robert Tormey is something of an expert on forced sales, having been dealing with them for more than twenty-five years as both a seller and a buyer. He was introduced to the concept in 1988. The forced sale in question involved a small financial services business in Santa Barbara, California, that had been started by three partners a few years earlier. Tormey, then in his early thirties, was one of them.

A numbers guy by training and inclination, he had joined Arthur Andersen out of business school and after becoming a CPA, moved on to Shearson Lehman/American Express, where he made so much money selling securities that in 1985 he decided to quit and go into business with two friends from work. "At Shearson, I had twenty to thirty people working for me," he said. "I figured, 'How hard can this be?'"

Harder than he imagined. Tormey soon realized he'd underestimated the difficulties of building a retail stockbrokerage business in a heavily regulated industry that was simultaneously undergoing radical change due to, among other things, the rise of discount brokerages like Charles Schwab. Fortunately, the business had two other services that mitigated the challenges on the retail side: an investment manager for wealthy individuals and a corporate finance arm, run by Tormey, that handled capital transactions for middle-market companies (loosely defined as companies with between $10 million and $500 million in annual revenues).

The firm was still getting itself established when calamity struck in the form of Black Monday. On that fateful day, Monday, October 19, 1987, the Dow Jones Industrial Average suffered its largest one-day percentage decline ever, plummeting 22.6 percent, and business ground to a halt at brokerages around the country.

None of the partners had seen it coming, and they weren't prepared for the turmoil that followed. "I realized I was in way over my head," said Tormey. "The retail side dried up overnight. Nobody wanted to even think about buying stocks. We were losing money in the brokerage every single month. My only thought was, 'How do we get rid of this thing?'"

The way out was a sale, but selling a brokerage in the aftermath of Black Monday was next to impossible. The industry was going through a massive contraction. The partners' best bet was to find a small or regional securities firm that wanted a retail presence in Santa Barbara. Tormey, meanwhile, was working long hours to prop up a business in which he knew he had no future. "That's when I learned what a forced sale is all about. I mean, you get to the point where the business has taken so much out of you that you just dream day and night of selling the damn thing."

The partners finally found a broker-dealer in Newport Beach that was willing to take the firm off their hands. Tormey left even before the sale was completed. "We basically got out for an assumption of the firm's liabilities," he said. "Our equity was worth almost nothing. I was tapped out putting money in."

The end of Tormey's early—and brief—career as an entrepreneur marked the beginning of his longer and far more successful career as a chief financial officer of and adviser to middle-market businesses. His specialty was helping troubled companies. Today he can tell story after story about the forced sales of struggling businesses, some of which he worked for, some of which he helped an employer acquire. One, for example, was a profitable, growing company with more than $30 million in sales whose owners decided to go into real estate development. The partners borrowed money from their company to make an equity investment in a new two-hundred-unit garden apartment complex, then secured a loan from a nonbank lender for the balance of the capital required. As often happens, the project ran into problems and delays. The owners, who were new to the construction game, hadn't foreseen them and so had left themselves exposed with no permanent lender to take out the nonbank lender at the expiration of their interim construction loan. By the time the complex opened, an international credit crunch had begun. To make matters worse, the opening was late, and the complex was only 40 percent occupied when the construction loan matured. The partners weren't able to line up a permanent lender and lacked the resources to finance the debt on their own. The finance company that had made the loan foreclosed on the property, and the owners lost their equity investment—that is, the money they'd borrowed from their company.

When they met with their CPA, he informed them that the company couldn't continue to carry the note receivable to them as an asset on its books because it had been secured by the equity in the foreclosed apartment building. The owners now had no secondary source of repayment other than their salaries from the company. Accordingly, under accounting rules, the company had to treat the money they'd just lost as a taxable dividend and take a charge to earnings and equity. That charge lowered their personal net worth and put them in default on a major loan from their primary bank. The bank proceeded to call the loan, forcing the sale of the company to one of its suppliers. The erstwhile partners, having squandered the most valuable asset they'd ever owned, sued each other.

That's one way owners can be forced to sell a business, though I wouldn't call it typical. There really isn't such a thing. The circumstances of these unhappy endings are seldom the same. Nevertheless, a common thread links them all: the owners' failure to prepare for the unexpected. Exactly why they've failed to prepare varies from case to case, as does the specific type of preparation that would have given them options other than to sell the company under the worst possible circumstances. But in each case some weakness or vulnerability has escaped the owner's attention. When exposed, a forced sale remained the only alternative to bankruptcy or liquidation.

How Bill Niman Lost His Company

Bill Niman's case is not typical either, but it does show how even smart, experienced businesspeople can be seduced by success and lulled into relaxing their guard. I'm referring here to the executives and investors who joined the company in the late 1990s. At the time, Niman Ranch was struggling. Founded in the early 1970s, the business had never been profitable and might well have suffered an early demise but for an amazing stroke of fortune in 1984. That's when the National Park Service decided to designate the ranch for inclusion in the Point Reyes National Seashore. The government paid Niman and his partner, Orville Schell, $1.3 million for their two hundred acres in Bolinas, north of San Francisco, while granting them the right to live on the land and farm it during their lifetimes and also allowing them to lease an additional eight hundred contiguous acres. A couple years later, Niman and Schell persuaded Susie Tompkins Buell, cofounder of the Esprit clothing company, to lend them $500,000. Between Buell's loan and the money from the government, they were able to cover the company's ongoing losses for the next decade. Meanwhile, the ranch's reputation grew, thanks mainly to the elite Bay Area restaurants that had begun putting its name on their menus.

By 1997, however, the money from Buell and the government was gone, and the business was dangerously close to insolvency. Then, out of the blue, Niman received a call from a serial Silicon Valley executive named Mike McConnell, who wanted to see if Niman had a job for his godson. "Bill said, 'Well, I don't really need people, but I've got a business opportunity,'" McConnell recalled. "He wanted to expand, and Orville didn't." McConnell, who'd already earned a fortune in technology, anted up $500,000, bought Schell out, and became Niman's partner. A few months later they were joined by a former Nestlé executive, Rob Hurlbut, who had contacted Niman seeking advice about a seafood business he wanted to start. Instead, Niman recruited him.

The arrival of McConnell and Hurlbut was a turning point. The new partners were businessmen, not ranchers like Niman. While they shared his values and believed in his mission, what really fascinated them was the opportunity to create a nationally recognized brand in a commodity food business. They joined the company at just the right time. Niman had begun working with an Iowa hog farmer named Paul Willis, who had his own vision of reviving traditional hog farming in the Midwest, where hundreds of thousands of family-owned hog farms had gone out of business or been absorbed into massive indoor pig factories. As Willis and Niman were putting together a network of suppliers, Whole Foods Market called to say it wanted to start purchasing free-range pork from the company for all of its stores. It was a huge opportunity for Niman Ranch, and not only because of the volume of sales involved. Pork had the potential to generate more profit than either beef or lamb, which in fact weren't generating any profit at all.

While Hurlbut focused on seizing the opportunity in pork, McConnell began raising the capital needed to grow. It was easy, he said. That was the era of the dot-com boom, and nowhere was the get-rich-quick fever more intense than in the San Francisco Bay Area. Although the company was making little, if any, money, profit wasn't all that important to investors back then. Brand and scalability were everything, and "first movers" had an edge. As a marginally profitable first mover with a strong brand and an apparently scalable business model, Niman Ranch became a hot property, and McConnell was able to raise about $11 million from seventy-five investors from 1998 to 2004.

Niman had some reservations about what the money was doing to the company's culture. "We stopped being careful and started spending money on corporate identity programs, attending trade shows, holding strategic planning sessions with outside facilitators—all the classic things—instead of being thrifty and acting like we were poor," he said. But he put his reservations aside. "I thought, 'What do I know? These guys are out in the business world seeing what other companies are doing. It must be the right thing.' And I have to admit that I was seduced by the notion of becoming a really big company and having a really big impact on the industry. Right to the end, the investment bankers were telling me, 'You'll sell it for $100 million. You'll probably get $30 million for your shares.' I was seduced by that too."

He certainly wasn't alone. Most of the business world had been swept up in the dot-com craze. Niman Ranch had all the qualities of a hot dot-com but one: It was a meat company, not an Internet company. The conventional wisdom at the time held that "brand equity"— measured by growth in sales—was like money in the bank. Niman Ranch had a lot of brand equity and was acquiring more each month, as sales rose rapidly. No one worried about the dearth of profits. "Whatever income we had, we would pour back into the company," Niman recalled. "Our entire focus was on increasing revenue."

In the real world, however, such a strategy works only if you have a business model that allows you to become profitable in the future, at a higher level of sales, and you must be able to reach that level before your capital runs out. Niman Ranch had a sustainable business model on the pork side of the business, which Hurlbut and Willis had developed, but not on the beef side, which was Niman's domain. Although Hurlbut tried to persuade the founder to apply the pork business model to the beef business, Niman wouldn't budge. "Bill would say, 'If you do that, you'll destroy the brand,'" said McConnell. "The board wasn't sure enough to override Bill."

But it's neither fair nor accurate to pin all the blame on Niman. The fund-raising had left him with just 12.5 percent of the stock at that point, and he was surrounded by experienced businesspeople—not just McConnell and Hurlbut but also the investors who controlled the board. They all should have recognized that an unprofitable business model was not sustainable, and yet no changes were made to it, even as the myths of the dot-com era began to explode all around them.

The moment of truth came in 2006. That year, Niman Ranch lost $4 million on about $60 million in sales and was almost out of cash, and the shareholders weren't willing to put any more in. The company's future depended on the value of its brand equity. The board had already decided to find out how much it was really worth. For six months or so, the company entertained a parade of potential acquirers. It soon became clear that Niman Ranch wasn't worth anywhere near what the shareholders had thought and what the investment bankers had encouraged them to believe. They got exactly one bid for the business, from Hilco Equity Partners, which offered to buy 43 percent of the stock and voting control for about $5 million.

With the prospect of bankruptcy staring them in the face, the shareholders, including Niman, were actually relieved that someone else was willing to invest in the business. Moreover, the leaders of Hilco and its subsidiary, Natural Food Holdings, seemed to embrace the Niman Ranch values and philosophy. Although they had no further need for Hurlbut and McConnell, they were adamant that they wanted Niman to stay on as chairman of the board and company spokesperson.

He agreed but insisted on having an employment contract defining the terms under which he could later leave. That turned out to be a wise precaution. Within a month of the sale in July 2006, the relationship began to come apart, and a year later Niman was gone.

He now believes his crucial mistake was to give up control to Hurlbut, McConnell, and the board. It's far from clear, however, that the result would have been different had he held on to it. What ultimately did him in, he admits, were "delusions of grandeur and a big payday." His was not the first exit to be spoiled by such temptations, nor will it be the last.

Is Your Business Sellable?

Now, you might well ask at this point, "How can I make sure I don't get pushed into a forced sale, given that the factors leading to one may be out of my control?" There are no guarantees, but you can gain a measure of security by building a business capable of responding and adapting to almost any circumstance. You do that by constantly looking for and addressing the business's weaknesses and vulnerabilities and by asking a lot of what-ifs. Jack Stack of SRC Holdings refers to the driving force behind the process as "creative paranoia," and—as Andrew Grove of Intel famously put it—"only the paranoid survive."

But there's a bright side to this particular type of paranoia: It's one of the best tools you can have for building the most value in a business and maximizing your odds of having the kind of exit you want. In a word, it improves your company's sellability, which is another condition for a happy ending to your journey.

I should clarify here what I mean by sellability. On one level, a company is sellable (or salable, as some prefer) if there's a buyer willing to acquire it. That's not saying much. After all, companies that wind up in forced sales are sellable in that sense. Then again, the vast majority of small businesses don't even rise to that low standard. According to a study by the U.S. Chamber of Commerce, just 20 percent of companies put up for sale are ultimately sold, meaning that four out of five prospective sellers walk away empty-handed. A much greater number of would-be sellers—by one estimate, 65 to 75 percent of owners who would like to sell—never even make it into the market. They learn early on that they have little or no chance of finding a buyer.

But you need more than a willing buyer to have a good exit. You also need to be in a position to choose when you will leave and who will own the company after you're gone. The latter will depend to some extent on the type of company you have. Many small businesses, for example, exist mainly to provide the owner with a way to earn a living. Some of these ventures may be sellable, but the pool of potential buyers for them is limited to family members, employees, or other people who want to be their own boss and are looking for a business to earn a living from. In many such cases, the owner's best course may be simply to forget about selling the business and instead stay with it as long as it continues to support his or her lifestyle, accumulating enough savings to live on after shutting it down.

Technology start-ups are also in a category of their own. Size and profitability have nothing to do with whether or not such businesses are sellable, according to one of the leading independent experts on exit strategies in tech companies, Basil Peters of Strategic Exits Corp. in Vancouver, British Columbia. The owners of tech companies cross the threshold of sellability, he said, when they prove the business model, not when they achieve a certain level of sales or have a certain amount of earnings.

For example, a recurring revenue business, such as a company that sells subscriptions to some type of service, needs to be able to document (1) gross margin per customer, (2) the length of time a customer remains a customer, and (3) the cost of customer acquisition. "In other words, how much a customer is worth and how much it costs to acquire one," he explained. "And actual data, not projections." Other types of businesses must prove the model using different metrics, with five or six elements in some cases. The idea, Peters said, is to be able to project credibly how much the business would be worth if an acquirer invested a given amount of capital. It then becomes possible to have a fact-based negotiation over value. Granted, other factors may come into play, such as competition and market trends, but you're beginning with a solid base of data that's more important to a buyer than the amount of revenue the company currently has or the amount of profit it's generating.

In fact, Peters argues that owners should seriously consider selling such a business as soon as the model has been proven. "It's always best to sell on an upward trend," he said. "You sell on the promise, not the reality. Once you have enough information to prove the model, that's often when you can get the best price. The danger, if you wait, is that you'll ride the value over the top. Most entrepreneurs do."

He has facts and figures to back up his argument, which is undoubtedly relevant to entrepreneurs who are in business because they love the process of starting, building, and selling companies and who aren't particularly interested in holding on to any particular company for an extended period of time. But that's not the case for the overwhelming majority of owners, and certainly not for those who've been in business for many years, or whose business model was proven long ago. Those people need to think about sellability differently.

What Sellers Sell and Buyers Buy

The first step is to understand exactly what you're selling when you sell a business: future cash flow. A buyer's initial motive for doing a deal may be something else—a desire, say, to boost earnings, enter a new market, fend off a competitor, or do an industry roll-up. In the final analysis, however, it's all about long-term cash flow. Every company that acquires another company wants and expects that its cash flow will be greater in the future by making the acquisition than it would have been if the acquisition had not happened. Venture capitalists, private equity groups, and angel investors have the same expectation. Family members or employees who acquire a business *should* have that expectation as well. If they're acquiring a company that's going to give them less cash flow in the future, there's a good chance that they're getting stuck with a lousy deal.

I suppose there may be exceptions to this rule, but I have a hard time imagining what they would be. You can't spend sales, after all, or profits, or market share, or synergy. They're all important, but they're concepts. Cash is king because it's the only thing you can spend. People buy businesses so that they'll eventually have more of it.

That's one reason why acquirers tend to value nontechnology companies based on their earnings before interest, taxes, depreciation, and amortization, or EBITDA, which is a rough measure of what's called "free cash flow." Think of it as the amount of cash a company generates in a year after paying all of its operating costs and expenses but before covering what it owes in taxes and interest (which another owner might not have to pay) and before deducting depreciation and amortization (which are accounting conventions reflecting the cost and life span of certain assets). It is thus a better reflection of the business's operating condition than, say, net earnings.*

Once you realize that you're selling future cash flow, you can deduce what most smart buyers will want to know about your business. First, they'll be interested in your current cash flow and the amount it's projected to grow in the coming years. Second, they'll gauge how much they can really count on those projections; that is, what's the risk of

---

* Technically, free cash flow is EBITDA minus the change in noncash working capital—mainly inventory and receivables—minus routine capital expenditures (often abbreviated to CAPEX). For simplicity's sake, however, both buyers and sellers generally discuss the value of businesses in multiples of EBITDA alone.

things going wrong? So if you're trying to improve your chances of selling your business, it's obvious what you need to do: Demonstrate the company's future growth potential and reduce the risk to the buyer. Since acquirers assess the risk by, among other things, closely examining a company's past performance, everything you do as you build your business will have an impact on your ability to sell it.

Granted, a buyer may come along who will view things differently. Another company might see a way your business could help it generate greater cash flow in the future, say, by giving it capabilities it doesn't already have or by providing access to a new market or by absorbing a competitor. Accordingly, this buyer would be less interested in your company's size and profitability than in other factors, such as the strength of your patents and trademarks or the transferability of your customer relationships. Such acquirers are known as strategic buyers, as opposed to financial buyers, which are mainly private equity groups of one sort or another. The former, as the name implies, are looking to help themselves strategically. The latter's aim is to grow any business they acquire and sell it for a lot more money in three to seven years. Not surprisingly, financial buyers tend to be easier to locate than strategic buyers, and the standards they use to evaluate potential acquisitions are more consistent from one deal to another.

Those standards are important for another reason: If you build your company with them in mind, not only will the business eventually be easier to sell, but it will become better, stronger, and more durable in the process. That's because financial buyers are among the most finicky and sophisticated acquirers around. They are accountable to their investors, who are interested only in the financial performance of their portfolios. So financial buyers have to be expert at identifying a company's weaknesses and vulnerabilities, as well as its unique strengths. And they have methods of evaluating potential acquisitions that business owners can use to identify the specific weaknesses and strengths of their own companies even if they have no intention of ever selling to a financial buyer. The future owners—family members, employees, or whoever—will be better off as a result.

Sellability Factors

Smart owners of private companies have long understood the value of learning how a professional investor evaluates a company. They have used methods ranging from having M&A (mergers and acquisitions) professionals conduct analyses of their businesses, to inviting them to sit on advisory boards, to actually taking trial runs through due diligence. A growing number of software tools are also available that can at least get you started on assessing the strengths and weaknesses of a business from an investor's perspective.

One program was developed by John Warrillow, who more or less stumbled across the market for such tools. As I noted in chapter 1, he embarked on a new career as a writer and speaker after selling his fourth company in 2008. Among other things, he wrote a book, *Built to Sell,* that tells the fictional story of an owner of an advertising firm who learns how to turn his unsellable business into one that can be sold. To promote the book, he set up a Web site, www.builttosell. com, and posted on it a sellability index—a simple quiz intended to give business owners a general idea of whether or not they have sellable companies. To his surprise, he began getting a steadily growing stream of notifications that people were using it. "It dawned on me these results should be telling me something," he said. He went to work creating a much better assessment tool, which he called The Sellability Score.

His is by no means the only one. B2B CFO in Mesa, Arizona; Core-Value Software in Norwich, Vermont; Inc. Navigator in Jasper, Georgia; and MAUS Business Systems in Brookvale, New South Wales, Australia, among others, have similar programs. These tools can help business owners with one of the most difficult and important tasks they face: learning to look at their companies objectively, through the eyes of an investor with no emotional ties to the business or its people. Owners who master that skill are far less likely to wind up in a forced sale than those who don't. They also have significantly greater control over what happens to them and their companies, both before and after they leave.

Let me hasten to add that none of these programs provides a road map to sellability. Nor can they guarantee that you'll someday be able to sell your company for top dollar. What they can do is give you a set of markers pointing the direction in which to go. Some do it with a dashboard you can use to track your progress on key variables. Others use a periodic assessment. They all do a pretty good job of highlighting key variables.

For example, The Sellability Score* has owners answer a series of questions about their businesses and then assigns an overall score as well as scores on each of eight factors that would affect a company's desirability to a typical investor. But the real value to most owners, I suspect, lies less in the scores than in the accompanying report, which includes tutorials on each of the eight factors.

The first factor is *financial performance.* The tutorial looks at the thought process of an investor in coming up with a price for a business. There's an exercise explaining how to calculate a company's "present value" and showing how it is affected by the degree of risk an investor perceives. Small companies carry a risk simply by virtue of their relative size. Hence the "small company discount."

---

* I've used The Sellability Score as an example here not because it is better than the other programs—I haven't studied all of them closely enough to know if it is or isn't—but because, unlike the others, it is free to company owners. Warrillow's revenue comes from the brokers, M&A lawyers, financial advisers, and investment bankers who pay him to be part of his network. After an owner fills out an online questionnaire, the system generates a report that is sent to an M&A professional, who contacts the owner, goes through it with him or her, and suggests ways to make the company more attractive to potential buyers, based on the vulnerabilities identified by the system.

The second factor is *growth potential*. This section carries the lesson a step further by demonstrating the effect that growth rates have on calculations of present value. The faster the company is projected to grow, the higher its present value. Thus, as noted previously, a business's scalability is a key factor for buyers, and the report suggests various ways that a business owner can think about scaling—by expanding geographically; by coming up with new products to offer existing customers; by finding new customers to fill unused capacity; and by adapting products or services from one culture to another.

The third factor is *overdependence*. (Warrillow calls it "The Switzerland Structure," alluding to the benefits of neutrality and independence.) The idea is to avoid the danger of being so dependent on any one customer, supplier, or employee that the loss of that customer, supplier, or employee would cripple the business. Investors look especially closely at customer concentration (the term of art), which they regard as a key vulnerability. If any one customer accounts for more than 15 percent of sales, they will discount the price accordingly.

The fourth factor is *cash flow*. The more a business can finance its growth with its own internally generated cash flow, the less it has to rely on outside capital. An acquirer will pay more for a company with less need of outside capital, and less for a company with more need of outside capital. (Warrillow refers to this as "The Valuation Teeter-Totter.") The report goes on to suggest ways that businesses can accumulate more cash by reducing collection times from customers and increasing payment times to suppliers.

The fifth factor is *recurring revenue*, which is important because it provides some assurance of future sales, thereby lowering the risk to a potential buyer and thus raising the business's value. Here Warrillow spells out six levels of recurring revenue, ranging from consumables that people have to keep buying (e.g., toothpaste, shampoo, toilet paper), to renewable subscriptions (e.g., newspapers and magazines), to sunk-money renewable subscriptions (e.g., Bloomberg Terminals), to automatically renewing subscriptions (e.g., document storage), to long-term contracts that lock the customer in for years at a time (e.g., wireless telephone service). The more assured the future revenue, the lower the risk and the higher the business's market value.

The sixth factor is *unique value proposition*. (Warrillow calls it "Monopoly Control.") The harder it is for competitors to copy what a company is offering, the less pressure there is to reduce prices. Warren Buffett talks about acquiring companies with a "moat" around them, ideally one that's wide enough and deep enough to keep competitors from entering your castle and stealing your customers. The moat is widest when you have an impregnable competitive advantage, which—again—reduces the risk to an acquirer and increases the business's value.

The seventh factor is *customer satisfaction*. What matters here is that the business has established a discipline for measuring customer satisfaction consistently and rigorously. Testimonials from happy customers won't do, nor do most customer satisfaction surveys make the grade. Warrillow follows the lead of many well-run companies, large and small, that have adopted the Net Promoter Score methodology developed by loyalty guru Fred Reichheld and presented in his best seller *The Ultimate Question*, which predicts your customers' likelihood of repurchasing from you and making referrals to you—two important drivers of growth—by their answers to one question: "On a scale of 1 to 10, how likely are you to refer our company to a friend or colleague?" Those answering with a 9 or 10 are considered promoters—that is, likely to buy again and refer others. A 7 or an 8 indicates a customer who's neutral, or "passively satisfied" in the Reichheld lingo. All the others are detractors. The Net Promoter Score is calculated by subtracting the percentage of detractors from the percentage of promoters. As Warrillow points out, the methodology works particularly well for small to midsized private companies in that (1) it's easy to implement; (2) it gives them a common language with investors; (3) it's cheap; and (4) it's predictive.

The eighth and final factor is *strength of the management team.* This is really about the owner's role in decision making. If all the key decisions are made by the owner, there will inevitably be big questions about the company's viability following his or her departure. A potential buyer would take an especially close look at relationships with customers, whose loyalty may be more to the owner than to the company. The better your company can function without you, the more sellable it will be.

Ultimately, of course, you're in the best position if you have a wide variety of potential buyers—financial, strategic, employees, managers, or family members—when it comes time to decide whom you will sell to. You can be fairly sure of having the full range by building a business that could be sold to a private equity group. If you have that option, you're likely to have all the others as well.

Learning from Private Equity

In the coming years, private equity groups (also known as PEGs) will be buying thousands and thousands of companies, if only because there is so much private equity around and the pressure on firms to invest it is so intense. That's actually one of the biggest problems the industry has struggled with in recent years. According to Bain & Co., private equity firms had in 2014 more than a trillion dollars of "dry powder"—that is, money they'd raised and had yet to invest. Investors had pledged that money because they want a better return than they can get from other sorts of investments, but they can get it only if the firms put the money to work in growing businesses. The longer it sits around, the unhappier the investors become, and they aren't shy about letting the firms know it. PEGs also face a time limit. If they don't invest the money in a given period (usually five years), they lose access to it, which in turn hurts their ability to raise funds in the future.

But that doesn't mean it's easy to sell to a private equity group. "PEGs will look at hundreds of businesses before investing," noted Robert Tormey, the forced sales expert, who has worked for and with more than thirty private equity firms in the past twenty years. "I've marketed two businesses through investment bankers. In the first case, our investment banker circulated over a hundred copies of the placement memorandum to qualified PEGs. We received five letters of intent, which was considered an enormous success. In the second instance, we also sent out more than a hundred memoranda and received three responses and one letter of intent. That's not unusual. For each business a PEG invests in, a hundred or more have been passed up."

The competition to cash out by selling to a PEG will only increase in the coming years, as retiring baby boomers—who by one estimate own nearly four million of the U.S. businesses that have employees— flood the market. From that perspective alone, it would make sense to learn what PEGs look for in a business and then to apply those lessons to your company, although I should note that PEGs seldom invest in companies with less than $5 million in EBITDA. That's the amount of annual cash flow required to secure the type of loan that allows a PEG to achieve the level of returns it has promised its investors, as explained below.

But you don't need $5 million in EBITDA to develop the disciplines and best practices valued by the most astute investors and acquirers. If you do, you'll have a stronger, more resilient, and more valuable company no matter what sort of exit you eventually choose. You'll also have better access to the capital you need to grow.

In an unpublished white paper titled "The Care and Feeding of Your Exit Strategy: Lessons Learned from Private Equity," Tormey recounted an experience he had as the CFO of a manufacturer that was owned by a PEG. The company was doing a roll-up—that is, buying a number of smaller companies in an industry and consolidating them in one larger entity. Tormey was in charge of corporate development, responsible for everything from identifying acquisition candidates to integrating the acquired businesses into the combined company. There was no shortage of potential acquirees. He and his colleagues looked at five or more possible deals for every one they closed.

In retrospect, he said, what interested him most was the effect that the buying process had on the way they ran their own company. As time went by, Tormey and his team increasingly adopted practices they would have liked to see in the businesses they acquired. "We focused on creating enterprise value in all of our actions and initiatives. We began to maximize EBITDA and didn't focus on tax savings as much. We jealously guarded our working capital, closely monitoring our accounts receivable and basing our purchasing decisions on terms rather than just price. By then, we'd come to appreciate the returns we could get from working capital and the ways we could use our cash flow to leverage additional borrowings. We also made sure we always had the infrastructure to support more acquisitions. As a result, we were able to grow from $8 million to $40 million in sales in twenty-four months."

In other words, when you adopt the practices that very smart and experienced acquirers (such as a PEG) want to see in a potential acquisition, you wind up with a business that has the wherewithal to achieve whatever goals you may have for it—whether or not you eventually decide to sell to one of those smart and experienced acquirers. Why? Because those practices give you access to capital. Not that access to capital is all that matters. But it's necessary for anyone with a dream that he or she aims to achieve through business. Without access to capital—either your own or someone else's—you simply don't get very far.

How Private Equity Works

Why, you might ask, do acquirers put such a high value on these management practices? Consider how a private equity group earns a profit on a deal. The goal, remember, is to grow the acquired business and sell it for a lot more money in three to seven years. Toward that end, the firm recapitalizes the business, investing some equity and then loading up on debt. That way, the investors can get a much bigger bang for their equity buck when the company is eventually sold.*

Securing the debt is key to the deal. In most cases, a big chunk of it is borrowed from a bank, though not in the form of a conventional bank loan. Rather, it's a special type of loan known as a highly leveraged transaction, or HLT. The guidelines for HLTs are set by federal regulators, and those rules are enshrined in the credit agreement, which is quite different from and more stringent than the agreement for a conventional loan.

For example, one of the covenants in a typical HLT credit agreement spells out the minimum EBITDA that the company must have during every three-month period, each one identified by date, for the entire length of the contract, which may run as long as seven to ten years. The level of financial discipline required to maintain the required levels of EBITDA is extremely rare in privately owned businesses. Just think about it for a moment. The company's owners are promising to have a certain minimum level of EBITDA every quarter for up to ten years in the future, and that promise is backed up by a long-term business plan detailing exactly how they and their managers intend to do it. If they miss their targets, the credit agreement will have to be amended, which will almost certainly cost them a lot of money. There is very little wiggle room. With an HLT, the owners and senior managers can't allow themselves the kinds of perks that owners of private businesses routinely take advantage of. There can be no more padding of the payroll with extra salaries as favors to friends or family members. No

---

* The principle is the same as using debt versus equity to buy, say, a $1 million house that doubles in value over a ten-year period. If the owners have put up the entire $1 million, they earn a 100 percent return on their investment when it is sold ten years later. If they've bought the house with $100,000 of their money and a $900,000 mortgage, they earn a 1,000 percent return ($2 million − $900,000 = $1.1 million).

sweetheart loans to the owner. No gimmicks to reduce EBITDA in the interest of avoiding taxes. On the contrary, the goal is to maximize EBITDA, and thus the value of the enterprise, at every opportunity.

Tormey noted in his white paper that some small-business advisers tell their clients not to worry about perks and tax avoidance strategies: If they track the money they take out, they can always add it back in when the time comes to sell, and they'll get the full value of the restated earnings. But that's bad advice, Tormey argued, for a variety of reasons. To begin with, the owner, by taking the money out, is depriving the company of cash it could be using to pursue growth opportunities, which means its EBITDA is lower than it could have been. Buyers may also reduce the multiple they're willing to pay, figuring that the owner's decisions about money indicate a dearth of better ways to spend it. Beyond that, the add-backs introduce an air of uncertainty into projections, which affects how both the buyer and the buyer's lender evaluate the risk involved and hence the amount of money they're willing to invest, further depressing the sale price.

But the most serious damage, Tormey contended, is to the culture. When owners use their businesses as personal piggy banks, they make it all but impossible to develop a culture of accountability in the company. Managers see how the owner is treating the company's cash and conclude, quite rightly, that he or she has an agenda besides growing the business and meeting key performance targets. The effect is to undermine financial discipline. If the person at the top is not exercising it, neither will anyone else.

You can run a business that way if you're not carrying much debt and the bank is not scrutinizing your every move. You can't do it, however, if you've borrowed a ton of money and signed an HLT credit agreement. That contract requires you to submit annual budgets and then monitor the variances as the year goes along. It demands that you have good cash controls and adhere strictly to the stipulated financial ratios. It makes the whole company accountable for financial results, meaning that all sales, marketing, and operational decisions must be reviewed from a financial perspective before being acted on.

"In short," Tormey concluded, "the constraints of the PEG's business force the company to adopt a host of best practices that debt-free family businesses don't need to follow. It is the best practices—rather than the leverage or the investor's business acumen—that create the outsized investment results PEGs are known for. The good news is that you don't need to borrow the money to borrow the practices."

Creating a Culture of Accountability

Tormey is surely correct that, in theory at least, any business can adopt the best practices required of highly leveraged companies and see similar results. But knowing what the best practices are and implementing them are two different things. You need, as he suggests, a culture of accountability. Developing one is the hard part. Martin Babinec discovered just how hard in 1995 after selling a controlling interest in his company, TriNet, based in San Leandro, California, to a publicly owned strategic buyer.

TriNet is a professional employer organization, or PEO, an outsourcer of the various tasks involved in managing a workforce. By serving as the employer of record for its customers, they are relieved of the burden of maintaining a human resources department and spared the headaches of being an employer. The business had been on the verge of bankruptcy in 1990, but a group of angel investors had bailed it out at the last minute. By early 1994 it was profitable and doing about $2.5 million in sales, having established a secure foothold in its target market of emerging growth technology companies.

But Babinec had belatedly recognized that to achieve long-term success as a PEO, a company had to be much larger. Economies of scale were crucial in, for example, buying health insurance at competitive rates and constantly upgrading the technology required to handle its customers' complex needs. As well as TriNet was doing, it was still relatively small. Opportunities for growth were plentiful, however. What wasn't plentiful was the capital TriNet would need to take advantage of them.

So Babinec and his CFO, Doug Devlin, began to search for outside funding, eventually winding up in a meeting with representatives of Select Appointments (Holdings) Ltd., a large, publicly traded staffing company based in London. Select's people indicated that they would pay a premium for a majority stake in TriNet. After consulting with his management team and his investors, Babinec decided to accept the offer, in large part because he knew from research he'd done that Select was not a typical acquirer. It didn't buy companies and strip out costs by centralizing as many functions as possible. Rather, it had a record of targeting well-run businesses in need of growth capital and guidance but with capable management teams that it would leave in place and allow to operate more or less autonomously. "In essence, we'd be running our own company," Babinec recalled.

They negotiated a deal whereby Select would get 50.1 percent of the stock in return for an investment of $3.9 million—$3 million to grow the business and an additional $900,000 that Babinec would use to settle his start-up debt, with enough left over to give his family a small cushion in case Select decided he was not up to the job and brought in a new CEO. That was a worst-case scenario he could live with. He'd still be a major shareholder, after all, with about 35 percent of the company's stock.

The two sides signed a letter of intent, and the formal due diligence process began. Select brought in the accounting firm of Deloitte & Touche, which came back with some words of caution. Given the inexperience of TriNet's management team, the auditors felt it was too risky for Select to invest the entire $3.9 million in one lump sum. They suggested that instead the investment should be made in stages, or "tranches," subject to the company meeting certain revenue and EBITDA targets. Babinec and his team thought the conditions were reasonable enough, and they had complete confidence in their ability to hit the targets. The deal closed, and the first tranche of $1 million was delivered.

It was as if a sluice gate had been opened. "We'd been working on our growth plan for two years, and now we finally had serious money," Babinec recalled. "We immediately ramped up our hiring and began executing the other elements of our plan." That was in July 1995. By December, the expanded TriNet team was in place and ready to move forward as soon as the second tranche was delivered.

The company had a problem, however. TriNet's business is somewhat cyclical. Many clients eventually outgrow the need for its services, and, for tax reasons, the terminations typically come at the end of the year. Early in December 1995, the company learned that it was losing three of its largest customers, representing almost 25 percent of its annual revenues. That was a bigger bite than the management team had expected, and it meant that TriNet would not hit the revenue target for the second tranche.

Missing it was obviously unfortunate, but hardly catastrophic, given that new accounts in the pipeline would soon make up for the loss. Prior to the Select deal, Babinec would have expressed his disappointment and moved on. But he couldn't move on now without the second tranche, and for that he needed the approval of Tony Martin, Select's CEO, who also served on TriNet's board of directors. "I called him and said, 'Tony, here's the story,'" Babinec recalled. "'We're very confident in our growth plan. We've hired some great people. We've ramped up the overhead as called for in the budget. All right, we've had a minor setback with the loss of these customers, but look at the sales pipeline. We think we're in good shape, and it makes sense to advance us this next tranche.'"

Tony Martin said no.

For Babinec, it was a rude awakening. "If you could imagine the excitement of finally being able to grow the company with capital we'd been working to get for the better part of two years. We're executing on our business plan. We've started building a true executive team. We are investing in systems. We are doing all the things we've been salivating to do for a very long time. Now we're going to run into a cash problem. The worst part was that we'd have to conduct a layoff. It made no sense to us, booting out people we had just hired and already started to train—especially since we had confidence we could restore the lost revenue. We all believed that, long-term, it would be much more detrimental to cut than to not cut."

But Martin was firm. "He said we had to meet our projections. This was about living in the world of public companies. When you set projections, you must meet them. Believe me, it was not a fun situation. The layoff especially was very difficult, very painful. I was devastated because I felt the failure of my leadership was putting a bunch of dedicated and hard-working team members out into the street through no fault of their own. But that was our new reality. We were now working for a public company, and this kind of thing came with the territory." Only in retrospect did Babinec come to appreciate the benefits of the experience. "I can see now that I was being taught a lesson. And not just me, but the whole management team, because we operated in a very collaborative and transparent way. Ever after that we were very, very careful about making sure that we would meet our numbers. Very careful."

Learning to live by their forecast was just the first step, though a big one, in creating a culture of accountability at TriNet. In time, Babinec came to see how important that was. His goal, after all, had been to build a company that could remain independent beyond his tenure as CEO, and beyond Select's tenure as controlling shareholder—a company that would at least have a chance to achieve enduring greatness. "What we learned from Select was public market discipline, and Tony Martin was my mentor," he reflected many years later, after he no longer had an active role in the business other than serving on the board. "Inevitably you have screw-ups. That's the whole thing because you learn from mistakes much more than you learn from successes. But over time we learned how to be a private company that runs like a public company. We upped our game. As a public company, you have to be highly transparent. You can't have any related-party transactions. You have to set expectations and meet them. It's not just about using a budget. You have to deliver on your budget, which is extremely difficult to learn how to do, especially when there's rapid growth after a large infusion of capital."

The rewards both for TriNet and for Babinec personally were enormous. Without that culture of accountability, for example, it's extremely doubtful that Babinec would have been able, in 1999, to move his family across the country to the small upstate town of Little Falls, New York, while continuing to serve as TriNet's CEO. He had grown up in Little Falls, and his parents still lived there with one of his sisters. Babinec and his wife, Krista, wanted their children to enjoy the benefits of small-town living and thought the schools were better than in California. The move meant a grueling commute for Babinec to TriNet's headquarters in San Leandro, but he considered the new environment for his family worth the price he would have to pay, and his board gave its blessing to his plan.

It's equally doubtful that without TriNet's track record he would have been able, in 2005, to orchestrate such a smooth transition of majority ownership to a leading private equity firm, General Atlantic (GA). Select had been acquired by a Dutch company, Vedior, and an American PEO no longer fit into its plans. It was therefore unwilling to invest the capital TriNet needed to keep growing. With Vedior's blessing, Babinec began a two-year search for a new owner that culminated in the sale of a majority interest to General Atlantic, which he considered the ideal partner.

GA's capital had the desired effect. TriNet began making acquisitions, with the result that its rate of growth accelerated tremendously.

That posed a dilemma for Babinec. He realized that with so much going on, it was increasingly important for TriNet to have a CEO who operated out of its headquarters in California, but he wasn't willing to move his family back there. He also understood that GA would probably want to take TriNet public at some point. While he supported that goal, he had reached a point in his life where he no longer wanted to be CEO of a public company. So in 2008 he and the board hired his successor, and Babinec continued as a full-time chairman, a post he held until the end of 2009, when he stepped down to make way for another board member he considered more qualified to play that role. Babinec remained on the board, however, to provide whatever assistance he could as TriNet made its way to an initial public offering. His continued presence on the board was also important to GA, since he knew the business so well and was still a major shareholder.

My point here is not to suggest that you need a culture of accountability to have a satisfying end to your business journey. In Babinec's case, it was essential, given the other choices he made along the way, including his decision to go into the PEO business in the first place and the subsequent necessity to bring in investors with deep pockets. But there are plenty of examples of private company owners who've had happy exits without adopting public company discipline, as he calls it. That said, you'll stand a much better chance of having such an exit if you do have a culture of accountability, if only because you'll be in the best possible position to decide to whom, when, and for how much your company will be sold.

And those are definitely conditions for finishing your journey in a way that allows you both to look back with a sense of pride and accomplishment and to look forward with confidence to whatever comes next. It's about having choices, which is the same as having control. The more options you have to choose from, the more control you'll have over the outcome. By the same token, the more choices—and control—you want, the more you need to focus on improving your company's sellability.

That's seldom a short-term proposition. With few exceptions, there is a direct correlation between the amount of time you spend preparing yourself and your company for your departure and the degree of flexibility and choice you will have when you finally decide to leave. Hence the next condition for a good exit: giving yourself enough time.

4

It's About Time . . . and Timing

> A good exit takes time—measured in years,
> not months.

Ashton Harrison first got serious about selling her high-end lighting company, Shades of Light, in 2005, when she and her husband, Dave, hired a broker to value the business. "It cost us $15,000, and it was wasted money," she recalled, sitting in her office behind her main store in Richmond, Virginia. "He was supposed to put together a prospectus and take it to investment bankers. But we realized early on he wasn't qualified." Her phone rang. She glanced at it. "Excuse me, I have to take this," she said.

The call was from the landlord of her clearance store across town. While she reassured him about the new owners who would be replacing her as the tenant in a month's time, I scanned the office. It was a disaster, with notebooks, catalogs, printouts, and lampshades strewn about, a spare bicycle frame here, a television monitor there. It looked like the aftermath of a tornado strike. Chaos, Harrison admits, is her natural habitat. "I'm ADD," she said. "Most entrepreneurs are ADD. It can be hard on employees, but it can help you if you're the boss, because you can track four things at the same time."

An intense blond woman with penetrating eyes and a dry sense of humor, Harrison attributes much of her success to her attention deficit (and hyperactivity) disorder. She also acknowledges it as the source of many of her problems. In any event, it did not keep her from starting and building a business that she sold in August 2011—a twenty-five-year adventure she then chronicled in a book, *From A.D.D. to CEO: A CEO's Journey from Chaos to Success.*

As with most entrepreneurs, exiting was the furthest thing from her mind when she started out. Newly married at age thirty-three, she intended to have children and raise a family. She also wanted to keep working as long as she didn't have to do a lot of traveling. In her previous job as vice president of a fast-growing Richmond-based furniture retailer, she'd traveled constantly. Aside from giving her a basic education in business—she'd worked her way up from secretary—the experience had sparked an idea for a company: selling directly to decorators and consumers the high-end lighting and lampshades that had previously been available only in wholesale markets. She decided the idea was worth pursuing, quit her job, and, with money from the sale of her stock in the furniture company, opened her first store in 1986.

Over the next nineteen years, Shades of Light grew to $12.5 million in annual sales as Harrison expanded into other product lines and distribution channels, opening two additional stores and launching a catalog operation and a Web site. The business had its ups and downs, but by 2002 it had achieved sustained profitability, whether because of or despite her attention deficit problems is hard to say. "When I think back to the early 2000s, I have pictures of the staff running in circles and our operation resembling a rudderless ship," she recalled. Nevertheless the company was profitable, which led her to flirt with selling in 2005. Flirting was about all she had time to do, as the business soon began losing money amid a raft of morale problems, customer complaints, and declining sales.

Even a competent broker would have had trouble finding a buyer for the company back then. Harrison admits that she'd lost whatever control of the business she'd once had. The signs were everywhere. Inventory records were a mess. Financial statements were late and full of mistakes. Employee theft of merchandise had become a chronic problem. One person was caught embezzling funds. Harrison spent her time putting out fires. "At the end of my day, I hadn't gotten to one thing on my to-do list, much less met with a single manager to set goals or obtain progress reports."

Finally she turned to a strategic consultant she'd heard about from a fellow attention-deficient CEO. The consultant's name was Steve Kimball, and one of his first questions to Harrison and her husband was, "When do you think you want to exit?"

"How about tomorrow?" said Dave. It was his wife's business, but he'd been her chief in-house adviser, and he was eager to get off the roller coaster. Harrison herself, however, knew that the company was in no shape to be sold and said so.

"Can you ride it for another three to five years?" Kimball asked. "We'll probably need at least that long to get the real value of the business going."

"Okay, great," she said. "Where do we start?"

The Long Road

It's natural, I suppose, to feel that you have all the time in the world to prepare for your exit if you're thinking the actual event is years, and maybe even decades, away. It's also natural—when you do finally turn your attention to it—to wonder how long it will take to get a deal done. In almost all cases, the process takes a lot longer than you expect, at least if you want to have a good exit. The key factor is the business's readiness for the type of exit you envision, including your concerns, if any, about the fate of the company after you're gone. As a rule, the more you care about having your business's culture, values, and modus operandi remain intact beyond your tenure, the more time you'll need to orchestrate a satisfactory transfer of ownership.

But even if you're just interested in getting the best deal you can as soon as possible, it's probably going to take years. That's one reason why Kimball, who specializes in helping owners grow businesses, not leave them, begins each engagement by asking about his client's exit plans, including both the time frame and the amount of money he or she would like to wind up with. "Most people never correlate their thinking about a growth strategy with what they want to get out at the end, whether it's three years, a year, or ten years from now," he said. "But that's critical information."

In Harrison's case, the first task was to turn the company around. Shades of Light had lost $500,000 on sales of $10.5 million in 2007. No one was going to pay a premium price for a struggling retailer with declining revenues that had intermittently experienced profitability in the past and showed little promise of achieving it in the future. To make matters worse, all signs pointed to big economic troubles ahead. Harrison had found that her business tracked the stock market with uncanny accuracy. By the time Kimball showed up, in mid-2008, the Dow Jones Industrial Average had fallen more than 20 percent from its high on October 11, 2007, officially signaling a bear market. Dave Harrison, who had previously made a living as a stockbroker, worried that a recession had already begun—and that the company might not be able to survive it. To placate him, Ashton had started putting together a three-stage crisis management plan, which Kimball helped her complete.

The first stage—Code Yellow—consisted of seventeen cost-saving measures that would come into play if the stock market dropped another 20 percent and stayed there for at least three weeks. The company would move to the next stage—Code Orange, consisting of twenty more such measures—if it became apparent that the economy was not bouncing back. The third stage was Code Red, which Harrison described as the final stage before liquidation. She didn't think she'd ever get there, but then no one anticipated the collapse of Lehman Brothers. As the economy cratered, Harrison implemented Code Yellow in November 2008, Code Orange in January, and Code Red in March 2009.

And yet in the midst of the worst economy since the Great Depression, as well as the worst crisis in the company's history, Harrison made important strides toward getting Shades of Light in shape to be sold. It was a tricky balancing act, requiring her to prepare for the worst at the same time that she was trying to put the company on a profitable growth trajectory.

Steve Kimball's main job was to help Harrison develop a growth plan and then keep her on track. She'd made it clear to him that she was concerned about her erratic attention span and her tendency to fly off in different directions. She wanted him to help her stay focused.

He began by getting her to step back and look at the business as a whole. With his assistance, she created a financial dashboard, which she began using to monitor the most critical numbers and to ask important questions about the business, such as whether or not she had the right products. In addition to lights and lampshades, the company was selling rugs and custom draperies, which were extremely labor-intensive. Kimball suggested that dropping the draperies would free up resources and allow the staff to focus on more promising areas of the business. Harrison had misgivings. Curtains accounted for 16 percent of sales—almost $1 million. Nevertheless, she listened to Kimball's reasoning and agreed to phase the line out over the next few months. "I was pretty scared," she said.

The catalog posed an even bigger problem. It was the core of the business. Harrison had hired a series of catalog consultants, all of whom had pushed her to send out an increasing number of catalogs. They'd told her not to worry about costs: The secret was to build the brand. She'd maximize the company's value, they said, by boosting her close rate and building her house file. She did extremely well on both counts. Meanwhile, catalog costs exploded to an outrageous 34 percent of sales, and the company struggled to survive.

With Kimball's encouragement, Harrison began mailing fewer catalogs, which allowed her to cut catalog costs by more than half, to 16 percent of sales. "There were some tough calls," Kimball said. "One I remember was just incredibly gutsy. It was in early 2009. I met with Ashton and Dave at their house on a Sunday. A new catalog was set to go to the printer the next day. The previous catalog hadn't brought in anywhere near the sales Ashton had expected. If she went ahead with the next one, she might not be able to cover the printing and postage costs. But if she delayed and didn't get the usual bump in cash flow that comes when a catalog hits, she might not be able to pay other bills. So the wrong call could cripple the business. Ashton decided to take the risk of waiting, and it turned out to be a great call that showed her how to improve the rhythm of her mailings and cut her costs. But the decision was gut-wrenching."

Cutting the catalog costs was actually just one element of a four-pronged strategy that ultimately resulted in changing the company's business model. The first part involved making sure the company was offering the right products and eliminating those—such as custom draperies—that were obstructing the business's path to profitability.

Part two called for turning Shades of Light from a catalog-driven business into a Web-driven business. Kimball suggested, for example, that Harrison show new products on the Web site first and then put the best-selling ones into the catalog, thereby boosting revenue from the former and cutting the cost of producing the latter. She grasped the concept immediately, but it took a year to change the thinking of an organization that had been built around selecting, photographing, and writing about products in a catalog.

The third component of the strategy had to do with increasing contract sales, especially to companies in the hospitality industry, such as restaurants and resorts. The goal was to double the sales volume in that category.

The fourth part involved what Harrison referred to as "exclusives": She would design a product, or see one she liked, and then get it developed and manufactured at far less cost than she would have had to pay elsewhere. Alternatively, she would negotiate with the manufacturer to have exclusive access to a product for an agreed-upon amount of time, or at a lower price than others could buy it for.

By the end of 2008, she had launched all four initiatives, even as the company was moving into Code Orange and Code Red territory. It was an impressive feat, as she was constantly being pulled in two directions. "That's how it felt, too," she said. "And it was hell, pure hell."

Stage Three: The Sale

As I noted in chapter 1, there are four stages in the exit process, and doing the deal comes not first or second, but third. It's preceded by the strategic phase, when you build into the company the qualities and characteristics that will allow you to have the kind of exit you want. Harrison didn't consciously enter that stage until the middle of 2008, after she had been in business for twenty-two years, at which point she found herself with an unsellable company. But Shades of Light did have strengths she could build upon, and she proceeded to do just that.

By the middle of 2009, the turnaround was well under way. Although sales declined that year to $8.6 million, down from $11.8 million in 2008, the company was once again in the black, registering a pretax profit of about $500,000. Meanwhile, there had been a fundamental shift in the business model. A company totally reliant on catalog sales, which were expensive to acquire, had become centered on online sales, which came in at a small fraction of the catalog costs. (As a result, the mail-order division's profits increased five and a half times from 2007 to 2011.) That Harrison had pulled this off in the middle of a terrible economy made the achievement even more remarkable— and gave her a nice story to tell whenever she was ready to sell the business.

In early 2010, she told Kimball that she was indeed ready.

"Do you know what you'll do after you sell?" he asked.

Previously, she hadn't had an answer to that question. This time she said, "I have a list of fifty things I want to do," and began rattling them off.

Of course, coming up with fifty things to do is not much of a challenge for a person with ADHD. Aside from writing a book, the items on her list were rather vague—spend more time with grandchildren, travel with Dave, improve at golf and tennis, and the like. Mainly, Harrison wanted to start the search for a buyer, because she thought the timing was right, and she feared she might lose the opportunity to sell at a good price if she waited. After the changes she'd made in the previous two years, she could present a potential buyer with a proven business model. The track record of that model, though not long, was impressive given the circumstances. Sales were on target to grow almost 25 percent—to $10.7 million—in 2010, while the net pretax profit margin was holding steady at more than 10 percent, well above the industry average. The company was also debt-free: Harrison had paid off almost all the debt it had accumulated during the lean times. Meanwhile, the contract sales initiative was gaining traction and would offer any new owner a substantial growth opportunity.

Kimball advised Harrison that she could probably sell the business for more money if she kept growing it for a couple more years. Then again, there was a risk that the economy could take a turn for the worse. And if she decided to make some long-term investments in the company—as she probably should be doing, given its level of profitability—its margins would likely shrink for a while, diminishing its market value. In any case, he said, she should come up with a ball-park number that she would be happy walking away with. She did, and Kimball then suggested they run it by some investment bankers to see if anyone was interested in shopping Shades of Light.

It had been five years since Harrison had last gone looking for someone to market the business for her. This time around, she was much more careful than she'd been in 2005. She and Dave interviewed five or six investment bankers and asked each to present a marketing plan. The process took four months. In the end they settled on two bankers, including one who said he had a potential buyer already. They agreed to let him serve as the intermediary for that buyer alone.

The selling process went on for another eight months or so, brought in a number of potential acquirers, and ultimately led to an offer that took all of them by surprise. They had already received a letter of in-tent (LOI) from one possible buyer, which Harrison was reluctant to accept because the deal would cost employees their jobs. Shortly there-after, Kimball got a phone call from Dave Harrison. He said, "Hey, Steve, you're not going to believe this, but we just got an LOI from the banker. He wants to buy the business himself." The banker was Bryan Johnson, a senior vice president of the main investment banking firm the Harrisons were using. Kimball said, "Are you kidding me?" Harri-son said, "No, really." He then told Kimball what was in the LOI. They agreed that the offer was better than any other they'd received.

It turned out that Johnson and another member of the firm, Chris Menasco, had been talking about acquiring a small business with the potential to grow and were thus on the lookout for the right oppor-tunity. These were not naïve buyers. They had both been involved in dozens of deals. They saw in Shades of Light a company that was finan-cially solid and could serve as a platform on which they could build something considerably larger. They also recognized what they might be missing: knowledge of the products, relationships with manufacturers, and a gift for designing new products that customers liked. Those were things that Ashton Harrison could bring to the party, and the would-be owners expressed interest in having her stay on after the sale as a consultant. She was amenable, even though it would mean putting off forty-nine of her fifty things. (She wrote the book anyway.)

The deal was not without risk for Harrison. A portion of the sale proceeds would come in the form of an earnout—that is, a percentage of revenues, paid over time—and the acquirers had no experience in running a business like Shades of Light. If the company got in trouble, Harrison might not get paid. So the two sides structured a purchase-and-sale agreement that would give her a substantial initial payment, a percentage of annual sales for four years (the earnout), and a royalty on her designs, based on how well the products sold. She would also be paid a salary. The deal provided her with enough up-front money to weather the worst-case scenario, should it come to pass. The terms also gave her plenty of incentive to stay involved after the sale.

At the end of July 2011, the papers were signed, and the ownership of Shades of Light officially changed hands. Of course, no sale is complete until the final payment is made—in Harrison's case, sometime in 2015. That's seven years after she began getting the company in shape to sell and ten years after she first decided it was time to get serious about doing a deal. Even then, she would not be through with her exit until she'd completed her transition to whatever would come next. Could she have exited faster? Sure, but probably not with a result nearly as agreeable as the one she wound up with.

How Long, Baby, How Long

On the question of time, let's begin with a general rule: The earlier you start preparing for an exit, the more likely it is that you'll have a happy one. The reason is fairly obvious. In developing the qualities that a buyer looks for in a potential acquisition—which are the same qualities that business owners should want to have in their companies—time is a critical factor. As we noted in chapter 3, you need, at the minimum, enough time to

- design and prove a business model,
- demonstrate its growth potential, and
- do whatever you can to reduce the risk to the buyer.

That's essentially what Ashton Harrison did in the three years from the start of her company's turnaround to the signing of the sale documents.

If you have greater ambitions for your business than she had for hers, you're probably going to need more time—maybe a lot more time. Among those greater ambitions, I would include selling to a private equity firm, going public, or building an enduring employee- or family-owned company capable of continuing and improving upon what you have begun. With any of those options, you will (in most cases) need time to

- form a strong management team,
- develop potential successors,
- foster a high-performance culture that enhances the productivity of employees, and
- implement the financial systems, disciplines, and best practices that give both lenders and investors confidence in the company's ability to make good use of any cash it receives and deliver the desired return.

Then, too, time is needed to grow a business to a size at which some options—notably, going public or raising private equity—become realistic. (Again, with the exception of certain tech businesses.) The general rule of thumb is that you should have EBITDA of about $25 million or more before considering an initial public offering. The economics simply don't make sense for businesses smaller than that. And as noted earlier, private equity groups generally don't invest in companies that can serve a platform for building a larger business unless its has at least $5 million in EBITDA—the amount of annual cash flow required to secure an HLT (highly leveraged transaction), which is the lifeblood of a typical private equity deal. On the other hand, private equity firms do buy smaller companies as so-called "accretive bolt-on acquisitions" to build the platform companies already in their portfolios.

Size will also affect your ability to get the attention of strategic buyers, as well as financial ones. "Buyers of businesses recognize that the time and energy invested in buying a small business is comparable to buying a larger one," notes Robert Tormey, the finance professional from chapter 3, who has participated in more than thirty such transactions, on both the buyer's and the seller's side. "Consequently, most institutional buyers, including PEGs, invest their energies trying to buy larger businesses."

Even if your business is already big enough to entertain a variety of exit options, it could still take years to get it in shape to be sold—unless, that is, you've been prudent enough to start preparing early in your journey. Again, Tormey: "Owners frequently underestimate the difficulty of selling a business and being able to exit while they are still young enough to enjoy the proceeds. Capital markets can be fickle. The search for a buyer may take one or two years. Market cycles can last five years or more, during which valuations may go up and down and the window of valuation may open and close quickly. After the sale, many buyers will expect a seller to remain active with the company for two or three years. Consequently, the exit process may be a five- or six-year affair from beginning to end." And bear in mind, he is referring here just to stage three of the exit process—the execution of the sale.

Tormey's point about "windows of valuation" is worth emphasizing. We've already seen examples of owners who were able to take advantage of such a window, though only because they had already spent years preparing for their exits. Ray Pagano, for one, might have had to wait a long time, or accept a much lower price, if he had not been able to sell his company, Videolarm, when he did. The deal closed on February 13, 2009, as the economy was tanking. According to CFO Janet Spaulding, who stayed with the company after the sale to Moog Inc., it almost didn't happen. "We made sure that we hit our targets in January," she said. "We could do it mainly because we were still filling orders that had been placed earlier. But in February there were almost no sales. Now that I've been with Moog for a few years and seen how decisions get made, I have no doubt that if the closing had happened a month later than it did, they would have called the deal off. Ray would never have gotten the price he got."

Norm Brodsky had a similar experience with his company, CitiStorage, in which he sold a majority to a so-called business development company (that is, a publicly traded private equity firm) in December 2007. He'd been working on a sale for more than two years and had already walked away from one deal because he'd lost trust in the would-be acquirer. But he'd kept on looking for a buyer because he realized that a window of valuation had opened wide. Records-storage companies like his were suddenly hot properties and private equity firms were beating down his door. The giant of records storage, Iron Mountain, had recently acquired one of his chief competitors at a multiple so high it had shocked everyone in the industry. Brodsky concluded that the market was either at or near its peak. If he didn't sell soon, it could be years, or even decades, before he'd have a similar opportunity. He was sixty-five years old, he reasoned, and he should strike while the iron was hot. It was a good thing he did. By the time the sale was consummated, the valuation window was almost closed.

As it turned out, Brodsky was even more fortunate than he'd realized to get the deal done when he did. CitiStorage handled records for a wide variety of businesses, but about 65 percent of its sales were with hospitals and other medical companies. Brodsky had focused on the medical field because all of his competitors were focusing on law offices and accounting firms. "We became experts in handling medical records," he said. "We knew the HIPAA [Health Insurance Portability and Accountability Act] privacy rules better than our prospects, and so we could teach them how to comply." As a result, CitiStorage had the medical market virtually to itself.

What he didn't anticipate was the speed of change from physical to electronic records. In the five years following the sale, this affected every market segment, but nowhere faster than in the medical field. For example, CitiStorage had been storing in its warehouses tens of thousands of boxes filled with X-rays on celluloid film. By 2012, celluloid X-rays scarcely existed anymore. Almost all medical images were digital and stored accordingly.

"I'd always figured that digital technology would eventually disrupt the box business, but I never imagined the change would come so soon and happen so rapidly," Brodsky said, looking back in 2013. "I see now that if I hadn't sold in 2007, technology would have destroyed a lot of the equity value I'd spent seventeen years building. Instead of starting new businesses now, I'd be working night and day to reinvent the old one." He was able to avoid that fate for one and only one reason: From the beginning, he had built the company with an eye toward selling it.

Circumstances beyond your control inevitably play a role in determining the best time for a sale. If you're planning to sell to a third party and you want to sell at the best time, you need to be prepared. "A deal happens when all the factors around it come together—current market conditions for money, current market conditions for your product, the buyer's and the seller's stages of development, and so on," said Barry Carlson, who, as I mentioned in chapter 1, sold his company, Parasun Technologies, a high-speed Internet service provider, in May 2007 for almost $15 million. "The timing has nothing to do with whether you want to do it then or not. It's just the right time to sell. You sell when the selling is good, not when you think you'd like to. Doing anything else, you run the risk of leaving a whole bunch of money on the table."

To put it another way, you're virtually assured of leaving a bunch of money on the table if you haven't put in the time required to prepare your company to sell. Exactly how much time that is varies from one company and one situation to another, but in most instances we're talking years.

Early Exits

There's a case to be made, however, that the time required is shrinking, and the most passionate—and persuasive—champion of that view is Canadian entrepreneur turned angel investor Basil Peters, whose ideas about sellability we discussed in chapter 3. He has written a fascinating book called *Early Exits*, which spells out how and why he believes the process of building and selling companies has changed since the turn of the century.

"The Internet has accelerated everything," he said. "It allows entrepreneurs to market and sell to hundreds of millions of prospects in just days, and it has accelerated almost every other aspect of the business life cycle as well. Entrepreneurs now have 'weekenders' where they build entire companies in a weekend." Well, maybe. It depends on what you consider an entire company. Peters pointed to a team of entrepreneurs in London who, on a lark, built a business in twenty-four hours and then sold it on eBay in ten days. (You can watch them doing it in a video at www.24hour-startup.com.) That business never had an employee, however, and disappeared almost as quickly as it was born.

Peters contends that this trend of early exits is widespread and being driven in part by fundamental changes in the way large companies handle their research and development. Many, he said, have concluded that while they aren't very good at innovating, they have the resources needed to take an existing product or service and scale it rapidly. Small companies, on the other hand, are good at innovating but have a tough time scaling. Accordingly, large companies have cut back on doing their own research and development and instead buy start-ups that have come up with the innovations they need. In effect, the giants outsource their R&D to these small companies.

Jeff Johnson is one entrepreneur who took advantage of such an opportunity to sell a young company, although that wasn't his intention starting out. A veteran of several large enterprises, he initially viewed Arcemus, the company that he and his partners launched in April 2001, as a potential lifestyle business. But he had spent most of his adult life to that point—he was thirty-five—consciously preparing himself to be CEO of his own business, and well-managed companies, he knew, are built with the attributes smart buyers look for in a potential acquisition, whether or not selling is part of the plan.

The idea for the start-up grew out of the experiences of Johnson and his partners at Network Solutions, a pioneer in the business of registering Internet domain names. The explosion of Internet use posed major problems for the legal departments of large companies. No matter how well they protected their employers' intellectual property in the physical world, they did not have the means to do the same in cyberspace. Johnson and his partners saw this vulnerability as a business opportunity. They created a variety of systems that allowed a client company to identify infringements of its intellectual property and to register and manage its portfolio of domain names, thereby preventing infringers from taking advantage of misspellings, word similarities, and other loopholes in a company's defenses. In return, the client paid Arcemus a recurring monthly fee.

As ingenious as the systems were, Johnson and his team had a tough time selling them at first. "Here we were, this new company, offering an innovative solution to the problem, trying to sign up these giant enterprises like Johnson & Johnson, New York Life, and BMW," Johnson said. "How do we prove that we're competent and can deliver what we promise? And how do they know we're going to be around five years from now? The first ten customers were incredibly hard to get. But by the end of the first year, we had gone well past the first ten customers and were into the second ten, and then the third ten."

At the same time, Johnson was becoming increasingly aware of opportunities for expansion—and frustrated that he didn't have the capital to take advantage of them. He and his team had financed their start-up the old-fashioned way—by bootstrapping. Subsequently, they'd raised about $100,000 from individuals. That had helped, but it wasn't nearly enough to make the big leap Johnson had in mind. "We thought we could do a kind of slingshot around the corner and leave everybody else behind," Johnson said. "But we needed more capital to do it."

The problem was that Arcemus was a dot-com, and in 2003 many investors hadn't yet recovered from the dot-com bust. After failing to raise the capital on acceptable terms from banks, venture capitalists, private equity groups, and angels, he concluded that a new approach was needed. "I said, 'Let's think about this differently. What business are we in?' I decided we weren't really in the domain name management business, or even in the intellectual property protection business. Our business was managing certain types of records and information for large organizations. So I said, 'Let's find out who the players are in records and information management.' The folks on the team looked at me like I had three heads." But Johnson was serious, and it didn't take him long to identify the leader in records management: Iron Mountain. A little research confirmed that it would be an ideal partner for Arcemus.

Johnson wasn't sure exactly what he was looking for, but he figured it was worth making inquiries. So he picked up a telephone and called

Iron Mountain's main number. When that didn't get him anywhere, he began reading proxy statements, eventually coming up with a name, which led to another name, which led to a senior executive named Ken Rubin. "I called him and introduced myself," Johnson recalled, "and he said, 'Jeff, I get thirty of these calls a week. You've got two minutes to tell me what you want to tell me, and then I'll let you know whether I'm interested in continuing the dialogue.' I said, 'That's fantastic. I only need one.' I explained as succinctly as possible what we did and why I thought we should be of strategic interest to Iron Mountain. He said, 'Keep talking.'"

And they did. The conversations went on for more than six months, both at the Boston headquarters of Iron Mountain and at Arcemus's facility in Sterling, Virginia, as well as by phone. Among other things, Johnson learned that Iron Mountain was already dabbling in the intellectual property arena, although the top executives weren't really sure what to do with the various capabilities and service offerings that the company had acquired. Johnson and his partners had plenty of ideas, and it soon became evident that the best way to take advantage of them was for Iron Mountain to buy Arcemus's assets and integrate the Arcemus team into its operations.

And so Johnson and his partners had an early exit as owners of Arcemus, which was rechristened Iron Mountain Intellectual Property Management. Johnson became a senior vice president of Iron Mountain and general manager of that business unit. The sale closed in early May 2004—barely three years after the company's founding and less than two years after the introduction of its first products.

Build to Flip or Build to Last?

Johnson had a compelling reason for selling his company so early into his journey, but should other entrepreneurs follow his example? Basil

Peters thinks that they would if they had a better understanding of the process. "I believe exits are the best part of being an entrepreneur or investor," he said. "It's when we get paid for all of our hard work and risk capital. Selling a business is usually the biggest financial transaction of a person's career. It's exciting and will certainly change your life. But people don't understand it—for the simple reason that it doesn't happen very often."

Peters's view is not without critics. Some people have accused him of promoting the gold rush mentality that took hold of Silicon Valley during the dot-com bubble of the late 1990s. "Built to flip" is the term that *Good to Great* author Jim Collins used to describe it in a famous essay he wrote for *Fast Company* magazine in March 2000. "An intriguing idea: No need to build a company, much less one with enduring value. Today, it's enough to pull together a good story, to implement the rough draft of an idea, and—presto!—instant wealth." Collins found it all quite appalling.

Peters has pushed back against the criticism, contending that the companies Collins wrote about with Jerry Porras in their classic *Built to Last*—such as Disney and Walmart—"are not the type of companies that can be started, thrive and prosper in the 21st century. It's just not possible to take decades to build a company anymore. . . . 'Built to flip' is not a dirty phase or unnatural act. To succeed today, I believe entrepreneurs must not only aspire to early exits, but design them into their corporate structures and corporate DNA."

That argument seems questionable at best. Plenty of entrepreneurs are still striving to build great companies both on and off the Internet, and they're still taking decades to do it. Look at Jeff Bezos of Amazon, or Larry Page and Sergey Brin of Google, or Fred Smith of Federal Express, or John Mackey of Whole Foods, to name just five. Nevertheless, I agree with Peters that there's nothing inherently wrong with planning for an early exit. Neither does Collins. His objection was to the pervasive climate of greed in Silicon Valley during the late 1990s. He acknowledged in his essay that "building to last is not for everyone or for every company—nor should it be."

It's also true, however, that Peters's examples are almost all Internet-based companies, which live in an alternate reality from the one occupied by the vast majority of private businesses. Yes, the fundamental rules of business still apply. Internet companies need positive cash flow as much as any other class of enterprise. But because they do business in cyberspace, online start-ups have the potential to reach a global market—that is, to grow—at a rate unimaginable outside the realm of the World Wide Web, and that potential changes the calculus when it comes to selling.

But that hardly means that every Web-based entrepreneur should work toward an early exit. Entrepreneur turned venture capitalist Peter Thiel tells a story about what he considers the most significant moment in the history of Facebook, in which he was the first outside investor. In July 2006, when Facebook was two years old and doing about $30 million in sales, Yahoo offered to buy the business for $1 billion. Soon afterward, Facebook's board—Thiel, twenty-two-year-old founder Mark Zuckerberg, and venture capitalist Jim Breyer—convened to discuss the offer. "Both Breyer and myself on balance thought we probably should take the money," recalled Thiel at the 2013 SXSW conference, as reported by *Inc.* magazine's Allison Fass. "But Zuckerberg started the meeting like, 'This is kind of a formality, just a quick board meeting, it shouldn't take more than ten minutes. We're obviously not going to sell here.'" Taken aback, Thiel suggested they should at least talk about it. A billion dollars was a lot of money, he noted, and Zuckerberg owned 25 percent of the stock. "I don't know what I could do with the money," Zuckerberg responded. "I'd just start another social networking site. I kind of like the one I already have."

When Thiel and Breyer pressed him, Zuckerberg allowed that he also thought the offer was too low. Yahoo had no vision of Facebook's future, he said, and therefore could not properly value something that did not yet exist. Thiel wasn't completely convinced but went along with the founder's decision, consoling himself in the knowledge that Yahoo had previously had two other billion-dollar offers turned down—to eBay and Google. Given that Zuckerberg, too, turned out to have made the right call, Thiel drew a lesson from the episode: "All of us have to work toward a definite future . . . that can motivate and inspire people to change the world. . . . The most successful businesses have an idea for the future that's very different from the present, and that's not fully valued."

Of course, only a tiny percentage of new businesses are destined to become the next Facebook, eBay, or Google, but Thiel's insight applies to any company that strives for greatness. By that, I mean a company that is committed to having a "distinctive impact on the world," as Jim Collins puts it. He uses a test to define distinctive impact: "If your company disappeared, would it leave a gaping hole that could not easily be filled by any other enterprise on the planet?"

Building such a business is necessarily a long-term undertaking. Collins, in fact, argues that to be considered truly great, a business must maintain superior performance and continue to have a distinctive impact through more than one generation of ownership and leadership. Its greatness, in other words, can't be dependent on any single person. Note that size does not enter the equation. A business of almost any size can have superior performance (in relation to its industry) and a distinctive impact. The much bigger challenge for private companies is to keep doing it for multiple generations. It's exceedingly rare for a company to pull that off. Only after the second transfer of ownership and leadership do you really know whether a company has discovered some sort of system or methodology that allows it to continue wearing its mantle of greatness independently of any individual leader or owner.

The handful of private companies I've found that have passed that test are all either family-owned or employee-owned. Granted, I did not look at every private employer in the United States. There are more than seven million, and no one keeps track of information that would allow us to identify those with an enduring high-performance culture. But I did search far and wide for examples using the resources available to me, and the only companies I found had one of those two ownership structures. That is to say, the founders of these companies had chosen to sell (or give) their stock either to their employees or to members of their families, and thereafter the stock had stayed inside the business, passing from one generation of owners to another.

My theory is that for a culture and modus operandi to last, they need guardians. In family businesses, the guardians are the family members and in employee-owned businesses, the employee-owners. Without one or the other, each successive buyer brings his or her own style of leadership and management. The odds of building an enduring, great company that way are slim. To be sure, the odds aren't that much better if the company is family- or employee-owned. After all, countless family businesses are utterly dysfunctional, and numerous employee-owned companies have gone downhill after the founder departed. Developing a durable high-performance culture takes many, many years. If the founder or principal owner doesn't start focusing on it early in his or her journey, there's little chance that the company will ever enjoy the benefits of having one.

In Search of Durability

So how *do* you create a high-performance culture capable of outlasting any single owner, leader, management team, technology, or product mix? No entrepreneur I know has thought longer about that question or delved deeper into it than Jack Stack, the cofounder and CEO of SRC Holdings Corp., based in Springfield, Missouri. His search for answers began in the mid-1980s, when he first realized that he and his partners had overlooked a crucial issue in deciding to set up an employee stock ownership plan for all of their "associates," as Stack calls them.

Back then, the business was known as Springfield ReManufacturing Corp. It was a spin-off of International Harvester, an eighty-year-old equipment manufacturer that had gone from the twenty-eighth spot on the Fortune 500 in 1979 to the brink of bankruptcy in 1982. Its factory in Springfield employed about 230 people, all engaged in the remanufacturing of replacement parts for Harvester's construction equipment. As the company closed down plants and sold assets around the world in a desperate attempt to cut expenditures and raise cash, Stack and twelve other managers, scared to lose their jobs in the middle of a recession, had submitted a bid to buy the Springfield facility. In early 1983, Harvester unexpectedly accepted it, whereupon Stack and his colleagues hastily put together one of the worst leveraged buyouts in history. At one point in its first year, SRC had an 89-to-1 debt-to-equity ratio, which was like buying an $8.9 million house with just $100,000 down. Banks normally consider a ratio above 2.5-to-1 to be extremely risky for an engine manufacturer.

Yet SRC survived and by 1985 was profitable and growing. Its debt-to-equity ratio had been brought down to a more reasonable (but still uncomfortably high) 5.1-to-1. The recovering economy had certainly helped, but what had saved the company in its darkest hour was Stack's radical idea about how to manage a business: Share financial information with people throughout the company, teach them what it means and how to use it, and make them equity partners. At SRC they called it "The Great Game of Business." It revolved around a bonus program, structured as a game that all the employees played over the course of a year with the goal of improving certain "critical numbers."

In the fall of 1985, Stack brought the employees together for one of the company's periodic meetings to talk about how the business was doing and the challenges that lay ahead. Part of the meeting inevitably focused on SRC's stock value, which had already risen from 10 cents at the launch to $8.46. As a result, a typical stake in the company's ESOP was worth about $23,000, which was enough to capture everyone's attention. People were suddenly curious to understand exactly how the ESOP worked, what it would take to increase the share price, when they would receive their money, and how much each stake might be worth then.

In answering their questions, Stack spent some time explaining the fundamentals of cash flow. He mentioned that a portion of the company's cash was tied up in inventory, such as connecting rods and engine cores. When he finished, an hourly employee raised his hand. He said he understood that most of the cash SRC generated was being reinvested in the company. He wasn't clear, however, what would happen when people retired. He noted that a lot of them were about the same age and might be retiring at the same time. Where was the money going to come from to cash them out of the ESOP? "Okay, so we've got a lot of cash tied up in connecting rods," he said. "We can't eat connecting rods."

Stack was speechless. It was a great question, and he'd never even thought about it. He had no idea how to answer. For that matter, he had no idea how big the problem was, or might become. He had started the ESOP because, he said, "giving ownership to the people who do the work has always seemed like the simplest way to run a business. It frees you to concentrate on productivity." Until that moment, however, he hadn't given any thought to paying his associates what they would be owed when they eventually left.

The future debt was a so-called contingent liability, and Stack, who was thirty-five years old at the time, realized he would have to stick around until he figured out how to deal with it. Earlier that year, in a poll of the thirteen original partners, he had responded that he intended to leave in about five years or so. He'd had no idea how he might do that; he'd just supposed he'd figure it out. Now, however, he could see that leaving might take a bit longer. For whatever reason—he blamed his Irish Catholic upbringing—he knew he wouldn't be able to live with himself if he cashed out and then watched the company fail due to decisions made while he was CEO.

Had he been as sophisticated about business back then as he later became, he would have understood just how monumental a task he had cut out for himself and how long it would take to finish what he'd started. His time line for exiting kept lengthening as he worked with his colleagues to develop routines, disciplines, and systems that he thought would someday allow him to leave "with a clean conscience," as he put it. Along the way, they hit on a plan that turned out to be a crucial part of the answer to the employee's question.

The solution actually began with an altogether different problem. In the course of remanufacturing diesel engines for its customers, SRC often had to replace a part known as an oil cooler. Stack figured that if the company learned how to remanufacture oil coolers, it could save about $215,000 a year. As an experiment, he and three other senior managers started a company outside SRC to do just that. They recruited someone from outside SRC to be the entrepreneur, and then the five of them invested $1,000 of their own money and borrowed $50,000 from SRC—thus creating their own highly leveraged transaction.

The experiment was a smashing success. Within a year, the new business, called Engines Plus, was completely filling SRC's need for oil coolers at a fraction of what the company had previously been paying. By the end of the second year, the value of Engine Plus's stock had increased more than 6,000 percent over what they'd paid for it. Stack and the other managers realized that, for ethical reasons, they had to sell their 75 percent share to SRC immediately, while the stock was still a bargain.

Aside from reducing oil cooler costs and demonstrating the power of leverage, Engines Plus suggested a way to grow SRC that would also provide a potential solution to the contingent liability problem. The parent company could continue to create these spin-off businesses, some of which could later be sold to raise the capital needed to cash out ESOP members who would be leaving in the future. Thus began the transformation of SRC into SRC Holdings Corp.

The company's track record since then bears witness to the effectiveness of both the strategy and the management methods they came up with. After losing $60,000 on sales of $16 million in 1983, SRC has been profitable every year thereafter—an unbroken string of thirty-one consecutive years as of this writing. Annual revenues during that time have grown to $528 million and net after-tax profits to $22 million, while the size of the workforce increased from 119 to 1202 employees. Along the way, the company has given birth to more than 65 other businesses. Some of the businesses it has sold; some it shut down; and some have become part of SRC Holdings. Most of the latter are led by general managers who've grown up in the SRC system. The value of the company's stock, meanwhile, has exploded. An investment of $10,000 at the founding would have been worth $39.7 million by January 2014.

Through it all, Stack's thinking about his exit continued to evolve. He would be content, he decided, if he could leave the next generation of employees with a company and a culture they could keep going for at least ten years if they chose to. "I believe a culture can survive if it has structure, but it has to be a hard structure, not a soft one," he said. "I don't think a soft, feel-good type of culture—one that's built around just having a warm and fuzzy atmosphere for employees—can survive the loss of the person who created it and protected it. There have to be disciplines, and you need courage. It takes guts to look at a balance sheet and an income statement, identify the weaknesses, and then do what you must do to be secure. And you can never stop doing it. You have to constantly work on security. The more you teach people that pattern of thinking, the better chance there is that the culture will be sustained. The disciplines you've created will keep it alive."

SRC's culture has evolved accordingly. At its heart is the Great

Game of Business, the company's version of open-book management. The Game begins every September with a forecasting process that gets the entire workforce involved in producing what is not so much an annual budget as a business plan, with a complete set of financial projections, broken down month by month. That plan serves as a kind of road map for the year ahead. By comparing the projected numbers to the actual numbers, the managers and employees can monitor their progress toward their quarterly and annual goals. They do the monitoring every week, identifying the deviations from the plan and then figuring out what to do about them.*

By 2010, Stack was convinced that the culture he and his colleagues had created was in fact sustainable. SRC had a rising generation of leaders who had grown up in the company. Many had joined out of college or high school. They all had been playing the Great Game of Business for so long that it had become second nature to them. Stack had no doubt they knew how to keep the culture strong. "I think it's automatic," he said. "They'll use our system because it makes sense, because they've had a part in developing it, and they will carry it on."

That left the question of how ownership would be transferred. Over the years, SRC had cashed out twelve of the original thirteen partners, one by one, paying them more than $50 million under the terms of their original shareholders' agreement. Stack had sold some of his stock along the way but still owned 15 percent of the company. Other individual shareholders accounted for 22 percent, with the remaining 63 percent owned by the ESOP. (An ESOP counts as one shareholder. Employees are members of the ESOP, rather than direct shareholders in the company.) After much deliberation—and over the dissent of some board members who thought the shareholders would earn a better return by selling to a third party—the decision was made to have the ESOP buy out the 37 percent of the stock it didn't already own.

---

* You can learn more about SRC's culture and systems in the two books Stack and I wrote together, *The Great Game of Business* and *A Stake in the Outcome*.

Because SRC Holdings had been reorganized as an S corporation, all of the company's profits would thereafter pass through to the ESOP as the sole shareholder. Taxes on those profits would thus be deferred until individual members cashed out. The result would be an immediate boost to the company's cash flow.

The sale to the ESOP closed on August 5, 2011. To finance the deal, SRC took on an additional $11 million in debt, to be paid off in ten years.

We won't know for another couple of generations, of course, exactly how successful Stack and his colleagues have been in building an enduring great company. What we do know is that he has needed the better part of three decades to lay the groundwork for one. The company today has all the qualities that even the most demanding of private equity buyers would look for: a proven business model, an enormous growth potential, a tested management team, four or five strong internal candidates to succeed Stack, an extraordinarily productive workforce, a deeply embedded culture of accountability, and all of the financial systems and best practices that any investor could hope for. That's no accident. Stack has long made a point of learning, and having his associates learn, how to view the business from the perspective of an outside investor.

I'm sure other companies have found other paths to durability. While some of those paths may not be quite as long as Stack's, I doubt that there are any significant shortcuts. Enduring greatness is not only rare in business, as Jim Collins has repeatedly demonstrated in his four books exploring the subject, but also extremely difficult to achieve, demanding as it does an unflagging discipline over long periods of time. Building a great, enduring business is not for everyone, and perhaps not for you. If it is, however, the lesson is clear: Start early.

Then again, you'd be wise to start early even if you don't intend to build a great, enduring business. Every exit is affected by the time allotted to plan for it. There are no guarantees of a happy ending, but you're far more likely to have one if you give yourself plenty of time.

5

Après Moi

> **In choosing a successor, leave enough time to be wrong.**

According to Roxanne Byrde,* the phone call she received in the fall of 2007 came at just the right time. She had recently turned sixty-five, and the subject of succession was very much on her mind. The caller was the son of a franchisee who had owned several of her company's franchises for forty years. Byrde had known the young man—we'll call him Harry—since he was seven years old and had watched him grow up to become president of his father's company. For the previous four years, he had also served on the company's franchisee advisory council, which met twice a year. At those meetings, Byrde had found him to be "an easygoing gentleman," which she liked because she was a rather easygoing gentlewoman herself. "He was a very, very nice young man and quiet, though not too quiet, but not outspoken," she said.

Consequently, she was receptive when Harry inquired whether she ever planned to sell her company. It had been founded by Byrde's

---

* The people and the company in this story have been disguised.

grandfather, and she had taken over after the death of her father, but neither her children nor those of her siblings had joined the business, which she considered a prerequisite for owning it. "I was extremely concerned about a big conglomerate coming in and buying it and laying off all the people who have made it what it is today," she said. "I wanted very much for the culture of the company to remain as close as it could be to what it is now. We have a very happy workforce, and I think that has been an important part of our success." With that in mind, she had previously talked to her lawyer about setting up an employee stock ownership plan (ESOP). He had discouraged her, saying that ESOPs were complicated and risky.

Harry's interest in buying the company seemed like an ideal solution, but Byrde wasn't willing to sell it to him outright. For one thing, she planned to work for at least another ten years, and she wanted to remain in charge while she did. Before ceding control, she had to be sure that she was ready and also that she had the right successor—that is, someone who would maintain the company's culture and values.

She was also aware that the right successor might not be able to afford to pay full value for the company. Harry certainly couldn't. With the help of her attorney, she came up with a plan whereby Harry would pay $1.5 million and receive five percent of the stock. In the following years, the company would gradually buy and retire the stock owned by Byrde, paying whatever the contemporaneous valuation was at the time of the sale. As the total number of shares outstanding declined, Harry's percentage of the ownership would automatically increase. Although it might take him a decade or more to become the sole owner, he would be buying a company worth at least $50 million for $1.5 million.

It was obviously a great deal for Harry, and it would achieve all of Byrde's goals, particularly with regard to succession. "I figured that I'd make him president after a couple of years, and two or three years later he would become CEO. Then a couple of years after that, I'd take off.

By the time I walked out the door, I'd barely be missed because he would be handling so much stuff."

Byrde was happy with the plan. She had so much confidence in it that she was skeptical of the need for the various conditions her lawyer wanted to include in the formal agreement, such as a clause giving her the authority to unilaterally terminate the deal within the first two years, at which point she could buy back Harry's stock at the price he'd paid for it. But the lawyer said it was just a normal, prudent precaution, and she went along.

In early 2008, Byrde announced the news to her employees. She told them that Harry was buying into the company and would eventually become its owner and president. "Everyone in the building was happy," she said. "The vice presidents had worked with him, and they were happy too. They all thought he was the perfect guy, and so did I."

Almost immediately, however, it became clear that Harry might not be as perfect as Byrde had thought. "He came on very strong with the employees," she said. "He'd say things like, 'I'm not here to be your friend. I'm here to get work done.' I had a number of discussions with him about not being rude to people. Of course, he didn't feel he was being rude. He thought he was just being up-front and telling people what he thought. I told him, 'That's fine, but you can't do that and just walk away, because you leave them in a heap. They don't even know if they have a job the next day. You have to give them a chance to respond, and then you have to listen.'"

Byrde considered the ability to listen a basic job requirement for managers. Ever since she'd become CEO, one of her top priorities had been to have a culture in which employees knew that management cared about them and listened to them. It wasn't one of Harry's priorities, however. He seemed more interested in his expense account. "The first time he tried to charge a dinner with his wife to the company, I was shocked, and I stopped it," Byrde said. "I'm very, very strict about how we spend the company's money. I do not take my family out for dinners on the company's dime. He told the other vice presidents that when he became owner, that policy was one of the first things he was going to change."

Meanwhile, the incidents with employees grew more frequent. "He turned into a completely different person than I knew before," Byrde said. "He'd say out in the office, to anybody who was around, 'There's too many people here, and we're losing money because of it. We need to cut this workforce.' Naturally, then the employees would all get nervous. It got to the point where I was bringing him in once a week and saying, 'You cannot do this.' He would come back with, 'I've been outspoken all my life, and it's gotten me this far, so I don't think I'm going to change.'"

For a long time, Byrde clung to the hope that Harry would eventually mend his ways, but the problems persisted. She tried talking to him. She tried writing him letters. After a year and a half with no visible change in his behavior, she decided she had to try something different. She called Harry into her office and told him he had six months to shape up. If they were having the same problems then that she had already brought to his attention at least fifty times, she would have to reconsider their whole arrangement.

Harry seemed to get the message, but Byrde was concerned that he might simply "go underground," as she put it, and hide his true feelings from her while modifying his behavior just enough to make her think he had changed. In any case, she felt that she needed an independent, objective assessment of the situation. A board member gave her the name of a family business consulting company. She hired one of its senior associates to advise her. The consultant proceeded to conduct extensive interviews with Byrde, Harry, and the other vice presidents and concluded that it was still possible to salvage the relationship.

With Christmas approaching, the consultant suggested that Harry and Byrde take a month to think about the changes they'd like to see. When they got back together in early 2010, he said, they should each bring a list of what they expected from the other person. They would then come up with a plan to rectify the situation and move forward.

They never got to the rectify stage, however. Byrde was feeling more and more pressure to take action. She told the consultant, "I've heard from so many people about what he's done, and I believe what they tell me. If I don't do something, they'll think I'm not listening to them."

What tipped the balance were reports she began getting from the company's area managers about Harry's franchisee recruitment techniques. They said he was telling new franchisees that he was already running the company and so they need not worry about any details they didn't like in the franchise agreement. They should just sign it as written, because he understood what they wanted and, as the owner, would make sure they got it later on.

The stories convinced Byrde that no matter what he said, Harry was not going to change. He had learned a mode of doing business typical of a certain type of small business—the kind that always remains small. His methods had worked for him in the past, and he wasn't open to learning why they would inevitably lead to disaster in a company as large as hers. More to the point, he didn't seem to care that some of those methods were clearly unethical. Her biggest fear was that after gaining control of the business he would crank up its profitability by laying off a lot of people and sell it to the highest bidder, reaping a $60 million or $70 million reward for his $1.5 million investment.

Byrde resolved that Harry had to go. She contacted the consultant and let him know her decision. He didn't give her an argument. When the three of them reconvened on January 4, 2010, she told Harry that she'd decided their initial plan wouldn't work and she would be moving on without him. As per their contract, the company would buy back his stock at the price he'd paid for it. He would also get three months— later increased to six months—of severance pay.

Inside the company, the news of Harry's departure was greeted with general relief, although some of the franchisees he'd recruited were confused and upset. Byrde sent representatives to visit them and as-suage any concerns they had. As for Byrde herself, she felt as though a hundred-pound weight had been lifted from her shoulders. "I was get-ting to the point that I was not wanting to come into work," she said. But she didn't have long to enjoy her newfound relief before realizing that she was right back where she had started—with no successor and no exit plan.

The Wrong Guy

There is a tendency in some quarters to equate exit planning with suc-cession planning, and I suppose the two are more or less synonymous for public companies. That's because ownership is separated from man-agement when a company goes public. Thereafter, public market inves-tors decide when to buy and sell its stock, and a change in the company's leadership may or may not factor into their decisions. Hence the major question—and often the only question—that needs to be addressed when the CEO of a public company exits is, who will be the next CEO?

Private companies are a different story. Whether or not a successor is even necessary depends largely on the type of exit you have in mind. If, like Roxanne Byrde, you want your business to remain independent, keep its culture, and continue to thrive after you leave, developing a successor is clearly crucial. On the other hand, if you're planning to sell to a strategic buyer, as Ray Pagano did, you may not need to have a successor in place. The acquirer often prefers to install one of its own managers at the helm.

But what if you don't know the type of buyer you will someday sell your company to? What if you just want to make sure that you'll have the widest variety of options when it comes time to move on—including the option to pursue other interests while continuing to own the company?

Unless you're on the "early exit" path championed by Basil Peters,

you'd be wise to start thinking about succession and developing potential successors as soon as possible. Let's leave aside the obvious reason
that without a successor you will put everyone you care about at risk
should you be laid low. From an exit standpoint, there are numerous
buyers who might like to acquire your company but only as long as they
don't have to run it. If you have solved the succession puzzle—that is, if
your business can operate perfectly well without you—you will thus
have more suitors and be in a better bargaining position when you
eventually go to sell your business.

Having the right person is essential, if only because the wrong
person can cause enormous harm, no matter how well the business has
been run in the past. Hence the importance of making sure that when
you anoint a successor, you're in a position to discover your mistake (if
you've made one) and limit the damage, as Roxanne Byrde did. Owners
get into trouble when they postpone the search for a successor until just
before they're ready to leave. They then bring in someone with good
credentials from outside the company and immediately move on without fully appreciating the risk they're taking. By the time they realize
their mistake, the damage has already been done.

Consider Jim O'Neal, the founder of O&S Trucking and the former
mayor of Springfield, Missouri. He had started out as a freight broker in
1981, when he was twenty-seven years old, but two years later teamed
up with Keith Stever (the "S" in O&S) to launch the trucking company. Even then, O'Neal was drawn to politics. In 1987 he ran for and
won a seat on the Springfield city council, which did not please his
partner, who made an offer to buy him out. O'Neal was able to scare up
enough money in thirty days to match the offer. Under the terms of
their buy-sell agreement, that meant he was awarded the company.
Stever immediately started his own trucking company, Stever Trucking, which he later sold and which O'Neal acquired from the new
owner in 2004. "So we got our 'S' back," he said.

In the meantime, he had built O&S into a profitable, growing business renowned for its culture and repeatedly honored with national awards for everything from safety to innovation. A committed practitioner of open-book management, he had set up an ESOP in 2000 and sold it 40 percent of his equity in 2003. By 2006, O&S was doing $68 million in sales with pretax profits of $1.8 million, which was excellent for the notoriously thin-margin industry.

To all outward appearances, the company was in great shape, but O'Neal had a nagging sense that problems lay ahead. "I'd been to a seminar, and I heard this question that kept rolling around in my mind: 'Is your business model going to be relevant three years from now?'" He also had concerns about how well his management team was functioning. To make matters worse, he began to detect signs of a slowing economy in late 2006—a full year before the official start of the recession. Trucking, he noted, tends to pick up changes in the level of economic activity before other industries.

Right about this time, O'Neal was preparing to assume the chairmanship of the Truckload Carriers Association (TCA), a sixty-eight-year-old organization with about a thousand members nationwide. It was a big job that he had spent four years preparing for as a member of TCA's officer corps. His election would happen at the national convention in March 2007, and his TCA duties would demand much of his time and attention for the following year. He had shared his concerns about O&S with his insurance broker, who had advised him to get an independent analysis of the situation. The broker had mentioned a consultant—we'll call him Vince—in whom he had great confidence. O'Neal had contacted Vince and arranged to meet him at the TCA convention in Las Vegas. The two talked there, and O'Neal hired Vince to do an assessment, make recommendations, come up with a plan, and suggest how it should be implemented.

O'Neal admits that he was thinking not only about changes he might need to make in the company but also about changes he might want to make in his own life. He'd been in business twenty-six years and was feeling a little burned out. He also had an itch to do other things—politics, travel, industry association work. He wasn't quite ready to sell the business and didn't think the timing was right in any case. But he figured that if he could "get the company managed correctly," as he put it, he'd have time to take on other pursuits and simultaneously make O&S more attractive to a buyer.

Vince finished his report in July 2007. It confirmed some of O'Neal's previous concerns and raised some new ones. His management team was as dysfunctional as he'd suspected. The rumor mill was running overtime. The business model did need to change to stay relevant. So did O&S's forecasting capabilities. For all the data that the company churned out, it was seriously lacking in the timely information needed to guide operations on a daily and weekly basis.

Overall, O'Neal thought Vince had done a good job. "His write-up was accurate and helpful," he said, looking back six years later. "I should have stopped right there. I should have thanked him and paid him and brought our core group together to go through it and deal with it."

Instead he made Vince CEO.

At that point, frankly, O'Neal had little choice. His chairmanship of the TCA was taking up even more of his time than he'd anticipated, and he desperately needed someone to mind the store. Vince was the only plausible candidate because O'Neal had never developed any potential successors internally. While O'Neal had known him just a few months and had never worked with him, Vince had run other businesses, including a short stint as CEO of another trucking company, and clearly understood O&S's problems.

For the next three years, Vince ran O&S while O'Neal pursued a new career. In December 2008, he announced his candidacy for mayor of Springfield and thereafter was consumed by the mayoral campaign through the election in April, which he won. He was then consumed by the demands of the office. When I visited him in October 2009, he was no longer involved in day-to-day operations. "I try to be here when

I can," he said, "I look at long-term strategy, but I don't know what's going on inside." Not that he minded. "This is what I wanted. I follow the action using the technology."

As for selling the company, "I'm in no hurry," he said. "I make good money and have a nice life. There's no compelling reason to change." He planned to run for another two-year term as mayor and remain active in the trucking industry. The largest industry group was the American Trucking Associations (ATA), and O'Neal aspired to become its chairman, which brought with it influence in Washington, D.C., and travel both in the United States and abroad. He thus had a great deal riding on his CEO. He expressed confidence to me that Vince could handle the responsibility.

I didn't know whether O'Neal was delusional, dangerously uninformed, or simply overoptimistic when I paid my visit in 2009, but it's clear in retrospect that O&S was already in trouble back then. Sales had dropped from the 2006 high of $68 million to $62 million in 2009, while the pretax profit of $1.8 million had turned into a loss of $300,000. In 2010, sales declined another $6 million to $56 million, and the company lost an additional $865,000. Its main problem, however, was cash flow, which grew so tight that O&S had to ask its lenders for forbearance while it tried to fix its problems.

Those problems piled up, one on top of the other. A change in the payment policies of the company's three largest customers in 2009 had cost O&S $900,000 in annual cash flow. The resulting cash crunch had forced O&S to start paying drivers the way the company was being paid by shippers. Driver turnover more than doubled in response. The result was that in the first quarter of 2010 the company found itself with sixty to eighty idle trucks at a time—about 20 to 25 percent of its fleet—from which it received no income but on which it had to continue making lease payments, creating another huge cash drain. Meanwhile, a rash of truck accidents two years in a row wound up costing O&S nearly $2 million due to the $300,000 deductible in its insurance policies. In the old days of sky-high driver morale, its safety record had warranted such a huge deductible. It should have been reduced, but wasn't.

Adding to all these problems was Vince's compensation. He had already cost the company more than $1 million, and O&S was in more trouble than ever. Toward the end of 2010, O'Neal told Vince he was resuming his duties as CEO. "The company can no longer afford both of us," O'Neal said. O&S continued to struggle for the next seventeen months, while O'Neal tried to balance his responsibilities as mayor, CEO, and father. In 2011, O&S recorded a loss of $2.1 million on sales of $45 million, and O'Neal had to ask creditors for forbearance once again. It wasn't enough. Although he was reelected as mayor in April 2011, he resigned halfway through his term, on May 7, 2012. Twenty-three days later O&S filed for protection from creditors under Chapter 11 of the U.S. Bankruptcy Code. In the filing, the company's assets were estimated to be less than $50,000 against liabilities of $10 million to $50 million.

Desperate for help, O'Neal turned to Prime Inc., a $1.2 billion national trucking company, also based in Springfield. "The building was on fire, and the only thing we could do was jump out of the window," said O'Neal. "When we did, the only person holding a net was [Prime's founder and president] Robert Low." Low offered him the opportunity to become part of a special program that allowed O&S to keep its corporate identity while becoming a contract carrier for Prime. In one fell swoop, the company got rid of most of its overhead and almost all of its trailers. From its high of about sixty employees, the office staff shrank to fourteen people. O'Neal considered it a great deal. "If we can put twenty to thirty more trucks and drivers on the road, we could put a million dollars a year in the bottom line," he said and then paused. "If only I'd done it two years earlier."

By then, O'Neal did not own his company anymore. He had sold all of his stock to his controller of twenty-seven years, Anita Christian, to protect O&S in case a creditor invoked one of the personal guarantees he'd had to sign, thereby forcing him to declare personal bankruptcy. If he hadn't sold, the stock would have been an asset the creditor could have gone after. The sale was permissible as long as he and Christian followed the rules on such transactions, meaning that she had to pay a fair market value for it and be under no obligation to sell the stock back to him in the future. "She can choose to sell it or keep it," O'Neal said. "I can offer to buy it back, but she doesn't have to take the offer. My number one priority at this point is the survival of the company and of everybody here, including me."

O'Neal remained president and CEO with a three-year employment contract set to end in 2017. "I have no idea what I'll do then," he said. Does he blame himself for what happened? "Yeah, it's hard not to. It just gnaws at me all the time." There are any number of mistakes he can point to. By far the largest, however, was the mistake of putting his company in the hands of a successor who turned out to lack the skills, the tools, and the experience needed to guide it through the worst economic downturn in more than seventy-five years. As CEO of a trucking company, Vince was "like a piano player in a marching band," O'Neal said. "He was definitely out of his depth."

But the fault, he realizes, doesn't lie with Vince. "I'm the guy who hired him, and I have to live with that. The fact is, I had a pretty nice company going, and I blew it, and I'm never going to get back to that spot again, and now I don't know what I'm going to do."

The Key Question

O'Neal and Byrde are hardly alone in having chosen the wrong successor the first time around. That mistake is far more common than most entrepreneurs realize. We see it happen repeatedly with public companies, and often the founder has to come back in to right the ship.

(See Steve Jobs at Apple, Howard Schultz at Starbucks, Michael Dell at Dell Computer, N. R. Narayana Murthy at Infosys, Charles Schwab at Charles Schwab, Richard Hayne at Urban Outfitters, Tom Leighton at Akamai Technologies, and Reid Hoffman at LinkedIn, among others.)

But sometimes coming back is not an option. I have a friend—I'll call him Daniel—who in 1992 founded an executive placement firm that grew to be the best-known and most highly regarded in its particular niche. In 2003, he began thinking about moving on. He believed that ten years was enough for any CEO; he was worn out by his rat-race life; he felt that the company needed a CEO with skills he didn't have; and he wanted to write a book and do some teaching. So he began an intensive succession planning process that lasted two years. The company, which had an independent board of directors, hired a top-notch executive recruiting firm. In February 2005, the board selected a partner from a Big Four accounting firm with a stellar résumé. I'll call him Ralph.

Within a year, Daniel realized that he and his fellow directors had made a mistake. Although Ralph followed his mandate to expand the range of services offered to clients, he quickly alienated many of Daniel's erstwhile colleagues with a management style that was hierarchical, lavish, and command-and-control. He created a whole level of bureaucracy that hadn't existed before. He began promoting people based more on loyalty than on performance. He packed the board with friends. Most important, he moved the firm away from what had been its core market, middle-market companies, while bringing on more and more big-company accounts. The holdovers from Daniel's era complained to him that Ralph was ruining the business. Many of them left.

Daniel sympathized with them, but he was in a quandary. He feared that if he got Ralph fired, he would gain a reputation as a founder who couldn't let go. The firm would then have a hard time finding a qualified person to replace Ralph. Daniel himself didn't want the job. He'd built the company once, and it had taken an enormous amount of hard work and self-sacrifice. He wasn't willing to start over again.

He was worried, however. He felt that the firm's growing reliance on big company accounts was dangerous. He knew that the companies would respond to any downturn in the economy the way they always do: by getting rid of the consultants. Yet there were limits to what he could do, in part because Ralph's strategy appeared to be paying off. The firm was growing fast. Revenues were up dramatically. Profits were down due to the much larger management staff and extravagances like corporate jets. Ralph argued that these expenditures were investments in the future. At some point, the profit curve would bend upward, he said, and the firm would begin raking in cash.

But the profit curve never got the chance. In December 2007, the Great Recession began and continued for more than eighteen months. As the economy deteriorated, the firm's big-company customers responded just as Daniel had feared. In 2009, the firm's revenues declined for the first time in its history.

By then, Daniel had been able to reshape the board, forcing Ralph's cronies off and replacing them with directors whose independence could not be doubted. It was the new board that had to decide what to do with the company. There was an offer on the table from a large, publicly traded company in a related business that had long lusted after the firm. The board decided to sell for a combination of cash and stock worth about $50 million. Although the press release announcing the sale indicated that Ralph would continue as president, he was gone in five months. As for Daniel, he estimated that the sale price would have been twice as much had the firm simply stayed on the course it had followed during its first thirteen years.

But the worst part for him was the demise of a great company that he had hoped would live on after him. It was only later—when he was explaining to me one day what had gone wrong—that he suddenly realized the key mistake he and his fellow board members had made: In interviewing Ralph as a potential successor, they had neglected to question him about his approach to management. As a result, they hadn't foreseen the drastic changes Ralph would make or considered their impact on the firm. During his tenure as CEO, Daniel had run a lean company with a flat management structure. He had also practiced his own form of open-book management. The firm was a partnership, and financial information was widely shared with partners and employees. Ralph, in contrast, kept the numbers closely guarded. Partners and employees who wanted to know how the company was doing could only guess.

The change had a number of predictable consequences. First, it drastically reduced mutual accountability and concentrated power at the top, which in turn led to a culture of favoritism. That culture inhibited frank discussions among the partners and staff—the kind of discussions that might have brought to light the pitfalls in Ralph's new strategy. Second, the loss of transparency removed one of the most effective barriers to profligate spending and fostered wastefulness throughout the business. Finally, it virtually guaranteed that the firm would lose some of its best people, who would not accept being left in the dark, particularly after having known so much about the company's finances previously.

Indeed, almost all of the internal factors that had contributed to the firm's decline could be traced back to the change in management philosophy, and yet the board members had never asked the one question that could have exposed the risk: How widely do you believe financial information should be shared and discussed with partners and employees? That is, do you practice open-book management? In retrospect, Daniel found it incredible that they could have missed it. They'd looked at Ralph's résumé, his references, his ability to handle himself in an interview, his ideas about the firm's future, his qualifications for accom-

plishing the strategic goals they were planning to set out for him—
everything but the way he intended to manage the company. The
oversight had cost Daniel and his partners millions of dollars and had
cost his firm its independence.

Second Chances and Backup Plans

Given how easy it is to hire the wrong successor, Roxanne Byrde—with
help from her lawyer—took exactly the right approach. What's most
important is not that her initial assessment of Harry was wrong, but
that she gave herself plenty of time to correct the mistake and recover
from it.

Of course, she still had a succession problem to deal with, as well
as some exit decisions to make. Her experience with Harry had at
least narrowed her list of potential acquirers. In the wake of it, she realized that she could never sell the company to anyone she didn't know
extremely well and trust implicitly. "So I started thinking about an
ESOP again," she said. "That was my only option as far as I was concerned."

This time, however, she decided to consult with an ESOP specialist
whose firm had a national reputation for its expertise in ESOPs. It was
clear to Byrde after their first meeting that her initial concerns about
ESOPs were completely unfounded. She could retain as much control
as she wanted after selling to one. The more that she learned, the more
enthusiastic she became.

It took almost a year to work out all the details, but in June 2011
Byrde sold 100 percent of the stock to the ESOP for the company's
assessed value of $40 million. At about the same time, the com-
pany became an S corporation and thus would henceforth enjoy the
same benefits of deferred taxation and improved cash flow available to

every S corporation with an ESOP as the sole owner.* "It cost us a bundle," Byrde said two years later. "But every time I made out another check to another attorney or banker, I would say to myself, 'Roxanne, it would have cost you more than this in broker fees to sell to someone else.'"

She had also found the person she expects will succeed her as CEO. "He was right under my nose," she said. Although only in his mid-forties at the time, George Williams had been at the company for seventeen years, starting as a quality manager and working his way up to vice president. Years before, his boss had talked to Byrde about Williams's CEO potential, but she didn't know him well, hadn't worked with him on a daily basis, and was soon swept up in her early enthusiasm for Harry. Once Harry was out of the picture, she decided she should look more closely at Williams. She did and became convinced that he was a very strong candidate. "I talked to a number of people," she said. "The franchisees think he's the greatest thing since sliced bread. He gets along wonderfully with everyone. He follows through. He does what he's supposed to. He's got a great mind. And he loves the culture."

In early 2013, Byrde announced that on February 1, Williams would become president and chief operating officer of the company. She said there would be an eight-year transition period during which he would take over more and more of her responsibilities. In 2020, he would become chairman and CEO.

A year and half later, Byrde had seen nothing that would cause her to change her mind. On the contrary, she was even more optimistic. "He has strengths that I don't have," she said. "I've got some good

---

* Profits of S corps are passed through to the shareholders and then taxed at the individual rate. When an ESOP, which isn't taxed, owns 100 percent of the stock, the cash that would otherwise have gone to taxes stays in the company and can be used to finance its growth. Not that the government loses the revenue forever: It eventually gets paid when employees leave and pay individual taxes on their ESOP distributions.

points, but he has got better points where I have weaknesses. I actually see the company being much more successful under his leadership."

I would like to think that Byrde has solved her succession problem, and maybe she has. But Robert Tormey, the forced sales expert we encountered in chapter 3, tells some sad stories about owners who thought they had their succession problem solved. There was, for example, the seventy-year-old founder who had sold his metal-stamping company to a leveraged ESOP (that is, an ESOP that finances the purchase by taking on a lot of debt to be paid back out of earnings). He had received a great price for the business—ten times EBITDA, with all the tax benefits that go along with such deals—and invested the proceeds in a variable annuity. In addition, he had bought the factory and real estate, which he was leasing back to the company. He figured that the combination of annuity and rent payments would assure him of a steady income in the future. As for succession, he had recruited a Harvard MBA to take over as CEO and provided him with stock options as an incentive to stick around. Other key managers received a similar deal.

All went well until March 2002, when the company's costs suddenly skyrocketed due to a new tariff on imported steel. Its largest customer promptly switched to a Mexican supplier that was not subject to the tariff. Almost overnight the company's sales plummeted to 30 percent of what they had been at the time of the sale to the ESOP. The MBA and most of his fellow managers soon figured out that the value of their equity would never recover. They quit. The founder realized he had to unwind the ESOP, whereupon he discovered that the tax consequences of doing it would be harsh. Suddenly he needed a lot of cash to pay off the ESOP loan, but the cash from the sale was tied up in his variable annuity, and he would incur significant penalties to retrieve it. And what about the building? He had borrowed $5 million to acquire it from the company, which had spent all the proceeds. The building itself was now worthless, partly because the tenant (his company) had not paid rent for two years and partly because it was designed for only one purpose: metal stamping.

The founder brought Tormey in to investigate the situation and figure out how best to deal with it. "There wasn't much that could be done," Tormey said.

He has many similar stories about small business owners who failed to prepare for the possibility that their best-laid succession plans would go awry. His advice: "Don't count on a single successor. Don't borrow money or guarantee indebtedness in order to secure your plan. Don't underestimate the risks that your business is subject to. Don't wait too long. Don't take your health for granted. Have a plan B! Have a plan C!"

Getting It Right

As many snares as there are on the path to hiring a worthy successor, some owners do manage to avoid them and find someone who not only can be a good steward of the business but can grow and strengthen it. Roxanne Byrde may turn out to be one of them. Martin Lightsey is already one of them, having successfully replaced himself in 2003 as CEO of Specialty Blades in Staunton, Virginia, the company he had founded eighteen years before.

Lightsey had been thinking about succession from the company's earliest days. "I knew he intended to step away from being CEO at some point because he began Specialty Blades talking about who would succeed him," said his wife, Linda. "Maybe not the first couple of years, because we weren't even sure it was going to work, but once it was up and going, it was clear to me that Martin planned to eventually step down."

Lightsey had the advantage of having participated in the leveraged buyout of his former employer, American Safety Razor (ASR), in 1977.

In 1980, he had sold some of his shares to buy land in Staunton and build a home there, in the beautiful Shenandoah Valley. He was thus familiar with liquidity events and knew that he would eventually have to create one for the angel investors who had put up $350,000 in seed capital. Some of the investors were former colleagues at ASR. Others were from his own circle of friends. The need to cash them out at some point automatically raised the possibility of a sale and therefore the question of succession. So did Lightsey's hope of building a company that could last beyond him.

In the beginning, however, he had to focus all his attention on getting Specialty Blades to the point where it would be self-sustaining—that is, able to survive on its own internally generated cash flow. An engineer by education, experience, and mind-set, he had come up with the idea for the company while working at ASR, where he ran the industrial and scalpel blade division. Among the products it made were blades that would typically go into machinery, such as devices for cutting synthetic fiber to specific lengths. The equipment used to make these so-called specialty blades was a modified version of the machinery used to make razor blades. Lightsey thought that by marrying computer numerical control (CNC) machine tool technology with razor blade technology, ASR could begin manufacturing a whole range of specialty blades that customers wanted but the existing equipment couldn't produce.

After investigating the idea for a year or so, he took it to his boss, the CEO of ASR. Although the CEO liked the concept, it did not fit into his plans for the company. Lightsey said he would like to pursue the project outside of ASR. The CEO didn't object—he ultimately became an investor in Specialty Blades—but since Lightsey had done his research as an ASR employee, the two had to establish ground rules governing which parts of the intellectual property behind the machine he could use. In the end, the CEO agreed to give him the freedom to use almost all of it as long as he pledged not to compete with ASR.

Starting a manufacturing company is an expensive proposition. Lightsey thought he would need about $1 million to reach breakeven cash flow. He took his business plan to about fifty potential investors. Only eleven people signed up, and Lightsey had to settle for $500,000— including $150,000 of his own money from the sale of his ASR stock— which was the least amount he felt he needed to move forward. "On paper it looked like it would work," he told me, looking back thirteen years later. "Of course, it had never been done before, so we couldn't know for sure. It took about a year longer than I thought it would."

It also took more money—$500,000 more, to be exact. He raised it by securing a bridge loan of $125,000 from a local community bank and doing a second round of equity investments from the original share-holders. Launched in 1985, Specialty Blades finally broke even on sales of $830,000 in 1990. The following year, it turned its first profit, $309,000, on sales of almost $1.5 million. Along the way, the company developed a high-performance culture that reflected Lightsey's beliefs about how companies ought to be run. "I thought there was oppor-tunity to do it better than we did at ASR, where we had a union shop. I thought if you could get people on the shop floor working in con-cert with people in management and vice versa, you would have a much more powerful proposition. We didn't have a name for it in the beginning, but we were an open-book management company from the get-go—from 1985 on."

By 1997, the company was earning almost $1.6 million on $6 mil-lion in sales; the median initial investment of $43,750 was valued at almost $350,000; and some of the shareholders wanted liquidity. Among the latter were Lightsey's two daughters, Dana and Jennifer, to whom he and Linda had gifted 70 percent of their stock in 1994 for estate planning reasons. They could see the value was rising rapidly and—by acquiring the stock at a low basis—the girls would benefit from the stock appreciation that lay ahead. In addition, Lightsey had feared, rightly, that if he and Linda waited too long the tax liability on their estate when they died would be huge and might force the daughters to sell the stock to the highest bidder, with potentially devastating consequences for the company.

The daughters had financial needs of their own, however, which they could relieve by selling some of their stock. The question was, to whom could they sell their shares? Specialty Blades needed all of its internally generated cash flow to fund its growth, and so it could not afford to buy them back. The alternative was to find new investors to buy out the old ones. Lightsey thought other people in Staunton might be interested in investing if given the chance. He consulted a securities lawyer about going public and quickly realized that Specialty Blades couldn't afford the cost of doing an initial public offering, let alone the ongoing legal and accounting fees of as much as $500,000 annually— too much for a business with less than $10 million per year in sales.

Lightsey was aware, however, that the community bank in Staunton was trading its shares locally. How was that possible? he wondered. The lawyer explained that Virginia securities law contained certain so-called exceptions that allowed companies in the commonwealth to offer stock to the public without having to register or file reports with the Securities and Exchange Commission. In addition to an exception for small banks, there was one that Specialty Blades could use provided it sold the stock only to Virginia residents and met certain other conditions.

Lightsey spent several months researching the subject and conferring with his board and his attorney. The shares were finally offered for sale in early 1999, and thirty-five or so Virginians paid $600,000 to purchase thirty thousand of them at $20 per share (the value that the board had settled on). The offering cost the company a mere $15,000, most of which went to legal fees. It was the first of three intrastate stock offerings that Specialty Blades would do over the next ten years.

By allowing shareholders to buy and sell their stock, the intrastate offering mechanism took off the table one major issue that Lightsey would face when he eventually decided to exit, namely, the transfer of ownership. The shareholders could decide for themselves whether and when to buy or sell. The transfer of leadership, however, was still very much his concern. As luck would have it, a possible solution to that challenge emerged right before the first intrastate offering, and again one of his daughters was involved.

After her college graduation, the Lightseys' eldest daughter, Dana, had moved to San Francisco. Through friends, she had met a recent graduate of Middlebury College in Vermont named Peter Harris, who was working at a small consulting firm, advising multinational corporations on strategies for entering the Chinese market. It was a job for which he was well qualified, having participated in Middlebury's renowned Chinese-language program and double-majored in mathematics and Chinese, which he spoke fluently. Soon he and Dana were dating.

As their relationship blossomed, Harris faced a career choice. He was already spending a lot of time in China. The next step was to do a three-year tour there. Instead he decided to go to business school, eventually settling on the Darden School of Business at the University of Virginia. "You can live close to your parents for two years," he told Dana. "You're never going to get that chance again." She agreed. In 1996, they moved to Virginia. Before classes started that fall, they got married at the Lightsey home in Staunton.

Harris had made a very good first impression on both Martin and Linda Lightsey, and the better they got to know him, the more they liked him. They had no doubt that he would have his pick of job opportunities when he graduated. Lightsey couldn't help thinking, however, what an asset he would be to Specialty Blades. During one of the Harrises' visits to Staunton in the late spring of 1997, Lightsey suggested that he and Peter take a walk. As they made their way through the woods near the house, he told his son-in-law that, if he had any interest in working for a small Virginia manufacturing company, Lightsey would be happy to talk to him about joining Specialty Blades. "I just wanted him to know the opportunity was available," Lightsey said. "I was not encouraging him to take me up on it, but if he was interested, I was open to the possibility, despite my strong opposition to nepotism. I said, 'Financially, you can do a lot better in investment banking or consulting. There is no room for million-dollar salaries in a small manufacturing business.'"

Until then, Harris said, the thought of joining Specialty Blades had never crossed his mind. But after mulling it over for a few days, he decided it might not be a bad idea. He told Lightsey that he'd like to have further discussions about the possibility. Lightsey was delighted. Harris—who had just completed his first year at Darden—was working at Carrier Corporation that summer. At one point, he mentioned to his boss, the company's head of strategic planning, that he was thinking about going to work for his father-in-law's $6-million-a-year manufacturing business. "Are you out of your mind?" the boss said. "We're going to put you in charge of Argentina!"

Harris, however, wanted to run something, not just be another climber on a corporate ladder. From that perspective Specialty Blades could be a good opportunity—under the right conditions. While his goal was to be CEO, he realized that he would have to come in as a novice and earn the job. If he did eventually get it, there could be no doubt in anyone's mind that he'd been named CEO because he was the best candidate, not because he was Lightsey's son-in-law. So that there were no misunderstandings Lightsey and Harris put together a document stipulating that Specialty Blades was not and would never become a family business, promotions would be based strictly on merit, and other relatives would be discouraged from applying for jobs.

Harris later joked that it was the worst job offer imaginable. "Martin basically said, 'Why don't you come here on an extended audition in which you will have all the problems of perceived nepotism and none of the benefits of actual nepotism. Anything you get will only come from your performance, and by the time we reach the end of this process, there's no guarantee you'll be given what you want. I am personally going to recuse myself because I have a conflict of interest. In the meantime, I am going to pay you less than you made before you went to business school.'"

In June 1998, Harris officially joined the company, starting out as a salesman of industrial blades. The person for whom the situation was hardest, Harris said, was his boss. "Even if I wasn't Martin's son-in-law, she had a very difficult task. I mean, you bring in somebody straight out of business school, with the express purpose of rotating him through various jobs to see what his full potential is. I wouldn't say it's an anointment, but it's a loaded set of circumstances."

Lightsey faced an altogether different challenge. He needed to make sure that, when the time came to name his successor, the board would have a legitimate choice. A year or so earlier, he had hired a new head of finance who he thought would make a strong candidate. There was also the company's operations manager at the time, who had been employee number two (after Lightsey) at Specialty Blades.

Harris started out behind the others. He began by educating himself about the basics of the business. "I ran machines with the operators," he said. "I spent a great deal of time talking with customers to understand their products." He learned to read blueprints. He became acquainted with manufacturing technologies. After a year or so, the company was restructured into business units. Harris worked as a manager in the medical blades unit for about a year before being promoted to operations manager of the whole company. Along the way, the perception of nepotism steadily diminished, partly because of his obvious ability and work ethic and partly because of his equally obvious independence: Of everyone in the company, he was the person most likely to challenge Lightsey.

In 2002, Lightsey decided it was time for a new CEO. He believed that Harris was ready and would make an excellent one. As promised, however, he recused himself and turned the selection over to the other members of the board. Harris and the former operations manager, now sales manager, were the only internal candidates for the top job by then, the CFO having indicated that he was not interested in the job. The board proceeded to interview them separately and had them each provide written answers to a long series of questions. If neither internal candidate had proven acceptable to the board, it had the option of looking outside the company, but the members chose not to. Instead they gave the nod to Harris.

It took about six months for Lightsey to wrap up the loose ends of his tenure as CEO. In early January 2003, he formally stepped down and left on a three-month vacation with his wife. "I made a lot of mistakes, but one thing I did right was not get in Peter's way," he said. "I gave him a free hand." Harris subsequently described the transition as "seamless."

In any company, the transition from founding CEO to successor has an enormous impact on the long-term success of the process, as both Lightsey and Harris appreciated. "It is not so much about the handoff of business activities," Harris said. "It's the handoff of the humans. The incumbent loyalists need to feel like it's okay to go to the next person and not still be beholden to the first person. If you get the handoff wrong, the organization will reject the new person like antibodies attacking a virus. That's why outsiders are so difficult to bring right in. In my case, the rest of the organization already knew me pretty well after five years."

To be sure, Lightsey wasn't completely out of the picture. He remained chairman of the board and on the payroll at half of his previous salary, and he continued to show up at the office five days a week for seven and a half years. Those years were extraordinarily eventful for the company. Lightsey's main contribution was to meet regularly with Harris to discuss big decisions and to prepare for the quarterly board meetings.

Harris spent a year or so settling into his job. Not until 2004 did a new vision for the company come into focus, and it involved a major reorientation of the company. Up to then, Specialty Blades had been an industrial blade manufacturer with a sideline in medical blades, but its industrial blade markets were not expanding, and might even start shrinking, while the medical area appeared set to take off. Everyone agreed that the company needed to shift its emphasis. One of the early steps was to give the medical part of the business its own name: Incision Tech.

The new strategy soon began to pay off. Sales more than doubled from 2003 to 2007, from $9.7 million to $21.1 million, and pretax profit increased from $2.1 million to $3.1 million. The following year, the company acquired a Rhode Island manufacturer in a related medical field—needles and metal tubes. A large infusion of capital was needed to complete the deal. After scouring the private equity market looking for a firm that would invest for the long term, the board selected a Swedish family office,* Axel Johnson, which bought 22 percent of the stock via a private placement. That same year, the company adopted the name Cadence in recognition that its range of products was far wider than industrial and specialty medical blades.

All of these developments confirmed to Lightsey what he had sensed way back when he first invited Harris to join Specialty Blades: "At that stage of the company, Peter was a much better CEO than I would have been. I enjoyed the technical side, but I'm not sure I would have ever gotten beyond blade-making. Peter has taken the company to places I probably would have never gotten."

Harris continued to pursue an aggressive growth strategy for Cadence. By 2011, the company was doing $4.4 million pretax on $41.5 million in sales and needed another large infusion of outside capital. Once again, Axel Johnson stepped up, increasing its stake to 40 percent. But the most important development that year was Harris's

---

* A family office is a private wealth management company that handles investments for a single family whose wealth has often accumulated over generations.

decision to hire his own potential successor. It followed a revelation he'd had a year or two earlier. "Before I embarked on this path, I did not think through how difficult it would be to exit the path," he told me in 2010. "I didn't understand that, by being the successful successor, I was going to inherit the founder succession problem. I've inherited the obligation to create a succession that is as good as our succession was, which is a tremendous hurdle."

The demands of the job were a factor in his decision to start looking, but he was also beginning to think that the company might be outgrowing him, as it had outgrown Lightsey before. At some point, Cadence would need a new CEO with the experience and know-how to run a much larger organization, and it couldn't be someone like Harris when he first joined the business. "This company is way too complicated now," he said.

Not that he wanted a CEO-for-hire who would immediately take over from him. "The two biggest things that I look for in human beings I want to work with are humility and self-purpose. The two most common traits of CEOs-for-hire are conceit and self-interest."

The ideal candidate would therefore be someone who had the qualifications to become CEO of a company of the type and size Cadence would be in a few years, but who would be willing to come in as chief operating officer, while leaving Harris the flexibility to decide exactly when he wanted to step down. A search firm he'd hired had already identified one person who appeared to fit the profile in every way but the last—Alan Connor, a vice president and general manager of orthopedic specialties for one of Cadence's customers, Microaire Surgical Instruments. After spending time at Cadence and talking with Harris, Connor came away impressed with both but unwilling to take the job under those circumstances. Harris reconsidered and went back to Connor, suggesting he join Cadence as president with responsibility for all operations. In April 2011, he did just that.

Exactly a year later, Lightsey gave up his title and responsibilities as chairman of the board, while remaining a director. With the second succession process under way, he felt it was time to make the change. He had stepped down as CEO ten years before, when he was about to turn sixty. Now approaching seventy, he was ready to pass the baton one last time. Harris was immediately elected to replace him.

In October 2012, the board announced that Connor had been selected as the new CEO. After the usual six-month transition, he formally assumed his new position, and Harris, who remained chairman of the board, moved on to a job as vice president and managing director of Axel Johnson. As for Lightsey, his journey was nearly complete. "I'm happy," he said. "I'm certainly not in the position of some of my friends who've accumulated wealth they'll never spend no matter how extravagantly they live, but we are very well-off relative to the rest of the world and live a very comfortable life. Fortunately, I do have my dignity and my pride still intact."

Indeed, he had accomplished what only a relative handful of founders achieve: building a great company and setting it up to carry on as an independent business long after him.

6

━━━━━━━━●●━━━━━━━━

Who You Gonna Call?

> **The best advice comes from people who've been through it themselves.**

The members dribbled in one by one: the serial entrepreneur in the midst of selling his fourth business, dealing with a regulatory change that had suddenly put the sale in jeopardy; the woman who had inherited a company from her father, built it into an industry leader, and was beginning to prepare for whatever would come next; the founder still haunted by his decision six years earlier to sell his company, thereby undermining what he cherished most about it: its intimate and vibrant culture; the family business owner who'd had what the rest of the group regarded as the perfect exit and was now financially independent, retired, dividing his time between three homes, filling his days with travel, sailing, golf, writing classes, and grandchildren—and yet unable to shake the feeling that he had lost something important and didn't know how to get it back. And five others.

They'd come from all over Chicagoland on a steamy afternoon in August 2010 to a sprawling white-brick ranch house overlooking a golf course in the woodsy green suburb of Inverness, Illinois—the home of

Dave Jackson, his wife, and their daughter. He'd been an early entrepreneur in the home health care business and sold his company in 1998. The following year and a half he recalled as the worst period of his business career, a time when he felt utterly alone, lost, and confused. That experience had played a major role in his decision in 2008 to start a new business, Evolve USA, with Bruce Leech, who'd had an equally difficult exit (as chronicled in chapter 2). It's a member organization for business owners who've sold, are thinking about selling, or are in the process of selling their companies. The people gathered in Jackson's screened-in veranda had been the first to sign up and had been meeting every month for the past two years.

Their mood was cheery as they went around the room doing their regular "check-ins," updating the group on personal and business developments since the last meeting. They listened and laughed and gave each other gentle digs, until it came time for the serial entrepreneur, Michael LeMonier, to check in. He had been struggling with a number of things lately, and a regulatory threat to his business, MedPro Staffing, was the least of them. He had also had to place his father-in-law in an assisted living facility, empty the old man's home, and put down his dog.

But LeMonier led off with another piece of news that he found even more distressing. It concerned someone he had met prior to embarking on his entrepreneurial career, when he was working as a regional manager for a national staffing firm. One of his branch managers had introduced him to a young employee, who he quickly recognized was destined for bigger things. "He was handsome, articulate, and incredibly bright, far smarter than me," LeMonier recalled. "He wound up replacing me in some of my jobs. I loved it, and I loved him. He lifted the whole team. Eventually he left and went on to start three related businesses that did extremely well. Their combined sales went from nothing to $220 million in eleven years. A couple of years ago, he sold to a private equity firm for $100 million, or so I've heard.

"In June, he hung himself. My wife and I went to the memorial service in downtown Chicago. I think everyone there was in shock. It was so confusing. I mean, how could the world have lost such an incredible person at such a young age? I asked his former partner what had happened. He said, 'He lost his sense of purpose.'"

Questions, Questions

People who've sold their businesses say that one of the biggest obstacles to a graceful transition is the change in the nature of the questions they're facing. Successful entrepreneurs tend to be highly goal-oriented, which works to their advantage in a business context, where they're focused on setting and achieving objectives, usually ones that are quantified. The questions they deal with all revolve around progress toward a goal. How far along are we? What's holding us back? When will we hit the target? And on and on.

But once you've sold and left the company, you suddenly find yourself in a place where quantifiable objectives are much less relevant. The most pressing questions you face are existential ones. Who am I? Why am I here? Where am I going? "Running a business day-to-day is a rat race, and there's a lot of stress associated with it," observed LeMonier. "But we deal with a different kind of stress in Evolve that has more to do with purpose and the meaning of life. That's a challenge. Until you sell the business, you don't have the privilege or responsibility of choice. You're supporting a family, or whatever. It's much more difficult to choose your purpose than to have life's realities choose you."

By the time the group sat down for dinner, the discussion had turned to money—specifically, how important is it, was it, or should it be to sell your business for as much money as possible?

"I had quite a struggle with that," said Ed Kaiser, who went to work at his father's company, Polyline Corp.—a distributor of recording tape reels and other media packaging products—in 1976, became its sole owner in 1993, and sold it eleven years later. "Some of the potential acquirers might have moved the company and put all the employees out of work. Fortunately, I was able to find a buyer who met my minimum dollar amount and kept everyone employed."

"It's a struggle for me because I haven't sold yet," said Jean Moran, whose company, LMI Packaging Solutions, makes coverings and labels, such as the foil tops for yogurt containers. "I have people who worked for me coming back and telling me, 'This company changed my life.' Selling something like that for the most money feels repulsive to me."

"I don't think selling a company for the most money is a bad or evil thing," said LeMonier. "There's nothing wrong with it provided you're mindful of what you choose to accomplish in the sale. You have to ask yourself, 'What are my priorities and goals?' My first goal in selling the company I own now is to economically and publicly thank my leadership team for what they've done. I'm going to maximize the dollars, but that's in order to take care of the team. I want to send them on in the best possible way."

Dave Hale was sitting across the table, listening intently but with a look of mild distaste on his face. At seventy-three, he was the oldest member of the group. His company, Scale-Tronix, is a leading designer and manufacturer of medical scales, which he and his business partner, Carolyn Lepler, founded in 1975. "I don't know," he said. "The idea of ending what I do is just a terrible thought. Exiting seems like dying to me. From the beginning, our whole goal has been to solve problems and take care of customers. That's what I love to do—solve people's problems. Maybe I'm weird, but to me 'exit' is a four-letter word."

"I have a friend like you who hated the idea of exiting," said LeMonier. "He's about to lose his home because he didn't plan. I too enjoy what I do, but I've always separated my passions and investments. My wife and kids, my community, my church—those are my passions. My business is an investment."

"My business is my passion," said Hale.

"Yes, but the frightening part for you and me is, what are we apart from our businesses?" LeMonier countered.

"I can't help but think about your friend who committed suicide because he lost his sense of purpose after he sold his company," said Jack Altschuler, who used to own a water treatment company. "I don't think we humans exist very well without a clear sense of purpose. If my only purpose is my business and I leave my business, I have no purpose."

"The question is, can I be more than my business purpose?" said LeMonier. "I believe I was put on the planet to do more than make a buck. But making a buck frees me to discover my purpose more deeply and more personally."

"Look at the age of this group," said Altschuler. They were all older than fifty, and some, like Hale, were quite a bit older. "Yeah, you have to make a buck to live, but is that the primary driver for any of us anymore?"

Help! I Need Somebody

The path to an exit can be a lonely one, which may help explain why so many owners avoid it as long as possible. The obvious danger they face is that they won't be ready when they're suddenly forced to make decisions they haven't thought much about in advance. The less obvious danger is that when they finally do reach that stage, they'll become overly dependent on the opinions of investment bankers, brokers, and other such exit specialists, whose interests are different from those of an owner. For the specialists, the transaction is the end of the road. Once they've reached it, they move on to another client. For the owner, the transaction is the beginning of whatever comes next, which will be greatly affected by the handling of the sale.

You can mitigate that danger by learning from owners who've

already been through an exit. Their perspective is particularly helpful in the first stage of the process, when you're exploring options, learning about pitfalls, and clarifying your thinking about what you want. Most people have to get such advice informally, through their personal networks of friends and acquaintances, if only because formal mechanisms are few and far between. Chicago-based Evolve is one of the first member organizations devoted to providing owners with the peer support they need during the transition from active owner to something else.

The idea for the organization grew out of the founders' own difficult transitions, in which they both struggled to find fulfillment and meaning in their lives after the sale of their businesses. We've already heard about Bruce Leech's search. Jackson said his quest began with a book called *Halftime*, by Bob Buford, who wrote about going "from success to significance." Jackson already had the success part pretty well covered. In nine years, FirstChoice Health Care—the home health care company he'd founded in 1989—had grown to about $10 million in sales, with 150 employees (mostly nurses). On paper, at least, it was worth several million dollars.

But the business wasn't fun anymore. He was having to focus more and more on operations, which he didn't enjoy. "Everything felt like work," he said. To make matters worse, changes to Medicare reimbursement formulas were about to tilt the competitive landscape in favor of larger companies. Jackson decided it was the right moment to sell. He began looking for a buyer, and in July 1998 sold FirstChoice to Baltimore-based Integrated Health Services, a Fortune 500 company.

At thirty-eight years old, with a modest amount of wealth for the first time in his life, Jackson now faced the challenge of figuring out what would come next, and moving from success to significance resonated with him. For the first two months after the sale, he commuted daily to the downtown office of the buyer, to help with the transition. "I can remember riding the train and reading that book over and over and over again," he said.

Of course, looking for significance doesn't necessarily lead to achieving it. Chances are you can't even define it unless you first have a pretty good idea of who you are. Jackson, like most of us, was still learning. What he didn't anticipate was the degree to which that learning process would be accelerated by the sale.

The first hint came on a trip he took with his wife, Claudia, to scenic Door County on the Wisconsin peninsula that juts out into Lake Michigan, about five hours north of Chicago. "It was the fall," he said. "We were driving up, and about the time we hit the peninsula, it dawned on me that nobody was looking for me. I didn't have a pager anymore because I didn't need one. Nobody needed to track me down. It felt weird. That was my first awareness that, oh my gosh, things have really changed. I hadn't realized up to then how important it was for me to feel needed. My ego had been built to thrive on people needing me, and that had suddenly been removed from my world."

But he didn't appreciate the full implications of his insight until after the holidays, when he decided he should get back to work. He had built an office in the basement of his house in Inverness. "I would get up at six o'clock, shower, get dressed, and go to the basement, and then I would sit down there and rearrange the pencils all day." He'd check his e-mail. He'd make calls to set up meetings. He'd put together lists of people to contact, things to do, and potential opportunities to pursue— but with no clear purpose in mind. "It was like playing business. I was searching for something, but I didn't know what. I realize now I was just trying to find a way to feel valued or important."

That period was a nightmare, he said, and it dragged on for more than a year. Month after month, he floundered, not understanding what exactly was wrong, or what to do, just knowing he was a mess. Finally, out of sheer desperation, he hit on an idea. "I said, 'What would I do if I was still in the business and faced with a challenge?'" The answer, he realized, was to develop a business plan. First, however, he had to figure out what the business would do. On a pad of paper, he drew a T and wrote down on one side what he was willing to do, and on the other what he wasn't willing to do. "The not-willing-to-do list turned out to be really helpful. I had things on it like not giving up control over my time and not forgoing family vacations. That list brought clarity to me. As soon as I saw I wasn't willing to give up control over my time, I could eliminate a whole bunch of stuff I'd been considering. That was the first big ah-ha."

Jackson gradually pulled himself out of his funk. Still in search of significance, he threw himself into charitable work, joining a group of businessmen who, under the auspices of the Christian humanitarian organization World Vision, were establishing big-box warehouses in inner cities to supply donated home remodeling products to low income people and the community centers and churches that served them. Around this time, he began getting calls from friends and acquaintances who owned businesses and wanted to learn about his experience of selling FirstChoice. They would sit down over breakfast or lunch and he'd tell his story. It didn't occur to him that he was actually providing a valuable service until he happened to meet a local investment adviser named Keith Cantrell, who suggested he charge for his time and advice. Though skeptical at first, Jackson screwed up his courage and began asking for compensation. People happily paid.

As he realized he'd stumbled on a new career path, his relationship with Cantrell blossomed. Jackson proceeded to purchase a one-third share of Cantrell's business, Evanston Advisers, in 2001, three years after selling FirstChoice. He fit right in. Most of the firm's clients and prospects were business owners. A growing number of them, moreover, were looking for someone to guide them through the exit process. Jackson obliged, becoming the lead adviser to dozens of exiting business owners in the coming years.

There was a pattern, he said. "For most of these owners, it was like doing a two-minute drill at the end of the fourth quarter, but without ever having practiced it or even played the game before. I could see so much, not just that they didn't know, but that they didn't know they didn't know. I'd tell them that they were bound to feel unsatisfied on the other side when they realized they hadn't maximized value, or maximized tax benefits, or dealt with their personal identity, or done the other things you should do to get ready. All that takes time."

He sensed that these owners had a need for something else, some kind of learning mechanism, though he wasn't sure what. Then he heard that a few members of TEC (now Vistage) in Chicago were forming an alumni group for people who'd sold their companies. He began attending meetings, where he met Leech. "The group found we had a lot of life-after-business issues in common," Jackson said. "We studied *Transitions* by William Bridges. It isn't focused on business owners, but it helped give us a common language and understanding of what was happening to each of us. It's a little bit like grieving. You go through stages of grieving, and once you are aware of the stage you're in, you can deal with it. Well, that is kind of what happened for this group."

Some members of the group approached TEC/Vistage about setting up groups of former business owners who had exited, or were planning to exit, their companies. Vistage demurred, whereupon Jackson and Leech launched Evolve.

Who Leads the Leader?

There are, of course, limits to the help that any peer group can provide its members. That's especially true of the exit process, because exiting is one of the few parts of the business experience that many owners do just once and relatively few do repeatedly. Almost everything else in business involves a lot of repetition, which is fortunate, because it allows you to get better as you go along. Your mistakes become learning mechanisms. Not that you can't also learn from the mistakes you make during an exit, but if there's no next time, they will become sources of regret rather than means of improvement. Hence the importance of having the right kind of help for whatever stage of the exit process you are in. The closer you get to the actual transaction, the more specialized the help needs to be.

A group like Evolve, for example, can play an invaluable role at any stage, and especially during stage one, the exploratory phase. But you need another type, and a higher level, of expertise in stage two, the strategic phase. That's when the focus turns to developing the key value drivers that will have a major impact not only on the price the company will eventually be able to command in the marketplace but on its ability to overcome the various threats every business encounters from time to time and build a record of steady growth.

To be sure, business owners should always be paying attention to those value drivers whether or not they're actively preparing for an exit. The situation changes, however, once you have a reasonably clear idea of when you want to leave and how much money you want to sell the company for. At that point, you need expert advice from a specialist in whatever type of sale you have in mind. If your plan is to sell to an outside party, for example, you need the assistance of someone who knows the market for companies like yours and can give you specific advice on the factors that will allow you to get the best possible deal. Ideally, that individual will serve as your lead adviser and principal guide at least as far as the transaction, and maybe beyond. The right person will do more to ensure a happy outcome than anyone other than you. The wrong person will put everything you've worked for in jeopardy.

Some owners, of course, choose to manage the whole process themselves. That's generally a terrible idea—for at least two reasons. To begin with, unless you've done it before, you probably aren't qualified to handle it and won't do a good job. Ashton Harrison, for one, would undoubtedly have had a miserable exit experience had she not retained the services of Steve Kimball. An even greater danger is that you'll wind up neglecting the business as the sale process unfolds. Managing the sale of a company is a big job that calls for knowledge and skills most business owners have never had reason to acquire. If you try to do it yourself, you'll have little time to do much else. Unless your company is able to operate at a peak level without you, the business's performance will suffer during this period, and you'll pay a steep price for its decline whether or not the deal ever gets done.

And yet, ironically enough, the best lead advisers are often former business owners who did manage the sale of their companies, and who learned how it should be done by making costly mistakes, beginning with the mistake of serving as their own lead managers on the sale. I must admit here to a strong bias in favor of lead advisers with some such background—that is, former business owners who have been through the sale process and its aftermath themselves—as opposed to brokers, investment bankers, lawyers, accountants, wealth managers, and other M&A specialists whose only business experience has been in consulting, advising, doing deals, or providing some other type of professional service. I'd be especially wary of the large Wall Street investment banking firms, which have a reputation for turning this type of work over to their least experienced employees—brand-new MBAs—as a test to see how well they do.

I don't mean to cast aspersions on M&A professionals in general. Many are excellent at what they do, and you will need the services of some of them at various points in the process. But M&A specialists who've never experienced an exit of their own will probably have certain blind spots, particularly when it comes to the emotionally charged issues that accompany any sale. They also tend to be so focused on the transaction that they give little thought to what comes afterward. Competent lead advisers who are former business owners will be acutely aware that the exit process doesn't end with the sale. They will also know when specialized services are needed and who should be brought in to provide them.

You should be equally careful in choosing a lead adviser if you decide to sell to your children or other family members, or to your employees via an employee stock ownership plan. I realize that you may have a hard time finding a former owner who has taken such an exit route and then moved on to a career of helping other owners follow in his or her footsteps. When former owners of family- or employee-owned companies become business advisers, the businesses they advise tend to be the ones they used to own. That should not deter you, however, from getting as much advice as possible from former owners who have chosen the type of exit you're interested in. Their views are often starkly different from those of lawyers, accountants, and other professional service providers.

Now, I know some of the latter will object that they, too, are business owners: They own and operate professional service firms. That's true, but you see the world differently if you own a company that sells something other than your specialized advice—as Bob Woosley discovered when he left his accounting firm to start a business.

Trained as a CPA, Woosley had begun his career at Price Waterhouse and in 1982 became the first professional employee hired by Atlanta-based Frazier & Deeter. Three years later he was promoted to partner, while Frazier & Deeter went on to become one of the hundred largest accounting firms in America and recipient of numerous awards for growing fast, providing exemplary service, being well managed, and creating a great place to work.

But Woosley had the entrepreneurial bug. In 2000, he left to start a company, iLumen, with a partner. Their idea was to automate the collection, analysis, and benchmarking of financial data for businesses, with an initial target market of accounting firms, which could use the technology to offer better service and develop closer ties to their clients. Later the company offered it to bankers for use with their customers and to franchisors for use with franchisees. After a successful ten-year run, Woosley stepped down as CEO, and in 2011 he returned to Frazier & Deeter to lead the firm's entrepreneurial consulting practice and direct its strategic growth initiatives.

By then, the firm had grown, and Woosley had changed. So had the advice he offered to his entrepreneur clients. "I'm almost embarrassed about some of the advice I gave before I did iLumen," he said. "I give much better business advice today."

As Woosley suggests, the experience of starting, running, and exiting a business changes the way that anyone—including a specialist like him—views the process. That's why you want a person with such experience to lead the process. But it takes a whole team to handle the many technical issues that arise, especially in stage three. Part of the lead adviser's job is to assemble and manage that team, which will include at least a lawyer and an accountant, and maybe an insurance professional and a wealth manager or financial planner. The latter becomes especially important in stage four, after a deal has been consummated and money has changed hands.

Whether or not those other experts have entrepreneurial experience is not important as long as the lead adviser does. Then again, there are some advantages in having an ex-entrepreneur lead manager who, like Woosley, is based in a law, accounting, or wealth management firm. Dave Jackson, for example, has some clients who are in no hurry to do a deal, and he can give them as much time as they need because his wealth management firm does not depend on the successful completion of a transaction to get paid.

As for business brokers and investment bankers, their primary role is to develop a market for the company being sold, find potential acquirers, and oversee the sales process. Sometimes you need them. Sometimes you don't. They are distinguished from one another primarily by the size of the deals they handle and the way they go about their business, although the line between them gets blurred because some brokers identify themselves as investment bankers.

Brokers are generally for smaller companies with less than $5 million in sales and $500,000 in EBITDA. They handle business sales the way real estate brokers handle home sales, advertising in newspapers and online and trying to consummate a deal with whoever responds. Many small-time brokers handle a lot of other stuff as well—houses, boats, commercial property, mobile homes, you name it—and don't know much about the companies they're representing. They're the ones who give the industry a bad name. The better business brokers handle only company sales and often focus on a particular industry, which they know inside and out.

Investment bankers, on the other hand, focus on clients whose companies have annual revenues of more than $5 million and EBITDA of more than $1 million. In most cases, the bankers' job is to identify and entice potential buyers, then set up and manage an auction. There are both specialists by industry and generalists among investment banks, as there are among business brokerages. It's hard to say whether one or the other is preferable from the seller's standpoint. You can get arguments on both sides. Fortunately, if you have a good lead adviser, he or she will know whether you need an investment banker at all, and if so, which ones would be best for your type of deal.

Obviously, for the seller, a tremendous amount is riding on the lead M&A adviser, especially when you consider the principal advantage that buyers have going into any negotiation: Many of them have done multiple deals, while the seller has often yet to do even one. An experienced lead adviser can level the playing field. The hard part for the adviser is to acquire the necessary experience in the first place.

The Education of an M&A Adviser

Basil Peters admits that his first exit experience was very nearly an unmitigated disaster. The company in question was Nexus Engineering, which he'd cofounded in 1982 during his final year of graduate school at the University of British Columbia in Vancouver. He started the business, he said, out of financial necessity, having run through every cent he could beg or borrow as he worked toward his PhD in electrical and computer engineering.

In the beginning, it had just been Peters and a classmate, Peter van der Gracht, working in a lab at the university, supported by two angel investors. What had caught their attention were the opportunities in satellite communications, whose commercial applications were just being developed. Cable television, they'd decided, was the wave of the future. They'd begun making the guts of cable boxes—specifically, the head-end equipment needed to take the signals from a satellite and turn them into data that could be transmitted on a coaxial cable.

Their bet on cable had turned out to be a winner. After ringing up about $250,000 in sales the first year, the company almost doubled in size annually, reaching about $25 million in 1989. As manufacturers, they had needed a lot of working capital to maintain that growth rate, but outside equity had been readily available. They had done two rounds of venture capital and then brought on three institutional investors.

The company's big break came in 1990, when Time Warner announced plans to build the world's first five-hundred-channel cable television system in New York City. The giants of the industry, Scientific Atlanta and General Instrument, said it couldn't be done; Peters and van der Gracht believed it could and managed to convince Time Warner's chief engineer that their design for cable boxes capable of handling all those channels would work. They were awarded the contract, much to the chagrin of their giant competitors, who made no secret of their belief that Nexus would fail. But Nexus didn't fail. It delivered the system eighteen months later and in one fell swoop leapfrogged its competitors' technology.

Those were good times for Peters, who had become a celebrity in the small world of British Columbia business, showered with awards and featured on magazine covers. Nexus was not only growing fast but spinning off new ventures—six of them to be exact, all under the Nexus umbrella. Peters and van der Gracht were busy and happy. "I remember most days just being consumed with all the stuff that you do to run a business every day," Peters said. "Occasionally, at night, I would worry that it all seemed to be going too well. I had the vague feeling that I was missing something big. But I'd brush those concerns aside and go back to work."

The first sign of trouble came right about the time Nexus landed the Time Warner contract. Peters received an unexpected phone call from Ted Rogers, the founder and CEO of Nexus's largest customer, Rogers Communications. "He told me not to worry," Peters recalled. "He said I'd be seeing media stories about problems with savings and loan associations in the United States. He just wanted to reassure me that he'd still have access to his construction loans, which were the source of the funds he used to buy our stuff." Peters didn't know what to make of this news, but after receiving similar calls over the next few days from customers in the United States and Europe, he decided he should inform his board and his bank, which was lending him money against his receivables, that his largest customers were all telling him not to worry—a sure sign that there was something to be worried about.

In fact, Nexus Engineering was feeling the tremors of the S&L crisis and the resulting collapse of the junk bond market. The entire cable industry, including all of Nexus's best customers, had become reliant on high-yield debt—that is, junk bonds—to finance growth. Among the buyers of these bonds were a handful of large savings and loans. In 1989, Congress had passed a law giving S&Ls five years to get rid of their junk bonds. Pretty soon everyone was selling their bonds, which made it impossible to issue new ones. The cable companies' major source of funding dried up almost overnight.

Nevertheless, Peters's customers kept telling him not to worry, and he kept passing their reassurances along to the bank. After six months, it moved the account to the special loans department, which monitored Nexus for a year and then called the loan. "It was like watching a car crash in slow motion because you've known it's coming for a year," Peters said. In the meantime, the economy had slid into recession, and Nexus's investors had begun asking him if he could help them get a little liquidity.

"I had no idea how to provide a little liquidity in a private company during a recession," he said. "I thought I only had one option: to find a buyer for one or more of our seven companies. That was an uncomfortable idea. We were growth junkies. Selling one had never occurred to us, which I now find amazing. I just can't believe we didn't have an exit strategy. We'd never discussed it. The board had never thought about it. I'd never even talked about it over lunch with my partner. It was one of the worst mistakes of my career." Like so many mistakes, moreover, it opened the door to a host of others. Fortunately, he also did a few things right and got a couple of lucky breaks, which enabled him to avoid, narrowly, a complete wipeout.

How *Not* to Sell a Business

Peters can identify twelve mistakes he made during his desperate attempt to line up a buyer. As noted above, **mistake #1** was his failure to formulate an exit strategy. **Mistake #2** was one of those he only became aware of many years later, when he learned that he'd actually had an alternative to selling Nexus. Instead, he could have done a secondary offering. "That's when new investors buy stock from founders or early investors," he explains. "In retrospect, I should have organized one during our boom years. It would have provided the founders and angels with some liquidity at pretty good share prices. It would also have allowed all of us to diversify, and it would have spared me the pressure I later had from shareholders at the worst possible time."

He committed **mistake #3** in deciding to spend all of his time managing the sale process, while van der Gracht handled the day-to-day operations of the business. "I worked really hard on it, often for sixteen hours a day, because we really needed to find a buyer," Peters said. "But I wasn't very good. To be honest, I really sucked at it. And the company was in pretty bad shape. Previously, we'd both worked twelve hours a day on the business. With me switching entirely to a non-revenue-generating external function, it didn't take long for the business, which was already suffering, to get even worse. So that was another lesson for me: The CEO should never lead the exit."

Their best bet, they thought, was to sell Nexus to a defense contractor looking for a nondefense business to get into after the Cold War's end. Peters did manage to find three potential buyers, which he thought proved the validity of their plan. That was **mistake #4**. "As I've since learned, interested prospects aren't necessarily serious prospects. They tend to drop off, one by one, with no reason given. They aren't angry or anything. They just stop returning your phone calls. That's what happened with our interested buyers, until there was just one left."

With a single prospect and cash running low, the company was flirting with bankruptcy. All it would take was the loss of that last buyer. Fortunately, one of Nexus's angel investors—who had experience in selling companies—realized how dire the situation was and stepped in. He suggested they leak word to Scientific Atlanta that Nexus was in play and might soon be acquired. Peters had never heard of such a thing. "How do we get the information to the right person?" he asked. The angel said they could hire someone to slip word to an appropriate executive. He happened to have a friend whose company did sales for Scientific Atlanta, and who could probably reach someone in a high enough position. They'd have to negotiate a price, but the guy would probably do it for a "finder's fee" of $10,000 to $20,000—in cash.

Peters thought the proposal sounded risky and doubted the board would go for it, given how little cash the company had in the bank. It later occurred to him that such a gambit would probably have been unnecessary if they'd been working with a professional M&A adviser, but they weren't: **mistake #5**. In any event, the board did approve the plan; a fee was agreed upon; and a paper bag with the cash was delivered to the intermediary, who made the phone call as promised. Peters had instructed him to tell his contact at Scientific Atlanta that a deal between Nexus and a large defense contractor was imminent. The idea was to imply that small and underfunded Nexus—which had nevertheless landed the big Time Warner contract—would soon have the capital to present a much more formidable challenge. The plan worked brilliantly. Within a day or so, Scientific Atlanta's acquisitions people got in touch with Peters, asking if there was still time to put in a bid. They then quickly came in with an offer significantly higher than the defense contractor's.

The defense contractor, for its part, was having second thoughts and soon stopped returning phone calls. If Scientific Atlanta hadn't been in the picture by then, the battle to save Nexus would have been lost—hence **mistake #6**: having only one bidder. "That's another absolute, always-applies lesson," Peters said. "If you find yourself in that situation, you need to slow the process down, back up, and try to get at least one other prospect. Every exit needs multiple bidders."

At the time, however, Peters was mainly feeling relieved that Scientific Atlanta appeared ready to do a deal. "We were saved, or so I thought," he said. "As the negotiations heated up, I actually started to feel a little bit optimistic about the future. I was so naïve, and about to learn another painful lesson."

The lesson grew out of **mistake #7**: his failure to check whether or not the major shareholders were aligned around a common goal. He just assumed they were and was thus baffled by strange comments that one of the venture capitalists made at a couple of board meetings. Peters began to get worried when other board members alerted him to lobbying the VC was doing behind the scenes.

The purpose of the lobbying later became quite clear. Two of Peters's key supporters on the board resigned after the VC convinced them they'd lose their homes if Nexus ran out of cash. "That was never true, and the VC knew it," said Peters. "I tried to talk them out of leaving, but he'd done such an effective job that I couldn't dissuade them. As a result, I lost a couple of good, loyal board members right when I needed them most."

Because of **mistake #8**—ignorance of his investors' needs—the VC's actions took him completely by surprise. "This was another critical failure of mine," he said. "The firm had invested at about $3.20 a share. I didn't know then, but completely understand now after being a VC for a few years, that there was no way they were going to vote for a sale that would give them less than a 10X return on their investment." But a sale at $32 or more per share wasn't even remotely possible at that point.

It slowly dawned on Peters that he was facing a full-fledged hostile takeover attempt. "I learned later that the venture firm had a well-developed plan. They had regular meetings about how to kill the sale. They wanted us to run into a cash crunch, and then they'd do a wash-out round of financing and recapitalize the business at a tenth of a cent per share, effectively wiping out the early shareholders. It's a well-known tactic. It's often how VCs make the best returns. But our angels and the founders would have lost everything we'd spent ten years working on."

The VCs used every trick in the book. At one point, for example, Nexus's CFO showed up ashen-faced in Peters's office to let him know that a director had demanded to see all of the CEO's expense reports for the past two years. "His face was white," Peters said. "I said, 'Don't worry. Give him what he wants.' I had always had one of the controllers do my expense reports. So I knew there was nothing improper about them. The VCs had some forensic guy go through the file, and they came back with a bunch of questions, but they didn't find anything they could use to discredit me."

At another point, Peters received a phone call from a person who worked for a large institutional investor that had loaned Nexus several million dollars in subordinated debt a few years earlier. The caller said that an outsider had made inquiries about buying the debt. Peters was stunned. Nexus, like many other companies at the time, was out of compliance with its loan covenants and could have been forced into bankruptcy, but the lender had given Peters time to work out a solution. By acquiring the debt, the VC firm could gain a club it could use to kill the sale.

Realizing he was in danger of losing the company because of his failure to anticipate his adversaries' moves—**mistake #9**—Peters caught the next plane to Toronto, where the institutional investor was located, and begged for an opportunity to plead his case before a senior executive. His wish was granted, and he tried to persuade the executive to reject the VC firm's offer. The executive listened politely and said little, but as Peters was leaving, he thought he saw him wink. "All the way home, I wondered whether I'd just received the most important signal of my life, or this guy had a nervous twitch," Peters said. Whichever it was, the lender evidently decided its interests would not be served by getting involved in a takeover battle and declined to sell Nexus's debt, thereby depriving the VCs of their shortcut to victory. It would come down to votes in the boardroom.

In the meantime, the sale process was slowly unfolding. Because Nexus was by then the second largest head-end manufacturer in the market, and Scientific Atlanta the largest, it was possible that the merger would need regulatory approval, and they decided as a precaution to apply for it. They eventually got it, but only after a long wait. By then Scientific American had submitted a letter of intent, leading to additional months of due diligence and negotiation over the detailed agreement that would be submitted to Nexus's board for approval. If the board didn't approve it, the deal would die.

Peters recalled the nine months leading up to that showdown as a pitched battle. By and large, it was waged behind the scenes. The venture capitalist continued to wine, dine, and woo the other board members. Peters did his own lobbying when he wasn't working on the sale, but he felt he was always playing defense. "Our venture capital investors were way better at this game than I was. I would learn what they were doing after they'd already done it, at which point I'd have to struggle just to catch up. Every time I thought I'd solved part of the problem, I'd discover there was another whole front that I hadn't been paying attention to and was losing ground on."

At times, his adversary's attempts at intimidation turned physical. "This VC was about six foot seven and three hundred pounds and a star rugby player. I'll never forget one meeting when he got up from his chair and came storming around the table in my direction, literally screaming and yelling the whole time. He leaned over me. I am sure he'd had garlic for lunch. I thought he might hit me, and I was preparing to block the punch if it came. Fortunately, it didn't."

In August 1992, the agreement with Scientific Atlanta was finally ready for a vote. Peters's wife happened to be pregnant with their second child, a girl, and due around the time of the crucial board meeting. Peters had been praying that the baby would delay her arrival, but she decided she couldn't wait and made her debut at about 4:30 a.m. on the day of the meeting after a long and difficult labor. Peters was there at the hospital to welcome her, having spent the whole night by his wife's side. At about 6:30 a.m. he left for the office—dressed in jeans, dead tired, and in need of a shower. Although the board meeting was scheduled to begin a couple of hours later, he figured he would explain the situation and get it postponed.

But the board members were no more inclined to wait than his daughter had been. They voted to proceed with the meeting, a decidedly bad omen. Peters was more nervous than ever. If the board rejected the Scientific Atlanta deal, he would almost certainly wind up with nothing to show for all he'd put into Nexus over the previous decade. As he looked around the table, he had no idea how the vote would go. A couple of directors had pointedly declined to reveal their intentions, saying only that they would do their fiduciary duty after going through all the information. He couldn't even count on one of his original angel investors, whom the VC had often referred to as deadweight but had also courted assiduously.

The meeting lasted half the day. Board members meticulously examined the draft agreement, clause by clause, discussing each point. Technically, the question was, should Nexus management move on to the next phase of the process, which involved hammering out the remaining details with Scientific Atlanta? When Peters finally called for a show of hands, he won by a single vote.

Heading home to take his shower, Peters felt an overwhelming sense of relief. Granted, there was still work to be done, but negotiations with Scientific Atlanta had gone smoothly up to that point, and he had no reason to believe they wouldn't remain amicable. He began to feel confident again, or at least confident enough to take a weekend off to spend with the baby. After all, the last big obstacle to the sale had been cleared, and the battle with the venture capital firm was over—which was **mistake #10**.

One of Nexus's lawyers mentioned the need for an "extraordinary" shareholders' meeting. Peters had assumed the vote by the board was definitive, but it turned out not to be. The board vote had merely been a recommendation to the shareholders that they should approve the sale. For the deal to be consummated, the shareholders themselves had to vote on it. There were about seventy of them—fifty who worked in the company plus twenty or so outside investors.

Peters figured the vote would be a formality and the meeting would be a perfect time to celebrate. He ordered two pallets of beer, had a crate loaded up with crackers and chips, and arranged for a stereo to be set up in the warehouse where the meeting would be held. "I thought it was going to be a pretty fun afternoon—right up until three partners from the venture capital fund walked in with their lawyer. I knew they weren't coming for the beer. My stomach fell through the floor. I was totally unprepared. I had obviously missed something important."

What he'd missed were the details about the number of votes required to approve the sale—**mistake #11**. In order to protect minority shareholders, the law mandated a supermajority, not a simple majority as Peters had assumed. The percentage that constituted a supermajority was specified in the company's articles of incorporation. Peters had never read the articles. He wasn't even sure what they were. The VCs and their lawyer had obtained a copy of them during the due diligence they'd conducted before investing. They announced before the assembled shareholders that they had enough votes to deny the other side its supermajority and thus they could block the sale.

It was the worst possible news, and it came as a bolt out of the blue. Peters was so distraught that he scarcely noticed when Nexus's lawyer got into a discussion with the venture capitalists about the percentage of votes required. As the meeting's official scrutineer, it was the lawyer's duty to take notes, count votes, and ensure that proper procedures were followed. He pointed out that the VCs were looking at an old version of the articles. He had actually updated the articles at a prior annual meeting that almost nobody had attended because nothing interesting had been on the agenda. Among the items changed was the one governing the percentage of votes needed to approve a sale. The percentage had been reduced.

The venture capitalists wanted to see the document. A couple of hours went by as people searched for the paperwork. Peters waited along with everyone else, but his mind was elsewhere. "I really wasn't paying attention," he said. "I just sat there thinking I was dead. I thought I had made a fatal mistake, and my whole life's work was down the drain. The wealth I'd built up on paper over ten years was gone."

Finally, the documents were delivered—and his lawyer was shown to be correct. According to the amended articles of incorporation, the sale could be approved with fewer votes than the venture capitalists had believed, and they didn't have enough votes to block it. Although Peters was too drained by then to feel elated, he had learned another important lesson: Repair any structural defects early. "It's a pain in the neck, but if you don't do it, you greatly diminish your chances of having a successful exit."

There was one other error he made, **mistake #12**, but he didn't discover it until the last minute—literally. Scientific Atlanta had called a meeting in Atlanta to deal with the remaining sticking points. Its representatives had indicated there would be no more meetings. They'd put in all the time they were going to. Nexus had to decide.

Peters realized that shareholder approval would be needed for any changes to the deal. So he had brought a dozen key people with him to ensure he would get it. For two full days, they'd met with Scientific Atlanta's crew of fifteen or twenty acquisition experts, going through a list of items one at a time. The weather outside was scorching, and the room was uncomfortably warm, despite air-conditioning. "It was also a stressful meeting," Peters recalled. "I was sweating. But we finally finished the last item on the list. I pushed back from the table and was preparing to go around to shake everyone's hand when the fellow across the table from me said, 'Oh, and there's one more thing.' You never want to hear those words at that point in a deal. I'm sure my heart stopped beating. He said, 'And we want Peters to come along for a year.'"

Now, Peters had taken great care throughout the negotiations that his name not appear on any organization chart and that he not be described as having any useful function in the business. He was looking forward to working in and on the five companies Nexus wasn't selling.

At least two of them, he believed, had exciting prospects. He intended to go home right after the meeting and start his new life. He had it all mapped out.

"I felt like a trapped animal," Peters said. "I had the feeling of being cornered in a canyon surrounded by guys with spears. I looked at the people I'd flown down with. They were all smiling and nodding. If I said yes, there'd be a big check coming their way. I realized I had no choice but to do the gentlemanly thing, but I heard my molars grinding as I nodded my head and tried to smile."

It was a small price to pay. The sale turned Peters from a cash-strapped entrepreneur into an independently wealthy man with invest-able capital. "And it was great," he said. "It changed my life. I got to spend a couple of years traveling around to places that had white, sandy beaches and blue water." But he was not without regrets, mainly over how costly his mistakes had been. "We rode the company over the top. We waited too long. We managed to sell it for about $2 a share. If we'd done it just a couple years earlier, on the upswing, I think we could have easily gotten $5 or $10 a share."

It took him ten years to understand everything he'd done wrong and even longer to learn what he should have done instead. He eventually concluded that only luck had saved him and most of his fellow share-holders from disaster. "We weren't so good that we could outsmart any-body. There were several points where we could have lost it all. We were just plain lucky to get by them. I did okay, but it was much too close. And I could have gotten us all several times as much money if only I'd thought about exiting when I should have, early on. We wouldn't have had to start cold and learn so much along the way. So I can't emphasize it enough: Every company needs a good exit strategy."

Yet, his regrets notwithstanding, Peters walked away from the Sci-entific Atlanta deal with something that proved even more valuable in the long run than the money he received—namely, an education. The sale turned out to be his entry-level training as an M&A adviser. By the time he began serving as the lead manager in the sale of other people's businesses, he had a good grasp of the process, and his skills continued to improve with experience. He was at the top of his game when he took on Parasun Technologies, the company founded by Barry Carlson, who was also its largest shareholder. That deal was as good an example as any of the way that the sale of a business ought to be handled.

Anatomy of a Good Deal

Barry Carlson is one of those people who becomes an entrepreneur by accident. A rock musician and former student radical, he married at nineteen, had children, and went to work in a circuit board factory. In 1976, when he learned that the owners planned to shut it down, he bought it for a dollar and turned it around. Six years later, he sold it back to the original owners for a fraction of the price that he believes he could have gotten if he'd known what he was doing.

Parasun was a spin-off from a company he worked for after the circuit board business. It was a small Internet service provider (ISP) called Mind Link! Communications, which was acquired in early 1996 by iStar Internet in an industry roll-up. For the next year and a half, while iStar went around buying other small ISPs, Carlson did various contract jobs and kept an eye open for business opportunities. iStar's business model was evolving during this time, and it became increasingly apparent to him that the company had no use for a substantial chunk of what had been Mind Link!'s business—the part that served customers in remote areas of British Columbia. He knew that the business, though unprofitable, had decent cash flow. More important, it had an excellent technical crew. He figured that he could use it as a platform on which to build a substantial company. He approached iStar's people about buying it for a nominal fee. They agreed.

It took Carlson's team two or three years to figure out exactly what to do with the business. Operating as ParaLynx Internet Inc., they focused on setting up marketing partnerships with radio stations, which they provided with the technical means to offer private-label Internet service to the station's customers. One of the radio stations also had a cable operation and asked ParaLynx for help in providing broadband Internet to its customers. It dawned on Carlson and his vice president of sales and marketing, Steven MacDonald, that they could do the same for the other four thousand or so independent cable television operators in North America, most of whom had neither the technical savvy nor the resources to offer broadband but whose customers were asking for it.

"We'd watched the @Home Network burn through almost $600 million trying to do the same thing backward," said Carlson. "They were selling their own service under their own brand and treating the cable guys as carriers. It didn't work because the cable operators didn't like anybody getting between them and their customers. We did the exact opposite. We said, 'You pay us $5,000 to install all this stuff in your facility, and we'll help you get this business launched under your name. You then pay us seven dollars a customer per month. The customers are yours, and you pay only for what you sell.' They loved it."

With the change in strategy came a change in name—ParaLynx Internet became Parasun Technologies—as well as a change in leadership. Carlson was stretched thin, due mainly to his simultaneous involvement with another growing business, a daily online comic strip for geeks called *User Friendly*. As it took up more and more of Carlson's time, MacDonald, the sales and marketing VP, worried about the effect on Parasun. "He sat me down one day and said, 'I can do a better job running this company full-time than you can part-time,'" Carlson said. "I thought about it and decided he was probably right." So he handed Parasun's reins over to MacDonald.

Under MacDonald's leadership, the new strategy proved very

successful, but also expensive, and twice he and Carlson tried to merge with public companies in hopes of making it easier to raise capital and provide liquidity for Parasun shareholders. The first attempt involved a publicly traded Internet service provider. When that didn't pan out, they tried for more than a year to do a so-called reverse takeover, or RTO, wherein a private company is acquired by the shell of a public company—that is, a publicly owned entity that has been hollowed out and is no longer producing either goods or services. By merging with a shell, a private company can go public without incurring the expense of doing an initial public offering. The process is not without risks, however. For one thing, the shell may have hidden liabilities. For another, the merged company may not be ready to take on the burdens of being public.

Fortunately, Carlson and MacDonald's RTO failed when the acquirer's financing fell through. They shed no tears, having realized by then that the merger was a really bad idea. Parasun simply wasn't big enough, and its products weren't sexy enough, to attract much interest from the public markets. What's more, public ownership would have subjected the company to added pressures that it might not have survived.

It was also becoming clear that Parasun might not need outside capital as desperately as they'd thought. After losing money for three years during the launch of the cable strategy, the company finally turned profitable and cash flow positive in the fall of 2002. By 2004, its margins were good enough to finance its growth internally. But it also had thirty-five shareholders by then, including eleven employees, and Carlson knew he had a responsibility to create a way for them to cash out at some point. He figured that the best way to get some liquidity for everyone was to sell the company. It would be an attractive acquisition, he believed, for a variety of strategic buyers, especially companies looking to get into the broadband Internet business.

I should note here that unlike Ray Pagano, Jack Stack, or several other owners we've mentioned, Carlson was not particularly concerned about what happened to the company after the sale. He wished his employees well. That's why he had given them stock. But he was an absentee owner at this point, had no strong ties to the culture, and assumed that, as usually happens, it would change under new ownership.

He cared very much, however, about getting as lucrative a deal as possible, both for himself and for the other shareholders. Having botched the sale of his first business, he wanted to be sure that this time he had a competent team guiding the process. He already had one such person on his board: David Raffa, an experienced securities and corporate finance attorney who was in the midst of transitioning to deal making and investing. Among other things, Raffa was involved in the launch of a new venture group called BC Advantage Funds. One of his cofounders was Basil Peters.

Peters had heard about Parasun and, partly because of his own background in the cable industry, was curious to know more. He asked Raffa for an introduction. When he went to visit the company, he liked what he saw. "At the time it wasn't yet profitable, but it was in an area I knew," Peters said. "I thought they were doing good work. It was one of those classic kind of start-ups, where you walk in and immediately get the sense of being in an exciting, early-stage company. People are energized and running around. It just had the right feel to it."

Peters also felt Parasun's growth strategy was sound. "I could see that they were doing a lot of the right things and capturing customers. And I believed they had a broad market. Every quarter the company was growing, so I knew they were going to be successful. It was just a question of how successful."

Carlson, for his part, wanted both Raffa and Peters to help with the sale of the company. They indicated they were willing to come in, but only if they would be investors as well as advisers. They also wanted a formal M&A advisory agreement giving them a mandate to find a buyer and the flexibility to manage the sale as they saw fit. As part of the deal, Peters would replace Carlson as chairman of the board.

Their proposal required some persuasion. "The terms of an M&A advisory agreement aren't complex, but they're also not easy to negotiate because it's such a big decision for the company," Peters said. "We spent quite a bit of time talking about it with Barry and Steven. After we had something we thought was fair, Barry went away, slept on it for a couple of days, and came back saying he wanted to have a cup of coffee just with me. He said, 'You know, Basil, I just want to be sure that we've structured this deal so that you're not going to make any money at all unless you make me a very large amount of money.' And I said, 'Yep, that's exactly our intention. That creates the alignment. That's what we want.' And he said, 'Okay, then I'm fine with this. Let's do it.'"

In the end, it took three years from the signing of the M&A advisory agreement to the sale of the company. During that time, Peters carefully avoided the mistakes he'd made in selling Nexus Engineering. Indeed, if you were to examine the two processes side by side, you'd find that they were almost polar opposites.

One of the first moves he and Raffa made, for example, was to organize an off-site strategic planning retreat to settle on an exit strategy and to check the alignment of the various stakeholders. As soon as they tried to do the former, it became clear that they didn't have the latter. Some people (especially early investors, including Carlson) wanted to sell as soon as possible, while others (especially MacDonald and his managers) felt that the company would be much more valuable in two or three years and the liquidity event should wait.

Peters and Raffa agreed that it was too soon to do a sale, but recognized that to get alignment, they'd have to provide a way for the early investors to sell some or all of their stock. Working with BC Advantage, they organized a secondary offering, recruiting private investors to join them in putting up about $500,000, which was then used to buy the stock of anyone who wanted to sell. They were able to raise the money, Peters noted, because (1) the price was reasonable, (2) there was a clear exit strategy, and (3) there was a good team in place already working to execute the exit. "When you have those three things, it's no longer a long-term, highly illiquid private investment you're asking for," he said. "It's like a bridge. And it was actually not hard to find buyers. We put together about a dozen of them." A year later, Parasun did another secondary offering, and Peters invested again, this time through his own angel fund.

Of course, it wasn't just the early investors whose needs had to be attended to. The key managers had to be on board as well. With that in mind, Carlson had earlier sat down with Raffa to put together an options package for MacDonald and the other senior people. Up to that point, they'd had only the same small equity position that all the employees had. The options, which vested over five years or immediately on a sale, gave each of them a much larger stake in the business.

It all took longer than Peters had expected, but the various stakeholders were finally lined up around a common exit strategy: to sell the company in late 2006 or early 2007—two years hence—for at least $10 million. The biggest challenge to meeting that goal, he believed, was the youth and inexperience of the management team. "While they were doing a good job, they still had a lot to learn. Our job, as a very active board, was to help develop the skills of the management team as rapidly as we could." No one was more active than the chairman himself. "There was one period, probably the better part of a year, when I'd literally meet with them once a week to focus on some aspect of the operations that was critical to achieving the goals." Peters said.

He calls these "mentoring" sessions, but the other participants had a more jaundiced view, and Carlson often heard about it. "Basil drove everybody with absolutely mindless determination," he said. "He forced everybody to focus and taught the inside guys what they had to do. He just wanted to make certain we were doing all the right stuff and hitting our sales projections and understood the business from end to end. Of course, in the trenches, it's never that easy. You get lucky some months, other months you don't. Basil didn't care. He said, 'We have to hit our numbers every month. That's what it's going to take to get the best dollar for this business.' And he forced that discipline on everybody. At the time he ruffled a bunch of feathers. But, dammit, it worked and everybody did well as a consequence. The people who went through it will tell you now that they are grateful to him, very grateful."

As critical as Parasun's operations were to the ultimate outcome, there was much more to be done before the company could be put on the market. The sellers had to hire an accounting firm to do an audit. In addition, they would need a lawyer who specialized in mergers and acquisitions. The team would then have to assemble a so-called deal book containing the key information for potential buyers. Specialists would have to review Parasun's corporate structure from top to bottom, examine employment and contractor agreements, and conduct an in-depth tax review. Peters had a checklist of more than fifty different tasks to complete—most of them quite time-consuming and technical—prior to contacting potential acquirers.

Fortunately, he had David Raffa at his side. The former lawyer had a longer history with the company than Peters, and his legal background made him ideally suited to handle the structuring, documenting, and negotiating. By the late spring of 2006, all the items on the checklist had been completed, and the company was projecting $12 million in sales in the coming year, up from $8 million the year before, with EBITDA of $2.2 million, up from $1.5 million. Peters and Raffa decided it was time to start looking for buyers.

Over a period of three or four months, they compiled a list of about a hundred potential candidates, including both strategic and financial buyers. They then sent each prospect a two-page letter containing an executive summary and overview of Parasun. It took another two or three months to contact the people on the list and qualify the ones who were interested. About seven or eight wound up signing the nondisclosure agreements that allowed them access to the deal book. Out of that group, three prospects expressed a desire to move forward—enough, Peters said, for "a pretty active auction"—and wound up submitting offers on both price and terms.

The question then became which one to accept, sparking a lively discussion in the board, with Carlson leaning toward one offer and Peters and Raffa leaning toward another. "Barry's instinct was to go with the first bid we'd received, which wasn't unreasonable," said Peters. "It was a perfectly legitimate buyer with a perfectly good price. But David and I thought that we could get a better price from one of the others. So we had some long discussions about the bird in the hand versus the one we believed was still out there in the bush."

Carlson ultimately deferred to his advisers' judgment and was happy he did. "It came down to two local companies," he said. "David and Basil got them both interested enough that they put offers on the table at the same time, and so we had a bit of a bidding war. Not in the formal auction sense. An offer would come in, and David and Basil would look at it, figure out what we'd probably get from the other guys, and decide who should call whom and say what. It was a real education for me, watching them earn their money. At one point, we had an offer we were content with, but Basil and David looked at it and said, 'Let's keep the working capital.' So they went back and said, 'Okay, we like the numbers, but, of course, we're going to keep all but a quarter of a million dollars in working capital.' The buyer said okay. That was an extra $1.6 million. I would have left it on the table. I would have just assumed that the bank account went with the company."

The winner was publicly owned Uniserve Communications Corp., another Canadian ISP. As soon as the price and terms were agreed to, Uniserve proceeded with its due diligence. By and large, it went smoothly, though there were a few glitches. Uniserve had financial issues of its own that threatened to derail the deal. Twice it put off the closing. When its people tried to delay it a third time, Raffa and Peters said no. "David in particular had been arguing against delays," said Carlson. "He said, 'Unless we push these guys, this deal could fall off the truck. They've had all the time they need. No more extensions.' I thought he was just being pissy about it. But it turned out he was absolutely right. He told me later, 'I've seen too many deals fall apart because there's a third extension, and everybody throws their hands up and decides it's never going to happen.'"

Parasun set a deadline of Thursday, May 24, 2007, to close the deal. Carlson, MacDonald, and Peters agree now that if it hadn't closed that day, the sale wouldn't have happened. For one thing, Uniserve wouldn't have been able to raise the money due to its financial problems. In addition, there was a dramatic drop in the exchange rate of U.S. for Canadian dollars, which hit Parasun hard because 80 percent of its revenues were in U.S. dollars and almost all of its expenses were in Canadian currency.

Fortunately for all of Parasun's shareholders, the deal did close that day—at 11:55 p.m. The official purchase price was $12.5 million, but after the working capital was added back and other adjustments made, the final proceeds came to $14.8 million, just shy of 50 percent more than both the original offer and the target price of $10 million that the Parasun shareholders had agreed to in the exit strategy they'd come up with in September 2005.

Carlson, Peters, and Raffa took their money and moved on, but MacDonald and his management team stayed with Parasun and soon were handed control of Uniserve's business operations as well. Despite their best efforts, the company's financial situation continued to deteriorate. In October 2008, less than eighteen months after acquiring Parasun, Uniserve sold it to a U.S. company, Integrated Broadband Services (IBBS), for about $20 million. IBBS wanted only the customer list. It fired the employees. That was not a serious problem for MacDonald and his fellow Parasun alumni. They'd already had their payday, thanks in no small measure to Peters and Raffa. "Basil and David designed and executed the exit perfectly," said MacDonald.

As for Carlson, he achieved everything he was looking for from the sale. He was able to because (1) he knew who he was, what he wanted, and why; (2) he had a sellable company; (3) he had given himself enough time to prepare and had also been blessed with a worthy successor; and (4) he'd had the benefit of an excellent exit team led by an experienced adviser who was himself a former entrepreneur. As we saw in chapter 1, he also had a smooth ride through the transition phase (a subject I'll address further in chapter 9). That, in turn, was possible in part because he had a clean conscience. He knew he'd done right by both his investors and his employees—which happens to be the next condition of a happy exit.

7

The People Part

No one builds a business alone. So what about everyone else?

On a misty, overcast April day in 2010, Jack Altschuler showed up at a video recording studio in Glen Ellyn, Illinois, for an interview about his exit from his first company, Maram Corp., an industrial water treatment company, which he'd founded in 1972. Twelve years had passed since he'd sold it to a competitor, and he had moved on to a new career in leadership training and public speaking, but as he talked about the selling experience under the bright video lights, it was obvious that parts of it were still vivid in his mind. Dressed in a striped shirt, open at the collar, and a dark V-neck sweater, he was explaining why due diligence, which had dragged on for months, had been so difficult.

One factor, he said, had been his intense desire to leave the business. It had been fun and exciting for many years, but the bloom was off the rose. He wanted out. "I was quite unhappy. There were problems, ordinary business problems, that I just didn't want to deal with any longer."

The hardest part, however, had been the need to keep it all secret.

Altschuler had hired an accountant and a lawyer to manage the process, and they'd strongly advised him not to let any of his fifteen employees know what was going on. "They seemed to have lots of good reasons for that," he said, "and I followed their advice. But it was very difficult. I'd always had an open-door policy, and there I was with the door closed and on the phone talking to people they didn't know. It raised a lot of eyebrows. I had more than one person come in and ask, 'Is everything all right? What's going on with the business? Hey, your door is closed quite a bit these days.' It was pretty awkward at times."

Awkwardness aside, the secrecy was completely at odds with the culture Altschuler had built, which emphasized loyalty, trust, camaraderie, and service. Indeed, an act of disloyalty by a key employee had played a role in Altschuler's decision to sell the business. "I'm the kind of guy who tends to trust very quickly and easily," he said. "If there's a crossing of that trust, a breach of loyalty, I feel it deeply. So when one of my people whom I had really invested a great deal in decided to leave and to do it in a less than forthright manner, I took it hard. It was a very difficult lesson. From then on, it just became less fun to run the business."

And yet during the months leading up to the sale of his company, Altschuler had found himself having to keep his employees in the dark about a decision that was bound to have a major impact on all of them. The obfuscation involved had felt uncomfortably like disloyalty.

Sitting on a barstool in the video studio, he revisited one incident in particular that was still troubling to him twelve years later. "It just stands out in stark, stark relief," he said. "We had made sure that all the correspondence from my legal team and the accounting folks came to my house rather than to the business. When there were invoices, nothing on them was supposed to identify the work involved. Instead, it would say something innocuous like, 'For services rendered.' The accounting firm, though, had made a mistake and put down, 'For services in conjunction with sale of the business to . . . ,' and named the buyer.

I reviewed it and didn't catch the mistake before passing it on to my office manager along with other bills that she was going to pay. I remember sitting at my desk and having her walk to my doorway holding the piece of paper and saying, 'Jack, are you selling Maram?' The shock in her face . . ." Altschuler paused. Some long-submerged emotion welled up inside him. He took a moment to compose himself.

"I can feel my heart jumping right now because I can see it, and feel it, and everything in that moment. I tried to do a little dance around it, not say anything, but there was just no escaping the fact that she had clear evidence of what was going on and I had to tell her. She returned to her desk and about ten minutes later came back with tears in her eyes and told me how betrayed she felt. She had been so loyal to me. Here I was selling the company and not even telling her about it. She just had this terrible sense of betrayal, and there was nothing I could do. It was just awful."

The announcement to the rest of the employees hadn't gone any better. "Right after the papers were signed, I called a company meeting, and everybody showed up in the conference room," he said. "Other than my office manager, no one knew what was going on, and you could feel the shock in the room when I told them. People were speechless. I can still see their faces and how painful it was for them. It was a very unhappy meeting." Altschuler told them that the acquirer was another water treatment company he'd chosen in part because its culture was similar to Maram's. Anyone who wanted to stay would have a job with the new owner. A few people asked questions. A few expressed their disbelief. Then they all took the twenty-minute ride to the buyer's shop. "We did a tour, and it was just the strangest experience," Altschuler said. "The shock was hanging over us like a cloud. I really did get more of that betrayal reaction from people both then and later on. It was a very difficult time because people had a lot of loyalty to me and they felt betrayed. And I felt terrible about the pain they were experiencing."

His discomfort notwithstanding, Altschuler never questioned his decision to sell Maram. If anything, he wished he'd done it sooner. "I knew I wasn't the best person to lead the company any longer," he said. "So I didn't feel guilty about it, but I did feel bad for my employees. If I were doing it again, I would have given them lots of advance notice, maybe even two years. I'd have said, 'Let's do this together so it works for everyone.' But it didn't even occur to me back then. I just didn't see it, and I simply followed the advice I was given."

The Lives of Others

Every owner's exit affects many more people than the owner, including investors, naturally, as well as the owner's family and the company's customers and suppliers, but it usually has the biggest impact on employees, who have depended on the business for their livelihood and who are most vulnerable to any changes that new ownership brings. In many cases, moreover, an exiting proprietor's own feelings about the deal after it's done will be strongly influenced by the way his or her former employees react to it, as well as by how they fare under the new owner.

Of the thousands of successful entrepreneurs I've met over the years, the vast majority care deeply about their employees, try hard to treat them fairly, and endeavor to provide them with a good working environment—partly because it's the decent thing to do, but also because it's smart business. As has been demonstrated time and again, employees will be more productive and take better care of customers when they know that the company they work for cares about them. And yet, ironically enough, an owner's success in creating such an environment can often make the process of leaving more difficult.

Jack Altschuler is hardly unique in this regard. His story parallels that of Dave Jackson, the cofounder of Evolve USA, whose difficult transition we chronicled in chapter 6. Jackson, too, had left employees in the dark about his plan to sell FirstChoice, his home health care business. After the deal was done and the money transferred, he called a staff meeting. "That was the first my people had heard of it, and it was bad," he said. It was bad in part because of the intimate—and highly productive—culture at FirstChoice, which Jackson believed had played a major role in the company's success. "We were close—very close," he said. "We had a family atmosphere in the company. So the news of the sale came as a complete shock. People felt I hadn't been honest with them. They felt betrayed. I wasn't prepared for that reaction. In my mind, they were getting a good deal. They'd have a much better benefits package, and no one was being laid off or taking a cut in pay. Our mistake was that we didn't give them time to process the news. The buyer's HR person immediately began shoving forms in front of them and having them fill out paperwork. That was really a tough day."

Even if your employees don't regard your decision to sell as a betrayal, the exit may still be a bittersweet experience, especially if you've succeeded in creating a high-performance culture. Jean Jodoin is a case in point. In 1989, he and three partners founded Facilitec, based in Elgin, Illinois, by combining two other companies—Spotless Touch, a kitchen exhaust cleaning company, and Grease Guard, a manufacturer of rooftop grease traps for restaurants. From the start, they made it a priority to develop a great culture around working hard, having fun, and delivering great results to every customer. "It went through the entire organization from the customer service person on the phone to the tech in the field. We looked at every customer contact as a way to differentiate ourselves."

The company grew fast, with annual sales reaching $10 million in ten years, and attracted the attention of potential buyers, including publicly traded Ecolab. In 1999, Ecolab made an informal offer that Facilitec turned down. But over time the relationship between the partners became strained. "It took the fun out of coming to work," Jodoin said. And so when Ecolab returned with a new offer, they decided to accept. Jodoin had mixed feelings at the closing. "It was exciting because we were cashing out and getting more money than we had ever seen in our lifetimes, but there was an equal amount of sadness about leaving the people behind. We had a couple hundred employees who were counting on us, and I personally believed I let them down that day. I felt I'd promised them we'd keep our company growing for many years, but instead I was leaving them with a new owner that I knew in my heart of hearts would never treat them as well as I would treat them, that would not look out for them and their families the way that I would look out for them and their families. That's the heartbreak that I felt that day."

Peace of Mind

Now, I assume that most owners would rather not feel heartbroken on the day their businesses are sold. I also assume that they'd prefer not to have their former employees view the sale as a betrayal of trust. The idea, after all, is to be able to walk away not only with your money, but also with your peace of mind. Peace of mind comes from, among other things, the knowledge that you've done right by the various people who've helped you reach the end of your journey successfully. So the question is, what exactly does "doing right" mean to you? Different people will have different answers, which is fine, but exiting owners would be wise to ask themselves that question early in the process.

Tony Hartl, the entrepreneur behind Dallas-based Planet Tan, was keenly aware of the effect his departure would have on his employees when he decided, in 2008, that it was time to move on. He had launched the business thirteen years before, at the age of twenty-six, with $50,000—$40,000 from an investor, $10,000 from his 401(k)—that he'd used to buy three locations from the nearly bankrupt tanning company he was working for at the time. After the purchase, there had been barely enough money left over to put up new signs, but that turned out to be all Hartl needed to get started. He pulled together a team and got them to work on scrubbing down and shining up every square inch of the salons. The idea, he said, was to have "hospital-clean" facilities with the most up-to-date equipment available.

As his cash flow improved, Hartl made a crucial decision—to grow by expanding established salons rather than following the usual practice of adding new locations as fast as possible. He felt that by having a few very large salons rather than a lot of smaller ones, he could create a better experience for customers while increasing his sales volume significantly faster than his labor costs. He turned out to be right. By 2007, Planet Tan had grown to sixteen locations, all in the Dallas–Fort Worth area, with about 170 employees. Its salons averaged almost $1 million in sales, versus an industry average of $200,000 per unit. More to the point, the company had the highest per capita sales per unit in the industry, and many of the salons boasted EBITDA of more than 50 percent.

Hartl had no doubt about the secret to Planet Tan's success: the quality of the staff and the strength of the culture. "We had a higher purpose, which was building this great organization," he said. "I always talked about us being the best businesspeople in our industry. My whole thing was, 'Look at these technology companies that are becoming world-famous. Well, we can do that in the retail space. We can do it by showing up early, leaving late, putting the customer's needs before our own.' That was the essence of it. We hired people that agreed with that, or thought they did, and then their behavior would let us know for sure."

Early on, Hartl had begun getting inquiries about selling, some from private equity groups and some from competitors. He had turned them all away, partly because he felt the company wasn't ready. Most of the stores were relatively new and needed time to mature to the point at which they'd be generating significant cash flow. Just as important, he wasn't ready. "I was just so young I couldn't think of doing anything else besides running a company," he said. "I was doing exactly what I wanted to do. I was making good money, and I was engaged in this meaningful work."

Yet, his passion for the business notwithstanding, Hartl did not plan to spend the rest of his life at Planet Tan. When he was in college, he had set a goal for himself: to work until he was forty and then do something else for a while. He fully intended to keep that promise, which meant, of course, eventually selling. Then again, he was determined not to let that intention get in the way of doing what was right for the business. He strongly believed in running it as if he were going to own it forever—that is, always making the decisions that would be best for the company in the long term. But even so, the prospect of selling before his forty-first birthday was always in the back of his mind.

And the clock was ticking. In November 2006, he turned thirty-nine. An active member of the Young Entrepreneurs' Organization (YEO, now just EO—the Entrepreneurs' Organization), Hartl regularly attended meetings of his Forum, or chapter, which brought in an outside speaker every quarter. In early 2007, the speaker was business broker David Hammer, who had recently helped one member sell his payroll company. In describing the process, Hammer emphasized the importance of "the book" (also known as the deal book, or the confidential information memorandum, or CIM)—that is, the marketing document laying out the company's history, finances, growth potential, and other factors of interest to a buyer. He noted that, selling aside, the book served as a reality check on an owner's often inflated view of the company's value. That in particular appealed to Hartl. Shortly thereafter, he hired Hammer to work with him and his senior executives to create a book for Planet Tan. He regarded it more as a reality check than a concrete step toward the sale of his company, and indeed it proved to be an eye-opening exercise.

"I didn't realize how hard it would be to create the book or how much information you have to put together," Hartl said. "It was really a big learning experience. I was on the fence about having an audit done, because of the cost—$30,000. But David said it was important, and so we went ahead. It turned out to be the best thirty grand I ever spent. We made some changes in our accounting processes that were great for the organization. But what really surprised me was how much credibility it gave us with banks. When you turn your financials in, it just separates you from everyone else. So we did the book, and it made me so proud of my organization. It was clear that we were a very well-run business in terms of all the key metrics. And then, in the midst of putting the book together, my biggest competitor approached me about selling."

The competitor, Palm Beach Tan, was a national chain based in Dallas. Hartl had become friends with its CEO, Brooks Reed, who had mentioned more than once that his company would be interested in buying Planet Tan should Hartl ever decide to sell. Once the book was ready, Hartl delivered a copy to his headquarters. The company responded by asking him to refrain from shopping the deal around. On Hammer's advice, he told Palm Beach that he intended to meet with some other interested parties but wouldn't start an auction process while it was preparing a formal offer.

A private equity firm had also expressed strong interest in buying a major stake in Planet Tan. Hartl met with its representatives and quickly concluded that such a deal held no appeal for him. He didn't need outside capital to grow the business and certainly didn't want a partner. What he did want was job security for his key people, especially the core group that had been with him for more than seven years. He also wanted a buyer to maintain the culture and the brand.

Much to his surprise, Palm Beach Tan agreed to all of his conditions. "They said they even wanted to keep the name Planet Tan on our salons and learn why our salons were able to do so much in revenue," said Hartl. "They said, 'Let's take the best of what you do, the best ideas, the best practices, and let's incorporate them in all our businesses.' That sounded fantastic to me."

As the talks moved forward, Hartl became increasingly focused on the effect a sale would have on his people, particularly those closest to him. He had brought a few of them into the selling process—because he needed their help, felt they had a right to know, and realized they might find out anyway. He promised them that they would not be left high and dry. He did not expect them to lose their jobs, but he assured them that if they did, he would hire them himself at the same salary and benefits and find something for them to do while they were job hunting. "Worst-case scenario, I'd buy another company. I thought the least I could do was to make sure they didn't have to worry about money."

By then, Hartl owned all the stock in Planet Tan, having long since bought out his early investors. He had thought about creating a phantom stock program for his managers and studied the compensation practices of Chick-fil-A and Outback Steakhouse with that in mind. He even had a plan on paper that he'd intended to roll out the following year. With a sale now imminent, there was no point in going to the expense and trouble of implementing it. Instead, he began thinking about other ways to ensure that his managers were properly rewarded.

At the same time, he was screwing up his courage to tell the rest of his more than 160 employees about the sale. "That was scary," he said. "I brought in a guy from YEO who had sold his company to walk me through the process. After that, I was still very scared. I did not sleep for a while. I worried how people would respond. Would they up and leave the company? What if they did and then the deal fell through? There were all these scenarios running through my head. But it didn't go bad—I think because of the trust I had with my team. They'd worked closely with me, and I think they believed in me. They knew I wasn't going to pull a Dr. Jekyll and Mr. Hyde, you know, all of a sudden become a different guy. But it was one of the most frightening conversations I've ever had to prepare for."

The sale closed on November 18, 2008—just thirteen days after his forty-first birthday. Although his managers didn't own stock in Planet Tan, Hartl made sure they benefited financially. "I gave them all bonuses," he said. "It was a total surprise to them. Hell, it made me feel better than they did. The bonuses went all the way to the district managers and the people running the stores. The biggest one was for a guy who had hired me in a previous job and then twice served as my acting CFO at Planet Tan. I handed him a pretty good check over dinner—six figures."

For Hartl, the sale was the culmination of a long and arduous but rewarding journey. Abandoned by his father before his second birthday, he had grown up in extreme poverty. His mother had worked two jobs to support him and his sister and was not always able to make ends meet. They had often gone hungry. So Hartl's success in becoming not just financially secure but independently wealthy was a triumph. "It was kind of an awesome moment," he said. "I was proud of myself. Maybe that's the word. I was proud because I knew it wasn't luck. It was almost twenty years of working my butt off, and being very focused, and never being a flake, never failing to honor my commitments. It went beyond my greatest imagination."

Later, there was sadness, when it sunk in what he'd lost—namely, his company, including the people he'd worked with. "It was like losing the best friend I'd ever had. Planet Tan was the best of everything for me. It made me a better person. It introduced me to people I would otherwise never have met. It gave me privileges and opportunities that I was so thankful and grateful for. It was just the best partner I could have ever dreamed of. Ever. Ever. Ever." Still, Hartl had peace of mind in knowing he'd done right by the people who had accompanied him on the journey.

Sharing the Wealth

To be sure, what gives one exiting owner peace of mind might give another heartburn. These decisions about what's owed to employees are highly personal. Unless you're a Simon Legree, you'll no doubt wish your former employees well after you and they go separate ways, but that doesn't necessarily mean you'll feel an obligation to share with them the proceeds of the sale. If you choose to, it's mainly a reflection of your own character and values and—as with Hartl—may boost your morale almost as much as it does that of the recipients.

Not that you should underestimate the goodwill created by sharing the wealth. I remember being in Springfield, Missouri, in 1994 when Bob Wehr Jr. and his son Jim sold their company, Aaron's Automotive Products, to an industry roll-up. Many companies get awards for being among the best places to work in their communities; in Springfield, Aaron's Automotive had had a reputation for being among the worst. So the employees were understandably taken aback when they received checks of $1,000 and up, along with expressions of gratitude, from the Wehrs following the sale. News of their generosity made the front page of the local newspaper, and they were showered with praise from all sides.

All of these issues look quite different, however, if your employees are also shareholders in the business, either individually or through an ESOP. Let's leave aside for the moment the question of creating an ESOP mainly for the purpose of cashing out the owner. The chances are that if you've shared ownership with employees as you've been building the company, you've had at least one and maybe a couple of different purposes in mind.

One would be to create alignment around the goal of maximizing equity value. That's the main reason equity sharing is so widespread among emerging growth companies and is often encouraged by venture capitalists and private equity investors. By giving employees a financial incentive, the theory goes, you get everyone working together to ensure a lucrative outcome for all when the liquidity event finally happens. Assuming you're able to achieve such alignment, the sale marks the successful completion of a journey that the entire workforce has been on—a result that everyone will presumably want to celebrate.

However, many owners who share equity have no plans to sell the company to a third party. While they may want alignment around maximizing equity value, it's not because their intention is to eventually have a big payday when everyone cashes out all at once. Rather, they do it because they believe they'll have a better business if all the employees think and act like owners and have a stake in the outcome. Some would also say broad employee ownership is a more accurate reflection of reality, and thus fairer. After all, it's not only founders and investors who create equity value in a business. The employees have a role in it as well. From that perspective, employee ownership is simply a way of ensuring they get a piece of the pie they've helped to bake.

That said, figuring out how to do right by employees isn't necessarily any easier for the top executives of employee-owned companies—who often are also the shareholders with the largest individual holdings—than it is for owners who hold on to 100 percent of the equity. The former have a fiduciary responsibility that they must take into account in making their decisions. Then again, they also have the satisfaction of knowing they are serving their fellow owner-employees as well as themselves. Consider Ed Zimmer.

When Employees Are Part Owners

In 2006, Zimmer was CEO of ECCO Group, based in Boise, Idaho, one of the world's leading manufacturers of backup alarms and amber warning lights for trucks, construction equipment, buses, and other commercial vehicles. The company (which I wrote about in my book *Small Giants*) had an ESOP that owned about 57 percent of its stock. The rest was owned by Zimmer and former CEO Jim Thompson, along with various executives and a single outside investor who had a 3 percent stake. Zimmer was getting ready for his annual fall leadership retreat when he got word that a major competitor, Britax PMG Ltd., was in play. At the retreat, he brought up the possibility of acquiring the divisions of Britax that ECCO competed against. It would be the largest acquisition the company had ever done and would require it, for the first time, to use its equity to obtain the necessary financing, in which case all the shareholders, including the ESOP, would be diluted. The team agreed that an acquisition was worth investigating.

By late December the Britax acquisition was off the table, but the investigation had brought to the light other issues that Zimmer felt obliged to address. He had learned, for example, that acquirers were paying much higher multiples of EBITDA for companies like ECCO than he'd realized. He calculated that the market price of his company's stock was as much as $300 per share, or three times its appraised value of about $100 per share. (The appraised value is determined at least once a year by an independent, outside valuation, as required by law.) That discovery created a quandary for him, which had to do with the contingent liabilities built into every ESOP, as we saw in chapter 4. Companies with ESOPs have an obligation to buy, at the appraised value, the ESOP shares of vested members when they leave. The payments can be spread out over time—in ECCO's case, it was seven years—but if a lot of people leave more or less simultaneously, the drain on cash flow can be substantial.

Zimmer was well aware that a significant percentage of ECCO's 250 U.S. employees had been with the company for twenty years or more and were approaching retirement age. For most of them, the ESOP account was their largest asset, worth more than their homes or their 401(k)s. Suppose they left in three to five years. It would be ten to twelve years before they received the final payments for their stock, and during that time all kinds of things could happen to put their money at risk. The economy could tank. The company could stumble. New technologies could change the competitive landscape. Unforeseeable events could intervene.

If the market value of ECCO's stock was really as high as Zimmer had estimated, it was conceivable that a buyer might pay enough for the company to give ESOP members as much cash today, risk-free, as they'd get in ten or twelve years, assuming the company continued to grow at its current rate. From that perspective, it might be irresponsible for him as a fiduciary not to look for a buyer. In any case, he had a difficult choice to make: Sell now and let all the shareholders and ESOP members capture immediately the value they'd created, or accept the risk of waiting, continuing to build the company, and keeping ownership—and control—in their own hands.

Then there were other factors to consider. While the ESOP was important to ECCO's U.S. employees, the company also had operations in Britain and Australia, representing almost 40 percent of the workforce, whose people could not be members of it. Zimmer had to weigh their interests as well. He also had to consider the company's future capital needs. He could see a couple of potential acquisitions of competitors that would strengthen ECCO but require more capital than the company could borrow. So even if it was not sold now, a piece of it might well have to be sold in the future to finance those deals.

And what about Zimmer's personal interests? Hard as he tried to focus only on what was best for the company and the employees as a whole, he couldn't escape the reality that he, too, was a shareholder, one of the largest, with a wife and two children. Almost all of their net worth was tied up in his ECCO stock. If disaster should strike the company, his family would suffer along with everyone else's.

After lengthy deliberations with his leadership team about what course to follow, Zimmer decided to let the market answer the question for them. If they found the right buyer who was willing to pay the right price—that is, at least three times ECCO's appraised value—they would move forward with a sale. Otherwise, they would remain independent. They were actually in a good position to test the market, he believed, because they had complete flexibility, not only in what type of deal they would do, but in whether or not to do a deal at all. If the offers they received were substantially below Zimmer's estimate of the market price, they could walk away and the company would be fine. They could therefore be extremely picky about the people they would do a deal with—or so he thought.

The first step was to find an investment bank to represent ECCO. Working his contacts, Zimmer got recommendations for six M&A firms familiar with the automotive market. He and his colleagues began interviewing them and quickly settled on Lincoln International, a global investment bank based in Chicago. "Everybody else spent the time talking about terms and fee structures and trying to impress us," he said. "These guys spent the time asking us questions and trying to understand our needs."

ECCO's people wanted to move quickly, partly because they didn't know how long the market would stay "frothy" (as their bankers put it) and valuations would stay high, and partly because they hoped to minimize their exposure to the industry rumor mill. It helped that they had a compelling story to tell potential acquirers. Not only did ECCO have a solid record of profitability and growth, and not only was it a longtime open-book practitioner with good systems, a strong management team, and a culture of accountability, but—even more important—it had several easily identifiable opportunities to double its size in the near future, provided it had the capital to take advantage of them.

In February 2007, work began on the deal book. Lincoln International put an analyst on it full-time. Like Hartl, Zimmer was both amazed and impressed by the time and effort required. "It wasn't just accounting and numbers," he said. "It was more, what's the story here? What's the value here? And they did a great job. I mean this book was really good." In May, Lincoln International sent out so-called teasers to about two hundred prospects, instructing them to send back signed confidentiality agreements (CAs) if they were interested in seeing the book. The bankers told Zimmer they would be "ecstatic" to get thirty CAs returned. They received eighty-two. After perusing the deal book, twenty-eight potential acquirers put in preliminary bids, ten of which were above the minimum offer that the ECCO team had said they could accept. They decided to continue the process with nine of them.

Zimmer had by then hired an independent fiduciary consultant, not connected to Lincoln, to advise him and later to certify that the process had produced the best outcome for the ESOP members. "I was thinking, 'This sale could really happen,'" Zimmer said. "We'd proved the value. It was above the market price I'd estimated, and there was a lot of interest. So now it's a matter of figuring out what was the very best scenario for everybody. In my mind, it was that we get a premium number and everybody keeps their jobs. But the consultant said, 'Now wait a minute, you have a fiduciary responsibility to the ESOP members and shareholders to get the maximum price for them, regardless of whether or not they lose their jobs.' I said, 'You're kidding.' And he said, 'No, I'm not. That's the way it is.' I said, 'Do you mean to tell me that if they get a number that's a couple bucks a share more and lose their jobs, that's a better deal?' And he said, 'You've got to get the best price for the shareholders.'"

Zimmer's elation about ECCO's situation immediately turned to anxiety about the fate of the employees. Had he set in motion a chain of events that would inadvertently cost them their jobs? He and his colleagues suddenly had a rooting interest among the various suitors. "We wanted a buyer who was not from our industry," he said. "We wanted someone who was looking at ECCO as a platform, and would leave it alone and grow it—as opposed to a competitor that might shut us down and suck us into its operations. As it turned out, the highest offers were from financial investors looking for growth."

All financial buyers aren't equal, however. A private equity group would finance the deal with a combination of equity and debt. "My concern there was that we could wind up paying $3 million or $4 million a year in interest, and they'd cut our operations and cut expenses, build up the EBITDA, and sell us again in a few years," Zimmer said. He'd seen this happen with a couple of competitors. Every three years or so, the company would get a new owner, CEO, and CFO, as well as a pile of debt. To raise the cash needed to make its interest payments, it would drop its prices 20 percent and sell off inventory at the end of each quarter. Its customers quickly caught on and waited to get the discount, while the company's competitors, including ECCO, picked off its best customers right and left between fire sales. Zimmer's fear was that ECCO might wind up in such a situation. "It scared us because we'd be obligated to accept the offer if it was the most money for shareholders."

The deal book had gone out in May 2007. The preliminary bids arrived in June. The management meetings took place over three weeks in July. Each one was a daylong affair. Zimmer would start, talking about ECCO's culture, core values, structure, and strategy. He was followed by all of the people who reported directly to him, except for the managing director of the Australian business, who couldn't attend. Each person focused on a different topic—markets, products, engineering, opportunities abroad, and so on. Zimmer also put together a panel to analyze the competition. The whole presentation took about six hours. The idea was not only to give potential acquirers a clear and comprehensive picture of the company, but also to let them hear directly from the members of the senior management team, the strength of which, Lincoln believed, would influence ECCO's value and thus the price that a buyer would be willing to pay. By the end, Zimmer said, they had become really good at it.

Although ostensibly a chance for acquirers to evaluate ECCO, these meetings were also an opportunity for the ECCO team to evaluate the acquirers. Zimmer had his eye on one in particular. In May, his main contact at Lincoln, Tom Williams, had called him and said that a copy of the deal book had been requested by a fifth-generation, family-owned, Philadelphia-based investment firm called Berwind. Originally a coal mining company, it had been transformed by its former CEO, Charles Graham Berwind Jr., into a diversified conglomerate of manufacturing and service businesses. "Tom said, 'We've never done a deal with them, but they've been on our radar screen for years,'" Zimmer said. "Apparently they were very selective. They had a very tight profile, and if a potential acquisition didn't fit it, they'd walk away. He said, 'It's Berkshire Hathaway on a small scale, and if we could get them to the finish line, they would be an ideal partner.' He knew how worried I was about becoming a short-term private equity play."

The first management meeting happened to be with Berwind, and the ECCO team came away duly impressed. "I probably liked them more than anybody else because I knew their model," said Zimmer. "After we did our presentations, they talked to us for an hour about why they'd be a good partner and what they'd bring to the party. And we all liked what they said. They had this multibillion-dollar-a-year business with about twenty-six people in corporate. So we knew they weren't operating any of their companies. They wouldn't know how. I also liked that they wouldn't put any debt on our balance sheet. They'd carry it in corporate. You don't do that if you're planning to flip a company. You'd only do it if you were planning to keep it."

Several of the other suitors made it clear that they did plan to load the company with debt and then flip it in a few years—and they viewed that as a selling point. Their idea was that the management team would continue to grow the company organically and, with the help of its new partners, do some acquisitions. Assuming ECCO continued to perform as it had in the past, it would be able to pay down the debt on schedule, which would cause the equity value to soar. The owners would then sell the new entity in three to five years, allowing all the shareholders, including senior managers, to make a fortune.

That opportunity held no appeal for Zimmer. While he intended to stay on as CEO after the sale if the new owners wanted him to, he was not at all interested in making a killing—especially not if many of his colleagues would become victims, as was likely in such a scenario. Among the various suitors, Berwind alone eschewed the build-to-flip plan. It wanted to use ECCO as a platform for creating an enduring business that it would hold on to indefinitely. The acquisition would open up new areas for Berwind's industrial division, including electronics manufacturing, commercial vehicles, and automotive. Zimmer knew from its track record that when one of Berwind's companies established itself in a certain market segment, it stayed there for a long, long time, and that scenario he found very appealing.

The nine prospective buyers had a couple of weeks following the final management presentation to submit their letters of intent (LOIs) with firm offers, after which one offer would be selected and due diligence would begin. Three of the nine companies let it be known that they would not submit LOIs. Then came a surprise: Berwind informed Lincoln International that it wanted to conduct due diligence before submitting its offer. That was highly unusual, but Lincoln passed along the request to Zimmer, who gave his approval not knowing exactly what to expect. Normally, due diligence takes weeks. To everyone's astonishment, Berwind completed it in two days. A dozen people—about evenly split between Berwind people and auditors from big accounting firms—flew in on two corporate jets. A few local accountants were also brought in. They began at 8 a.m. one morning and left at 6 p.m. the next afternoon.

Evidently they liked what they found at ECCO. When the offers were formally submitted in early August, Berwind had increased from its preliminary offer. Although one other offer was a bit higher, Berwind asserted that it could close the deal in fifteen days, rather than the usual sixty days. Even more important, its offer was the only one not contingent on getting financing. Zimmer's independent fiduciary consultant agreed that, as a result, Berwind's offer was clearly best for the shareholders.

In fact, the ability of the five others to obtain financing had just become highly problematic. Right about the time they were putting in their bids, a liquidity crisis hit global financial markets, brought on by the bursting of the U.S. housing bubble and the collapse of the subprime mortgage industry. Suddenly it became much, much more difficult for all types of borrowers to get funding.

Zimmer didn't immediately appreciate just how much the economic landscape had changed. He was greatly relieved that Berwind's offer had spared him from pressure to accept one of the others. But until all the papers were signed and the money transferred, there was always a possibility that the deal could fall through—which meant that losing bidders still had a chance to get the rebound, as it were. Lincoln kept the other suitors informed while ECCO's lawyers and Berwind's lawyers started drafting the final purchase agreement. Meanwhile, first one, then another, then another of the suitors pulled out, saying they could no longer secure the financing they would need to do the deal. Berwind, which didn't require outside financing, was eventually the only one left standing. "They could have pulled the deal at any point, because the economic environment had changed so radically, but they didn't," said Zimmer.

In the midst of all this, Zimmer's sister, who had been struggling with cancer, took a turn for the worse. She was also the mother of one of his key managers, Chris Thompson, and the ex-wife of former CEO Jim Thompson, who was still a major shareholder. Fortunately, ECCO had a highly competent CFO, George Forbes, who was able to keep the sale process moving forward while Zimmer focused on the family crisis. The closing was scheduled for September 10, 2007. At 5 a.m. that morning, Zimmer's sister died. He called the CEO of Berwind, Michael McLelland, who told him to take his time. "He said, 'Do what you have to do. We're not going anywhere,'" said Zimmer. So the deal closed a few days later than anticipated, and for an amount of money—$340 per share—that was well over three times the company's appraised value.

From a financial perspective, it was an extraordinarily good deal for all the employee-owners, who got to keep their jobs in the bargain. At that point, however, not even Zimmer had any idea just how fortunate they were. Knowing what we do now about what transpired in the U.S. economy in the following years, we can say definitively that had ECCO not been sold to Berwind at that moment, the employee-owners would have had to wait a long, long time before such an opportunity would present itself again, and that's assuming disaster would not have struck in the meantime—by no means a certainty.

After the Sale

It's worth noting that, unlike Hartl and most other owners, Zimmer didn't have any concerns about telling employees the company had been sold. They already knew that a sale was in the works. Six months earlier, on the same day that the teasers had gone out, Zimmer had called a company meeting and told everyone what was happening. Because ECCO was an open-book company, and its employees well versed in the financials, he was able to explain in detail why the management team had decided the time was right to test the market. People knew that the share price was about $100, based on the latest valuation, and most of them understood the difference between an appraisal value and a market value. Zimmer told them that he thought the latter might be as much as $300 a share, and that the company would not be sold if it turned out to be much less. All the ESOP members knew how many shares they had and so could easily calculate what a sale would mean to them personally. Zimmer reminded those whose shares hadn't yet vested that they'd vest immediately in the event of a sale.

Zimmer said the response was positive overall. "There were a lot of questions. People were mainly concerned that a competitor might buy us and close us or move us. I said, 'We all have to have some faith that whoever pays that kind of price for this company won't want to ruin it. They'll want to make it better. Because they'll be spending a boatload of money, which they wouldn't do if the plan was to kill it.' People understood the logic and were very supportive."

As the sales process unfolded, Zimmer continued to update employees on each step of the process at the company's regular monthly meetings. Between meetings, the leadership team kept their ears open for rumors. Whenever they got wind of one, they'd respond, usually by taking people aside and asking them to spell out their concerns. Zimmer also put together a panel of employee representatives, one from each department, and met with them every two weeks to answer any questions they had themselves or had heard from others.

As a result of these efforts to keep employees in the loop, there was very little drama when the deal finally closed. Zimmer admits that things might not have gone so smoothly if the final offer had been less than $300 per share. "If we'd been at, say, $290 a share, I might have had some ESOP people saying, 'I want my money.' I would have been really conflicted between what I should do for myself and what obligation I had to the ESOP and the other employees. But the final price was such a clear success that there was no doubt about what we should do." Indeed, more than one hundred ESOP members (out of 250 U.S. employees altogether) had payouts of over $100,000.

Initially, at least, Zimmer was the only employee whose job changed very much—in some ways that he enjoyed and in others that he didn't. He loved the opportunity to do acquisitions. Within the first five months, he negotiated two deals, both of which closed in February 2008. In May, he went shopping again, this time for a company that could take ECCO into the so-called red-and-blue market—that is, North American police cars. After being turned down by one potential acquiree, he arranged the purchase of another. That deal closed on December 31, 2008.

Much less fun than doing acquisitions was the experience of setting up the in-depth financial reporting that Berwind demanded of its portfolio companies. As careful as ECCO had always been in projecting and tracking its numbers, the information it provided didn't have anywhere near the level of detail that Berwind expected. With the sale closing in September 2007, Zimmer was immediately thrust into the torment of budgeting for 2008. "The process was really gut-wrenching," he said.

It didn't help that the economy was entering the depths of the Great Recession. The original equipment manufacturers (OEMs) among ECCO's customers had all cut their orders back at least 50 percent. Its second largest customer, Caterpillar, had cut back 70 percent. In April, Zimmer bowed to the inevitable and ordered the first major layoff in the company's thirty-six-year history. More than 15 percent of the workforce was let go. Some of those who lost their jobs were bitter and faulted the change in ownership. "The ECCO of old—the small giant they once were—would have gone about it in a whole different manner with information about the decisions leading up to the layoffs, recommendations of counseling, and just plain caring," said one of them. "The new ECCO-Berwind did not even give a hint of what was to

come. Groups of employees from all areas were summoned to the conference room on a Monday morning and handed their termination
paperwork."

Zimmer didn't dispute that ECCO's culture had changed somewhat
following the sale, but insisted that he would actually have had to lay
off many more people if Berwind hadn't been in the picture. Nor would
he have handled it differently in the past. The layoff was done quickly
and without much notice, he said, in hopes of minimizing fear in the
workforce, which can be dangerously debilitating when the threat of
layoffs drags on for months. Better to do it all at once and get it over
with.

Next to firing people, Zimmer's least enjoyable responsibility was
the constant reporting that Berwind required. He was the only CEO of
a Berwind company without an MBA and a background in accounting,
and he wasn't used to tracking the numbers as closely as his boss required. "Before the sale, a variance from budget of 1 percent might not
get any scrutiny at all," Zimmer said. "But it would require hours or
even days of analysis to explain it in the Berwind world." More than
once he told his boss that he thought Berwind would be happier with
someone else as CEO of ECCO, but each time the boss talked him out
of quitting.

Zimmer had been advised by a friend who had sold his own company to stay at ECCO at least until Berwind had released the portion of
the sale proceeds (about $4 million) being held in escrow pending reso-
lution of the so-called representations and warranties that are part of
every purchase and sale contract.* Though the money was supposed to
be paid in March 2009, it had been delayed pending resolution of some

* The clause in the contract specifying the seller's "representations and warranties" is often
referred to as the "survival clause," and for good reason. It spells out what assurances the
seller has and hasn't given the buyer about various factors that affect the company's value
but whose impact won't be known until sometime after the sale. In other words, it identifies
potential risks in the valuation and says who is responsible for what. It also serves as a kind
of statute of limitations by setting the amount of time for which these assurances will be in
force.

outstanding issues. The two sides finally reached an agreement in August, and the remaining funds were distributed to the ECCO shareholders, including members of the ESOP.

It took a little time for Zimmer to realize the significance of that event to him personally. He had long felt he'd be ready to leave when he had enough of his own capital in liquid investments that his family could live indefinitely on the returns with no change in lifestyle. He had even come up with a number, though he hadn't thought about it for a while. "I had my head down, doing what needed to be done, and all of a sudden I look up after the escrow is released and realize, 'Hey, I'm there!'"

Shortly thereafter, he received a call from his boss, who said he would be flying to Boise the next week to start planning for 2010. He also brought up a touchy subject. "He thought I hadn't been traveling enough," Zimmer said. "He wanted me to start spending more time on the road, especially with our companies in England and Australia." Zimmer hung up the phone and sat thinking about the future. He realized his boss had a point. Although he was spending sixty-five nights a year away from home, the company did need him to do more traveling. The problem was he had lost all enthusiasm for it. An hour later, he called his boss back and said he'd made up his mind to retire. Maybe it was the tone in his voice, but his boss didn't put up an argument this time.

On October 15, 2009, he stepped down as ECCO's CEO, a position he'd held for more than twenty years. What he felt, he said, was a mixture of pride and relief. "I was proud of what we'd accomplished. The company was stronger than ever and in good hands." The relief came from knowing he'd done exceptionally well by his associates, and now the business was someone else's responsibility.

Friends, Fools, and Family Investors

Deciding what you owe to employees may be a matter of choice, but what you owe to investors generally isn't. When you take other people's money to use in building your business, you make a promise—usually explicit, sometimes implicit—to give them a good return on their investment. If the money comes in the form of a loan, you owe them repayment with mutually agreed-upon interest. An equity investment is different, because it's worth nothing in the event of failure, and sometimes worth nothing even in the event of success. (See Bill Niman, chapter 3.) Equity investors are taking a lot more risk, and thus putting a lot more trust in you to do right by them. Along with that trust comes responsibility, and it weighs most heavily on entrepreneurs who have counted on the investments of friends and family.

Few entrepreneurs I know have had to bear a greater burden in that regard than Gary Hirshberg, who cofounded Stonyfield Farm, best known for its organic yogurt, with Samuel Kaymen in 1983. By the time he sold a majority stake to Groupe Danone in the early 2000s, the company had 297 shareholders. About a hundred of those were employees who had received stock options along the way. The rest were individual investors, including the friends, acquaintances, and relatives who had kept Stonyfield afloat in its early days, when the company lost money year after year for almost a decade. Others had invested but had come to Hirshberg at some point saying they needed cash, and he had found people to buy their stock.

The abundance of shareholders was a direct result of the implausible way that Stonyfield became a viable business. Indeed, it was pretty much accidental that the company got started at all. Kaymen had a 501(c)3 not-for-profit in New Hampshire called the Rural Education Center. Hirshberg, who was executive director of another environmental not-for-profit on Cape Cod, served on Kaymen's board. Board members used to eat Kaymen's (especially delicious) homemade yogurt as they brainstormed about ways to raise money for the center. Finally, one said, "Why don't we try selling Samuel's yogurt?" Kaymen began doing just that in April 1983. In June, Hirshberg agreed to join him full-time but first had some loose ends to tie up. When he finally arrived in September, he found a huge stack of unopened envelopes in his new office. His first task was to open them and separate the checks from the bills—or so he thought. He quickly discovered there were no checks, only bills amounting to about $75,000. "In other words, I'd basically been on the job for about four hours, and we were already bankrupt," he said. "So I did what any self-respecting entrepreneur does: I called my mother and borrowed $30,000 from her. Then I proceeded to work with friends and family and folks from all over at finding the rest." He kept doing it, moreover, for the next eighteen years.

In the very beginning, the thought of providing his benefactors with an exit never entered his mind. "We were just trying to fund our farming school. I don't think I even knew what an exit was. I barely knew what a balance sheet was." It was an investment adviser to some wealthy people who introduced him to the concept in 1984. Hirshberg was working on his first private placement, which would raise $200,000 privately from a group of investors. The investors' adviser naturally wanted to know how his clients would get their money back. "I never really gave him an answer. I think I was just so flaky that he eventually gave up asking. That became my M.O. I did a $500,000 equity round in 1986 and a $2.3 million equity round between 1989 and 1990, and I was very busy finding exits for people who needed to get out, but never once in all those years did I put in writing an obligation to provide anybody with an exit."

Not that Hirshberg was unaware of his responsibilities to his investors, but by avoiding a commitment to any single investor, he was free to do what he thought was best for all of his investors. "That's an immensely important point," he said. "I wasn't accountable to anyone other than everyone, and so no single person had any control over me. I never had to sign away my life. Because of that, everything else became possible."

But never underestimate the importance of being lucky rather than smart. Hirshberg admits that he didn't intentionally avoid investors who would have forced him to commit to a specific exit plan. "We went through a period from 1987 to 1990 when we were losing $25,000 a week. I had to replace that with equity capital. I wasn't against getting institutional money. No one would invest in me. They looked at us, and here we were in the yogurt business, which was barely even a category. Not only that, but the organic yogurt business, which was thoroughly threatening and bizarre to these guys."

You may wonder how he was able to get any equity funding at all, let alone the $10 million that he estimates he raised during the nine years that Stonyfield was operating at a loss with its survival very much in doubt. For openers, it took a lot of work. Although he wound up with 297 shareholders, Hirshberg estimates that he talked to more than a thousand potential investors. It helped that his family had skin in the game. "Remember, the very first investor was my mother. That is not an incidental point. When you've got friends and family, especially mothers—and even worse, I had my mother-in-law deep into the company—it commands a certain degree of attention to these issues, and I obviously felt obligated to see that they got a return. And the people who invested knew full well that my mother and mother-in-law were in. So everyone could be confident that I'd take care of my shareholders."

While it may have reassured investors that Hirshberg's mother and mother-in-law were also at risk, their vulnerability had the opposite effect on his wife, Meg Cadoux Hirshberg, who wrote about her experience with scorching honesty in her excellent book *For Better or For Work*. She was well aware in those early years just how desperate Stonyfield's financial situation was. "[It] tied my stomach in knots," she wrote.

"There was no escaping scowling creditors, mountains of debt, and looming bankruptcy." To get by, even to make payroll, Gary leaned heavily on Meg's mother, Doris, who eventually became the third largest shareholder (after the two founders), with an illiquid investment of more than $1 million in Stonyfield that she might never get back. Meg grew increasingly distressed about the risk her mother was taking. Gary would ask for money, and Meg would plead with Doris not to do it, but she would always invest anyway, saying, "Meggie, I'm a big girl. I know what I'm doing, and it's going to work." That just increased Meg's anxiety. "They're both insane, I'd think. The two people I love most are nuts. I saw my family"—her brothers had also invested—"as financial innocents whom Gary and I were leading to slaughter."

To be sure, the outlook improved markedly when Stonyfield finally reached breakeven in 1992. The company was doing about $10 million in sales by then. Meanwhile, some early investors were coming to Hirshberg looking to cash out. Many had invested as little as $5,000 when their children were young. Now their children were going to college; their stock had become much more valuable; and they needed money. Hirshberg, for his part, had a policy of finding an exit for any investor who wanted out. "That was probably the smartest thing I did in the early days," he said. "Every November I would send a letter to the shareholders and say, 'If you would like to exit in the next year, please let me know.'

"I consider it a best practice. First of all, it's excellent PR, because it tells your shareholders that you have their interests in mind and can buy them out if and when they need to leave. Secondly, you remove the bad apples. I always say, the last investor I want is somebody who always wants out. And by getting rid of those people, by getting their capital replaced or reduced, you relieve yourself of that pressure."

To fulfill his promise, Hirshberg played matchmaker. He began attending financial conferences of investment banks like Silicon Valley's Hambrecht & Quist and Boston's Adams, Harkness & Hill, where he looked for buyers to match with sellers, while also keeping Stonyfield on the investment community's radar. "That's another benefit," he said. "My attending all those conferences was not only great learning for me and great for my shareholders, but I also got to expand the community of people interested in Stonyfield." Once he'd found a buyer, he would introduce the person to the seller and let them work out the terms. He didn't need to get more involved. There was enough trading going on that the market usually dictated the price.

Over the years, the dynamics of the process changed. "As we got bigger, the numbers got bigger," Hirshberg said. "We went from $5,000 investors to investors of $500,000 or more. Of course, they were more sophisticated, and I began dealing with more and more lawyers who were demanding more and more things. Because we were performing, and we were a desirable investment, we ultimately could get our way. I wouldn't necessarily recommend what we did to other people, because it was exhausting. But if you can avoid either institutional investors or acquiescing to things that don't feel right to you, you can create the conditions where the exit is on your terms, not on somebody else's terms."

Among the new shareholders were some professional money managers. One in particular came with a substantial amount of money from a group of global investors. "He brought me his term sheet with all the usual bells and whistles, but by then I definitely did not have to give in. It frustrated him to no end. I didn't even give him a board seat, although I did invite him to attend board meetings, which turned out to be a good move, because he didn't feel left out. He agitated a lot for selling the business. He was difficult to the point where several board members asked whether I really wanted to have him keep attending, because it was getting monotonous. But I was okay with it because I didn't have an obligation to do anything."

That was because nobody other than Kaymen, Hirshberg, and Meg's mother owned more than a small percentage of the stock. The voting power of the impatient money manager was only about 7 percent. Hirshberg's stake was about 20 percent. He and Kaymen had stopped being majority shareholders early on, and later, due to a series of near disasters, their percentages had dropped to the low double digits through dilution. They'd subsequently asked for and received stock options, which had allowed them to earn their way back up. They, plus Doris Cadoux, had voting control.

But although Hirshberg wasn't obliged to do anything, he did in fact want to find an exit for his investors, and sooner rather than later. A growing number of them were coming to him with requests to sell. By the mid-1990s, as much as $1 million of stock was changing hands every year, in ten to fifteen different transactions. He himself was spending up to 70 percent of his time locating buyers and working on deals, and the prospect of not having to do it anymore was appealing. Even when he wasn't making markets, he lived with the constant stress of knowing that almost three hundred people were waiting for an eventual liquidity event and counting on him to make sure they got a good deal when it happened. Many of them were people to whom he felt a personal debt—not only his mother, mother-in-law, and other family members, but also his cofounder, Kaymen, who was approaching his seventieth birthday and thinking about retirement, and the farmer who had accepted $5,000 in stock in lieu of payment for milk and thereby allowed Stonyfield to stay in business back in the early days. And the seller of dairy equipment who also took stock for payment at a critical point in the journey. And the owner of a public relations firm who did the same.

And so in 1998 Hirshberg began to seriously explore his selling options, which brought him face-to-face with the potential hazards of each one—and brings us to the next condition of a happy exit: knowing your buyer.

8

———•◆•———

Caveat Venditor

> **Make sure you know why potential buyers want to acquire your company.**

"Everything you do in business is preparing for the endgame, whether you know it or not," notes Gary Hirshberg, the chairman and cofounder of Stonyfield Farm. "A lot of us don't know it because we are so focused on survival."

He should know. Only by luck was he still a master of his fate in 1998 when he began looking for a way to cash out his 297 shareholders. Because he hadn't been able to secure funding from professional investors in the 1980s, when Stonyfield was constantly on the brink of bankruptcy, he had considerable freedom to decide which option was best for his shareholders, the company, and himself.

Hirshberg had long assumed he would eventually follow in the footsteps of his friends Ben Cohen and Jerry Greenfield, who had done an initial public offering of Ben & Jerry's Homemade, their Vermont-based ice-cream company, when it was just six years old. Having decided the time to act had arrived, he began to take the preliminary steps toward an IPO, forming a shareholder committee to oversee the process and interviewing potential investment banking firms to lead it. He had already selected Adams, Harkness & Hill and was about to hire it when he got a call from Cohen, whose company had become the target of a hostile takeover attempt by publicly owned Dreyer's Grand Ice Cream, based in Oakland, California. Cohen was desperately trying to pull together a group of private investors to serve as white knights and save Ben & Jerry's from Dreyer's. Hirshberg was happy to join the effort, but Cohen's predicament immediately soured him on the prospect of going public. "Once Ben & Jerry's received the offer from Dreyer's, the company was in play," he said. "Ben no longer had a choice of whether to sell. It was how to sell. In other words, he was negotiating without all the cards in his hand."*

That came as a revelation. "For some reason, I'd never taken in that going public was selling the company. I'd attended all these conferences put on by investment bankers. They hosted and toasted us and made us feel like the bee's knees. But no one ever said, 'When you go public, you're selling the company.' I don't think many of us realize that. But I saw it from the front-row seat working with Ben to fend off this hostile takeover."

Hirshberg's response was to switch gears and begin talking to investment bankers about finding a company to acquire Stonyfield, with certain conditions, one of which was that he would remain in control. It was a thoroughly unrealistic expectation. Hirshberg himself owned about 20 percent of the stock and employees had another 5 percent. All the other shareholders he intended to cash out. So he was asking an acquirer to purchase 75 percent of the stock and leave him in charge. "That's not possible," said Jim Gold, a managing director of Lazard Frères & Co., "but I'd love to help you try and do it."

---

* Some analysts dispute the contention that Ben & Jerry's had no choice but to be sold once a potential buyer entered the picture. (See Antony Page and Robert A. Katz, "The Truth About Ben & Jerry's," *Stanford Social Innovation Review*, Fall 2012.) Be that as it may, there's little doubt that Cohen and his board believed the company had to be sold or face debilitating shareholder lawsuits.

"That means you're my guy," Hirshberg said.

He had a pretty good idea of the kind of acquirer he wanted. "I was looking for a company that could bring synergy and make us more effective and efficient. We saw the market moving toward organic and natural. We thought, correctly, that it was going to get more competitive and difficult, and we really wanted somebody who could bring us distribution clout, sales clout, manufacturing expertise, or something, and also leave me fully in charge. And on top of that, I wanted a top multiple for my shareholders. Fortunately, I wasn't under pressure from them to do a deal. Unlike Ben, I had all the time in the world. There were a couple of professional investors who kept asking, 'What are you going to do?' But they owned only a small percentage of the stock and had no clout. They were just a nuisance. I had the full support of the board. In fact, I had shareholders who had seen what was happening with Ben & Jerry's and absolutely did not want me to do a deal."

Among the first potential acquirers that Gold put Hirshberg in touch with was Groupe Danone, the Paris-based global leader in fresh dairy products, among other things. He'd met the company's head of M&A in Lazard's New York City offices. The offer he received was so low that he didn't even respond to it. He kept looking. "From 1998 to 2001, I talked to about twenty large companies," he said. "You probably couldn't even name a major corporation with a perishable food business that I didn't talk to. By the end, it was looking as though Jim Gold's prediction was right—that what I wanted was impossible."

But in the fall of 2000 Danone contacted Gold and asked whether Hirshberg might be willing to reconsider. Gold responded that Danone's original offer was much too low and, in any event, Hirshberg would do a deal only if he could remain in charge and run Stonyfield without interference from the parent company. Far from scaring Danone off, Hirshberg's condition was right in line with the thinking of Danone's chairman and CEO, Franck Riboud. He was well aware that his company had no experience in the organic yogurt business and didn't understand it. He thought he and his people had a lot to learn from the Americans. Hirshberg had to stay if Danone was to get what Riboud wanted out of the acquisition—and Riboud was willing to pay a lot more for Stonyfield if Hirshberg would remain in charge.

The negotiations then began in earnest, and as always, the devil was in the details. It took a whole year to work out the terms of the deal. Hundreds of questions presented themselves: What would happen if Hirshberg was not able to go on for some reason? What if Stonyfield's performance didn't meet expectations? What if Danone got into a business that contradicted Stonyfield's values—for example, toxic waste? What if Danone was acquired by PepsiCo, or by Altria, parent company of Philip Morris, or by some other entity that would undermine Stonyfield's credibility with its consumers? And on and on.

Then, of course, there were the fundamental issues of governance, ownership, and succession. How could Stonyfield's autonomy be preserved while simultaneously protecting the interests of Danone's shareholders? Would Hirshberg and his managers own Danone stock or hold on to their Stonyfield stock? In the latter instance, would they receive dividends, and if so, how would that work? And how long would the agreement between the two companies remain in force? What would happen when it ended? How could it be amended? How would Hirshberg's successor be chosen? The list seemed endless.

As the two sides waded through the issues, Hirshberg had moments when he despaired of their ability to resolve all of them. Several times he was on the verge of walking away. He credits his lawyer, Stephen L. Palmer of K&L Gates, and his negotiating partner, Danone's then head of M&A, Nicolas Moulin, with keeping the process alive. "Nicolas was a magician," Hirshberg said. "We've become friends, but he was my enemy for a time there. I learned later that he had orders to get the deal done, but I didn't know that, and so I was negotiating for my life. We'd reach a point where I'd say, 'Look, it's not working. I have to go home and think about everything.' And Nicolas, who was deft as well as enormously talented, would say, 'Why don't you go out, take a walk, and clear your mind. And before you fly home'—we were in New York—'come back in two hours and see if we can't solve it.' By the time I came back, he'd have worked it out. Because he's a genius. That must have happened ten or twenty times."

Part of the problem was that there were no role models for such a deal, or at least none that Hirshberg, Palmer, and Moulin knew of. Seldom if ever has the owner or major shareholder of a privately owned company been in a position to demand the guaranteed level of independence after the sale that Hirshberg was insisting on. Equally rare was the willingness of a giant, publicly traded company to grant it. That came directly from the CEO, Franck Riboud, who considered the deal critical to his company's future and was determined to make it happen. He left the negotiating to Moulin but followed the talks closely and stepped in at crucial moments. "One time in particular I was ready to give up on the deal," Hirshberg said. "I was done. And I had lunch with Franck, and he brought me back. I'm sure it's obvious, but I just have to say it: If it wasn't for Franck, if I didn't have support at the very top, this wouldn't have worked. This wasn't some guy in M&A persuading the people at the top to do it. This was the person at the top saying we're going to do it."

Riboud's determination to do a deal began with his recognition that Stonyfield had come up with a business model fundamentally different from Danone's, and it worked at least as well, maybe better. Danone's model was standard for consumer products companies: Keep your cost of goods as low as possible and your gross margins as high as possible, then use your gross profit to market like crazy and do heavy advertising to reach more and more people and get them to buy more and more product. In the process, you create—or hope to create—brand loyalty. Because of Stonyfield's decision to compete on quality, as well as its commitment to supporting family farmers, its cost of goods was higher and its gross margins lower than Danone's. As a result, Stonyfield didn't have the cash flow that would have allowed it to rely on advertising and other traditional marketing tools to build the brand. And yet survey after survey showed that the brand loyalty of Stonyfield's customers was significantly greater than that of other yogurt companies. "When our consumers go into a supermarket, they don't look for yogurt," Hirshberg said. "They look for Stonyfield." What's more, its net margins were either equal to or better than those of Danone's various businesses. Hence Riboud's eagerness to learn all he could about Stonyfield's model.

Hirshberg had his own ulterior motives. "I was negotiating to take care of my shareholders, but I also wanted to be free from worrying about them so that I could really concentrate on taking Stonyfield to the next level. Even though Danone was a big multinational, and certainly not an organic foods company, I was betting that I could do sort of an aikido move with them, where I would be able to channel their assets, their strengths, to aid and abet my mission while at the same time leaving me free to run with it. In addition, I was hoping to implant some of our DNA in Danone. That goes way beyond being organic. A lot of organic companies do the absolute minimum to qualify as organic. They're not building trust and authenticity. Our authenticity is in our DNA. We are fully transparent. Our consumers trust us, but we have to earn that trust every day. I don't take it for granted."

By the fall of 2001, Stonyfield and Danone finally had a deal. It wasn't simple; the purchase-and-sale agreement itself was several inches thick, with a long list of mutual obligations and what-if scenarios. Under the agreed terms, Stonyfield would remain a separate entity, and Danone—which was paying a reported $125 million—would own about 75 percent of the stock, to be purchased from the outside shareholders. "They gave us the top multiple," Hirshberg said. "I can't say what it was, but trust me: It was the best among the deals happening at that time. So I could look my shareholders in the eye and know I'd done fine by them."

Hirshberg, his managers, and his employees would retain the remaining 25 percent of the stock, but he would control three of the five seats on the board. In exchange, Danone would have three vetoes: It could nix any acquisition it didn't approve of; it could kill any capital expenditure over $1 million; and it could overrule any budget that exceeded certain agreed-upon parameters. The second one turned out to be the most important, although Hirshberg didn't realize it at the time. Stonyfield, whose annual revenues were $85 million, had never had a capital expenditure greater than $1 million. Within a few years, however, Hirshberg was having to seek approval for almost every capital expenditure—and usually getting it.

Aside from the vetoes, Danone wanted some protection should Hirshberg prove unable to keep growing Stonyfield's top line. So the two sides came up with a formula for determining the minimum acceptable growth rate, year by year, for the duration of the contract, which ran until 2016. (It was renewable thereafter.) Hirshberg would retain his majority control of the board only as long as he met that standard. He, on the other hand, wanted protection in case events beyond his control—say, a plane from the airport next door crashing into his factory—caused Stonyfield to have a terrible year. They decided that he would not lose his majority unless the company had two bad years in a row, and if it had one bad year, revenue improvements would thereafter be measured off the down year, not the year before.

To top it all off, the deal would unfold in two stages. In stage one, Danone would buy a 40 percent share in Stonyfield, and the stock of the selling shareholders would be put in escrow. Danone would then have two years to do about a dozen things, such as including Stonyfield in large food service contracts and helping it with manufacturing. Hirshberg would decide whether or not Danone had fulfilled its commitments in a satisfactory manner. If so, Danone would be permitted to buy the rest of the outside shareholders' stock. If not, it would remain a minority owner, and the contract would be null and void.

Hirshberg said he needed the trial period for the sake of his own credibility with customers. "I knew a lot of my natural foods consumers would be suspicious of the deal and might think that I'd sold out to The Man. The two-year trial allowed me to say in good faith that I would decide when and whether to complete this transaction. But it was great for me too, because I was nervous about these guys. I didn't know who they were, and I couldn't believe that we'd thought of everything. And I had friends, sophisticated businesspeople, who were saying this would never work. But those two years really gave me confidence. Danone earned my trust. I guess the lesson is to date before getting married."

Thirteen years later, Hirshberg had no regrets. Stonyfield's revenues were approaching $400 million; the relationship with Danone was stronger than ever; and he was in the midst of planning his exit. He had already relinquished the post of CEO in January 2012 and become chairman, but his initial successor—Walt Freese, a former CEO of Ben & Jerry's—hadn't worked out. Hirshberg had let him go after less than a year. He had then brought in his second successor, Esteve Torrens, a Danone executive who had previously served as general manager of Stonyfield Europe and then as the company's vice president of marketing and thus was well known to Hirshberg. "So I learned how important it is to work with someone before you make the person your successor," he said.

Looking back, Hirshberg reflected on what he'd done right in the run-up to the sale. "The simple lesson is, 'If you don't ask, you don't get.' It sounds trite and basic, but if I could tell you how many times that's the whole story right there. And it's ironic because entrepreneurs are pretty good at asking, but most people are limited by what they think is possible, and that's a darn shame because there is no reason to be. If my deal proves nothing else, it's that anything is possible when two parties want to get together."

That's one lesson, for sure. But there's another one, at least as important: Hirshberg took nothing for granted in negotiating the deal and didn't let flattery or money distract him from finding out exactly what Danone was looking to get out of the acquisition. Even then, he took the precaution of insisting on the trial period.

Granted, luck played a role. It always does. Among other things, Hirshberg was lucky to have Riboud and Moulin as his negotiating partners. But good luck never guarantees success. What counts is the ability to earn a high "return on luck" (to borrow Jim Collins's phrase). Hirshberg earned his by doing the same degree of due diligence on Danone as Danone did on Stonyfield.

Let the Seller Beware

I find it remarkable how many owners don't dig deeply into the reasons a would-be acquirer wants to own the business being sold. I suppose it's because they're focused on what they're going to get out of the sale. That's natural, and the dynamics of selling tend to encourage it: You seek offers; you receive offers; you qualify them and choose the one you like most; you do what you can to keep it from getting whittled down during due diligence. All of your emotional energy goes toward seeing that the deal gets done.

What you may miss is that the would-be acquirers are in selling mode as well. They sell their trustworthiness, their goodwill, their visions of the future, their ability to provide the right "fit," their high opinion of your people, and so on. No doubt many buyers are sincere about all that, but it's not hard to find examples of owners who feel afterward that they've been misled or even—dare I say it—lied to. And they may be justified: Promises are sometimes made and then broken, and contractual obligations are sometimes ignored. By then, moreover, it's usually too late: Most of an owner's power evaporates as soon as the deal closes.

Owners who have happy exits manage to avoid those nasty surprises, partly by determining in advance what is really motivating the buyer, and therefore what it is likely to do after the sale. Others find out the hard way—after the deal is done. Bobby Martin is one of the latter.

Martin had been a young salesman for NationsBank (later Bank of America), barely out of college, when he got the idea for his business. As a "commercial calling officer" based in Wilmington, North Carolina, he visited companies in the area and tried to interest them in the bank's various products and services. The companies he sold to operated in a wide variety of industries. and ranged in size from five to several hundred employees. In one day, he might call on an injection molding company, a restaurant chain, and an HVAC servicer. He found that the more he knew about the prospect's industry, the better the sales conversations would go.

So he made a habit of doing in-depth research on the industry in question before each sales call and coming armed with five to ten questions based on what he'd learned. "Let's say I was calling on a plastics manufacturer," he said. "I might find out that the cost of resin and other raw materials had risen 25 percent in the last twelve months. I'd go in and sit with the president and say, 'I understand resin prices have gone up 25 percent in the past year. How has that affected your working capital?' Or, 'How has that affected your borrowings on your line of credit?' The president would say, 'How do you know so much about this stuff?'" Salespeople from other banks would come in and talk about the weather, or sports, or whatever.

Martin took the same approach in his more formal PowerPoint presentations to the senior managers of a potential customer. He'd lay out the challenges that companies in their industry were facing and mold his sales pitch accordingly. Without that kind of information, his competitors were left to talk in general terms about what their banks could offer.

Martin's sales technique proved extremely effective and significantly increased the number of accounts he was bringing in. "But I had the entrepreneurial spirit," he said. "I was the one always bucking the bank's policies, not because they were bad, just because it was my nature." It wasn't long before he began thinking about turning what he was doing into a business. He realized that not only would the methodology work for other banks, but just about any company with businesses clients in a variety of different industries could adapt it for their own use. In 1999, he quit his job at NationsBank and began working on a business plan for a company he called First Research. It would be a subscription ser-vice providing up-to-date industry reports geared to the needs of sales-people.

Martin realized that he would have to spend most of his time selling the service and would therefore need a partner who could do the re-search and prepare the reports. The logical partner was a business that already provided industry information to customers. None of the com-panies he contacted were interested, but a prospect in Boston gave him a list of people who might be able to help him. One of them, Ingo Winzer, had a company in Wellesley, Massachusetts, called Local Market Monitor, which analyzed real estate markets around the country. Martin decided to give him a call.

"It was the luckiest phone call of my life," Martin said. "Because he is a good person and extremely smart, and he knew how to compile the industry information in a very clear, concise, and accurate manner. And he has a great reputation." The author of numerous articles, Winzer was frequently cited as an authority on housing and real estate in the *Wall Street Journal*, *Barron's*, and other publications.

Martin made him an offer: Winzer would join First Research as a cofounder and executive vice president/research and write up the first thirty reports, and Martin would give him 35 percent of the stock. Winzer agreed. "It took us six to twelve months to write those thirty reports," Martin said. "Then I just started hawking them around."

Like most start-ups, First Research was desperate for cash flow in the beginning, and the partners took whatever business they could get, whether or not it had anything to do with the company they intended to build. As long as Winzer could produce it, Martin would sell it. Little by little, the company's cash flow improved. Rather than paying themselves, Martin and Winzer used the extra cash to bring on another partner in March 2000, one of Martin's former colleagues from NationsBank, a salesman named Wil Brawley, to whom they gave 10 percent of the equity. "That was the second smartest thing I ever did," said Martin. "The smartest was to partner with Ingo." He and Brawley, as former bank salespeople, could be particularly effective in selling the service to banks, and that's where they concentrated their attention for the next couple of years.

Nothing in business is more exciting than a successful start-up, and everyone at First Research was having fun as the company took off in the early 2000s. The idea of selling it could not have been further from the owners' minds. "People would ask us what our exit strategy was, and Ingo, Wil, and I just laughed," said Martin. "We thought that was the goofiest thing in the world—to start a business with the intention of selling it. We were too ignorant to have an exit strategy, and we really didn't want one. We focused 110 percent on our customers and our product. Everything else was just a distraction."

As little interest as they had in exiting, they couldn't completely ignore the buzz they were generating as the company grew. By 2006, First Research had about forty employees and $6.5 million in revenue. Its salespeople had spread out beyond banks to other companies that sold products and services in multiple industries, including software and accounting. Martin and his partners would occasionally be approached about selling the business. "So we had a general idea of what the business was worth," Martin said. "But if you're growing and happy and have no intention of selling—which was the case with us—you just put it all out of your mind and keep going."

That summer he was manning the First Research booth at a trade show in Boston when a business development person from Hoover's, the business research company, stopped by. After looking through the company's materials and talking with Martin, she was duly impressed. "This is great," she said. "It would work really well with Hoover's. We should buy you."

When she got back to her office, she called the president of Hoover's to tell him about First Research. Shortly thereafter, Martin got a call from the business development people at Dun & Bradstreet, which owned Hoover's. They said they wanted to explore ways the companies might work together. Next, the president flew to Raleigh, where First Research was based, with the ostensible purpose of continuing the conversation. "I was pretty sure what they had in mind," Martin said. "You don't fly the president down to talk about partnerships. Even so, that was how I was going to approach it. I had no intention of selling, but everything is for sale, right?"

When people say that "everything is for sale," they're also saying that enough money trumps all other considerations, which begs a question: How much is enough? Martin talked it over with his partners. They decided that they probably couldn't refuse an offer in the vicinity of $30 million.

They were in no hurry to solicit that offer, however. First Research was in great shape, and they were having fun. Sales were growing and operating margins were excellent. Martin admits that managing the workforce was becoming more challenging as the number of employees approached fifty. But he liked the culture. "It had a real sense of freedom to it. It was self-motivated. It had a lot of personality. It was young, energetic. There was no turnover to speak of. I paid pretty well, and there was a fun atmosphere. We'd go on a retreat every year to a cool place. And one of our mottos was, 'Work to live, not live to work.' We were really into forty- or fifty-hour workweeks. I wasn't impressed with anybody who works seventy hours a week. I felt, 'Get a life, man.'"

Nevertheless, Martin held fast to his view that everything is for sale at the right price. Hoover's and D&B, for their part, continued to court him after the president's visit, during which Martin had politely declined an offer to merge. Finally, they asked Martin what it would take to do a deal. He mentioned his figure. Discussions ensued. They ultimately settled on $26.5 million, of which $22.5 million was to be paid at closing.

Martin said that he was a bit concerned about what might happen to First Research's culture after the sale, but the amount of money involved was too much to pass up. "That's what it came down to, to tell you the truth," he said. "It provided flexibility for the future, and it was also a nice payout for everybody. We didn't just keep it all for Ingo, Wil, and me. We had a deferred compensation plan for the employees that let them benefit from any increase in the company's value, and they did well financially."

Due diligence began as soon as the letter of intent was signed. Although it took less than three months, Martin said it was extremely stressful, in part because he made the classic mistake of trying to manage the process while continuing to run the business. "They came in with a billion questions," he said. "So I had two full-time jobs, which took its toll on my family." By then, he was married with one child and another on the way. "It was also stressful that I wasn't able to tell the employees why I was in all of these meetings with people in suits. Keeping it secret was very important because of SEC regulations, but our culture was built around transparency and openness. It became very obvious by the end that I was not being transparent or open. But I just couldn't be due to regulations."

The closing, in March 2007, was difficult as well. Because a lot of First Research's customers had nonassignment clauses in their contracts, Martin had to make sure they wouldn't leave after the transfer of ownership. "That was really exhausting. I was dealing with their legal departments, which was messy and awkward." The deferred compensation plan added another awkward wrinkle. On the day of the closing, employees had to be told about the sale, and before receiving their checks they were required to sign documents releasing the company from liability. They were then asked to keep quiet until D&B's share-holders had been notified of the merger.

But all of that stress and awkwardness was nothing compared to what Martin went through as the inevitable consequences of the sale unfolded. He remembers the aftermath as months of agony. He became so distraught that he began seeing a psychotherapist for the first time in his life. At one point he found himself hooked up to a treadmill for a stress test his doctor had ordered to make sure his heart was all right. In retrospect, it was clear that Martin had gone into the sale emotionally unprepared for the changes it would bring. That was mainly because in the period leading up to it he'd never thought through why Dun & Bradstreet was so interested in doing the deal and what would actually happen when Hoover's and First Research were merged.

He didn't anticipate, for example, the complications that would arise when Hoover's began distributing First Research's products through its own sales channels. How were salespeople to be compensated? Who would be credited with the sale if salespeople from both companies had relationships with the customers in question? How would the two sales forces work together? Such questions were entirely foreseeable, as was the likelihood that there would be confusion and personal anguish as things were sorted out. But Martin hadn't foreseen any of it. As a result, the level of anguish that his former employees were now feeling took him by surprise, and he suffered along with them.

"It was like their world was turned upside down," he said. "Everything had changed. It was new management. I was no longer in charge. They would tell me about the difficult emotional things they were experiencing because of the merger. I would feel their pain to the point where I was stressed tremendously about what they were going through."

But none of these things would have come as a surprise if he had taken a clear-eyed view of D&B's motivation for doing the deal. After all, it didn't really need First Reseach's workforce or even its customer base. What the acquirer did need was the intellectual property—specifically, the system Martin had developed for enhancing the productivity of salespeople who were selling to businesses in a variety of different industries. Of course, D&B wanted the cash flow that came with the intellectual property, but once the latter had been transferred to Hoover's and integrated into its product mix, it would have the goose as well as the golden eggs, and the acquisition could be considered a success.

Martin wound up leaving fifteen months after the sale. By then, he wasn't in quite so much agony as he had been earlier, but he didn't yet feel "normal," as he put it. By "normal," he meant that he could talk to his former employees—about 80 percent of whom either left or were let go—and feel sympathy without actually suffering along with them. It required another few months to reach that point.

It took him longer, much longer, to figure out whether or not he regretted selling the business. In the meantime, he had enough money to ensure that he would never have to work again. He had taken up writing and was working on a book about entrepreneurship. He said he loved the writing process, but he also loved building things. He figured he would probably want to build something again—maybe a not-for-profit. Would he ever want to build another for-profit business like First Research? "I don't know, man. I don't know if I would start a business if I'd have to suffer like that again. But maybe the second time around would be easier because I'd understand it better." In 2010, he started another industry research company, Vertical IQ, that is thriving today and has hired several former employees of First Research.

Thanks but No Thanks

Hirshberg and Martin obviously represent extremes of experience among owners who sell their businesses to other companies. They also approached their respective deals with radically different agendas. Hirshberg wanted his company to continue as an independent entity with the same mission, workforce, and leadership that it had before the sale. Martin was simply selling for an amount of money he felt he couldn't pass up. But he cared more than he realized about the fate of his employees going forward, as he discovered afterward. That's definitely the worst time to find out.

So we're back to the message of chapter 2 on the paramount importance of knowing who you are, what you want, and why, but with a corollary: It's equally important to know those same things about a potential acquirer. If, like Hirshberg, you care passionately about having your company retain its culture and identity after the sale, he has demonstrated a way to do it other than going public, selling to managers and employees, or passing it along to family members. He believes, moreover, that other mission-driven companies can emulate what he did, although it's hard to imagine how his model would work without a Franck Riboud in charge of the acquiring company.

In any case, Hirshberg is hardly typical. Many more owners are closer to Bobby Martin's end of the spectrum, in that they care about the fate of their employees and companies following the sale but aren't interested in having the businesses remain independent entities that they control. They look for a buyer with a similar culture and perhaps an openness to trying some of the methods that have worked well for them, in hopes that their employees will be happy and their systems validated. Sometimes they succeed. Ray Pagano, the founder of Videolarm (chapter 1), is a case in point. Often, however, owners believe they've found the right match, only to be disappointed later on.

Jeff Huenink was twenty-six, and just a couple of years out of college, when he first went into business. His company was called Sun Services of America Inc., and it was based in Tampa, Florida. He'd launched it in 1983 with the purchase of a small mom-and-pop company (for $180,000) that leased coin-operated industrial laundry equipment. Two years later, he did his next acquisition, buying a company in the same business, and discovered that it was doing much better than the previous owner had believed—and was therefore worth much more than Huenink had paid—because someone had been taking a huge number of coins from the laundry machines. He wound up earning his investment back in six months.

That deal opened his eyes to the potential for building a highly profitable company by purchasing small, undervalued businesses in the industry and then operating them as they should have been run all along. Over the next fifteen years, he grew Sun Services mainly by doing exactly that. Through his active involvement in the industry association—he joined the board and later served as its president—he was able to develop an extensive network of contacts for identifying companies that might be for sale. When a good prospect turned up, he moved aggressively to acquire it. At its peak, Sun Services had $10 million in annual revenue and employed thirty people. They were an unusually productive and efficient group. The company's sales per employee and operating margins were well above the industry averages. "We did more with less," he said. "We had very low overhead and were very productive. So we could compensate our people very well."

The company prospered for more than a decade, but by the late 1990s Huenink was beginning to think it was time to get out. "The industry was very mature, and I was frustrated because it was becoming increasingly difficult to make good acquisitions," he said. "And frankly I was not sure how long it would be before our technology became outdated. So I thought, 'You know, it's a great business. I really like it, but is this something I want to do the rest of my life?'"

At the same time, the public equity markets were booming, and cash businesses like his, with steady, recurring income, were attractive investments. Good deals were hard to find precisely because acquirers were willing to pay multiples as high as twelve times EBITDA. "I thought this was probably a once-in-a-lifetime opportunity," he said. He considered various options. One was to do a roll-up with some other laundry equipment leasing businesses and then to take the combined entity public. Another was simply to sell to one of the companies pursuing him. He decided the latter was the best course.

Huenink negotiated with two potential acquirers. In the end, he chose one of his competitors, Mac-Gray, based in Waltham, Massachusetts. When the deal closed in April 1997, it was still private but planning an IPO, which was part of the appeal for Huenink. The purchase price was $14 million, of which about $7.6 million was in Mac-Gray stock. Huenink figured that when Mac-Gray went public, he would benefit from the high multiples in the public markets. But to protect himself in case the company stayed private or its shares failed to appreciate in value as much as he expected, he negotiated a put, which gave him the right to sell the stock back to Mac-Gray at an agreed-upon price. In effect, it guaranteed a minimum value for his stock.

But mainly, he said, he decided to sell to Mac-Gray, rather than the other suitor, because of the cultural fit. Not only was Mac-Gray's culture similar to Sun Services', but its executives made a point of wanting to adopt and adapt his methods and systems. They had marveled at the productivity and efficiency of his workforce. Sun Services had per-unit operating costs that were half of their own. Huenink was happy to help them make the necessary changes, which, if nothing else, would enhance the value of his Mac-Gray stock.

It soon became apparent, however, that Mac-Gray's senior managers weren't going to implement the changes after all. Huenink realized what was stopping them. "It would have been very hard for them to do," he said. "They would have had to become a lot less top-heavy and change their whole compensation system and way of managing. They had a different way of doing things. It wasn't how I would have done it, but it was their company, and they preferred their way to mine. Which was fine. There are a lot of ways to succeed in business."

That said, he disagreed strongly enough with how the company was being run that he decided to cash out in December 1998. By then, Mac-Gray had gone public, but his stock in the company was languishing below the floor established by his put. He decided to exercise it, which he admits was like "dropping a small nuclear device" on the company.

Huenink later came to realize that his experience was not unique. "I've heard the same thing from several friends who have sold or merged their companies," he said. "Before the sale, the acquiring company says how much it likes how you operate and wants to do it too. But it never happens. I think that's because it's sort of admitting that someone else is better or smarter. That's a pretty tough thing for anybody to admit."

When Your Investors Turn Against You

As Huenink's experience shows, there are limits to your ability to know exactly what a strategic acquirer will do with your company, culture, and employees following the acquisition. As a general rule, it's best to assume that the more you care about what happens afterward, the more cautious you need to be. In the vast majority of cases, the strategic acquirer's culture will dominate, and yours will disappear. What happens to your employees will depend largely on their ability to adjust to the change—unless you've made arrangements beforehand to see that they are taken care of.

But what about financial acquirers? You would think it would be easier to predict their behavior, if only because their interests are so clearly defined. The vast majority are investing other people's money, after all, which means they have to think constantly about getting the return they need to keep their customers happy and turning their highly illiquid holdings into cash. You can expect that they will make decisions—and insist that you make decisions—based on those imperatives, even if the decisions aren't necessarily in the best interests of the company in the long term.

If only their motives were always so clear.

The technology world is rife with stories of entrepreneurs who thought they understood what their investors wanted, only to get blind-sided. Consider a software entrepreneur I know—I'll call her Joan—who suddenly began having troubles with one of her venture investors in 2009, following the onset of the Great Recession. The relationship, which had been fine up to then, became especially rancorous after the venture capital firm placed one of its junior staff people—we'll call him Marty—on the board. In board meetings, he treated Joan with disrespect bordering on contempt and went out of his way to pick fights with her. Outside the meetings, Marty tried to undermine Joan with her staff. For months, the VC did everything he could to make Joan's life miserable and largely succeeded.

The last straw was Marty's reversal on an acquisition that would have significantly boosted the company's value. After giving the deal a green light, he changed his mind on the day of the signing and blocked it. "It just destroyed my reputation in the marketplace," Joan said. Fed up, she went to see Marty's boss, who was one of the VC firm's founders. They hammered out a deal whereby the VC firm would approve the acquisition on three conditions. First, Joan had to resign her position as chairman of the board, although she could temporarily remain CEO. Second, she would have eighteen months to arrange for her company to be acquired. Third, she would agree to step down as CEO if the VC firm asked her to sell at that time and she refused.

The deal cleared up some, but not all, of Joan's questions about what she had been going through. "It was all about control," she said. "They wanted to get out and were scared that I wouldn't agree to sell the company." But she still couldn't figure out why the firm was in such a hurry to sell or why it kept putting obstacles in the way of improvements that would increase the company's value and therefore the value of the firm's holdings.

It was an investor in a friend's company who came up with the key to the mystery. The friend had mentioned Joan's problems to the investor, who had responded, "Look at the distribution." By that he meant check how the distribution of the proceeds from the company's sale would vary depending on the price an acquirer paid.

Joan asked her investment banker to do the calculation, and suddenly it all became clear to her. In return for its investment, the VC firm had received preferred stock that entitled it to get a fixed payout if the sale price was between $30 million and $80 million. The other private equity investors had a similar deal. Holders of common stock, including Joan herself, would receive a distribution only after the preferred stockholders had been paid. If the total sale proceeds exceeded $80 million, however, the preferred stock would be converted to common stock, and the money would be divided according to the number of shares each shareholder owned.

So from the VC firm's viewpoint, it made no difference whether the company sold for $30 million, $80 million, or anything in between. The firm's payout would be the same. Yes, its share of the proceeds would increase above $80 million, but the difference wasn't big enough to justify waiting for the company's value to rise to that level, especially given the inherent risks in any delay.

"That was the big ah-ha moment," Joan said. "If I had realized that earlier, I would have dealt with the situation much differently."

Joan could also see why the VC firm hadn't explained its position. Because it had a seat on the board, it had a fiduciary responsibility to represent the interests of all the shareholders. Had it ever admitted its true motivation, it would have opened itself to a lawsuit. Joan tested her theory on the VC firm's cofounder. "I told him, 'I've finally figured out your motivation.' And I explained what I had learned. All he said was, 'You've got your math right.'"

A Tale of Two Buyers

Joan was scarcely the first entrepreneur to discover that private equity investors have their own agendas, and that the reasons for their behavior may not be visible to the naked eye. Nor was she the first to be subjected to the harsh methods that some of them will use to get their way. Her experience, in fact, was no worse than the gauntlet that Basil Peters (chapter 6) had to run when he sold Nexus Engineering. In Silicon Valley, such stories are legion. There is even a Web site, thefunded .com, devoted to rating investment groups and telling stories about experiences, mostly bad ones, with investors. Its founder, Adeo Ressi, is a serial entrepreneur whose own stories of dealing with venture capitalists are particularly hair-raising.

On the other hand, there are at least as many VCs and private equity groups that add tremendous value to the companies they invest in and make it possible for entrepreneurs to have exactly the sort of exit they're looking for. Martin Babinec (chapter 3), for one, sings the praises of the value that private equity firm General Atlantic brought as majority shareholder of TriNet, above and beyond the contribution of the capital it provided. And there are thousands of other examples.

Still, it's true that you sometimes have to dig deep to divine the motives of financial buyers and investors. However irrational their actions may sometimes seem on the surface, there is usually a rational explanation for their behavior underneath, and the closer you can get to it, the better off you'll be. Ideally, of course, you do that before you sell the company. And make no mistake: The decision to take the private equity investment is almost always a decision to sell the company within seven years.

Paul Spiegelman faced such a quandary in 2009 when he began thinking about selling equity in Beryl Health. He and his two brothers had founded the company in 1985, working from a cot in a tiny conference room in their father's Los Angeles law office. Back then it was called Emergency Response Systems (ERS) and was centered around a device developed by Spiegelman's older brother, Mark, to help hospitals monitor high-risk patients twenty-four hours a day, seven days a week. The Spiegelman brothers would take turns sitting next to the alert screen waiting for a distress call from someone who had one of the devices. Spiegelman said they ate a lot of pizza and watched a lot of television.

Their course began to change in 1986. One of their clients, who worked at a local hospital, wanted to offer patients a telephone number they could call to get a referral to a doctor. Realizing the Spiegelman brothers had a lot of free time on their hands, she inquired if they would be willing to handle the calls. The hospital would pay them a monthly stipend of $3,000. They jumped at the chance and were thus introduced to the business that would eventually become Beryl Health.

In the beginning it was all quite primitive. "We'd basically answer the phone and read the names of different doctors off index cards," Spiegelman wrote in his book *Why Is Everyone Smiling?* "But it was clear to us right away that every hospital in the country would eventually need to offer this service if it wanted to bond with its community."

The brothers' big break came in 1995. They had managed to get themselves included in a project being conducted by Columbia/HCA (now Hospital Corporation of America) to develop a company-wide customer strategy, including physician referral. Given that Columbia/HCA was the largest for-profit operator of health care facilities in the world, it was a huge opportunity, and the brothers spent nine solid months crafting the best proposal they were capable of. Despite the long odds that a tiny, unknown company like theirs would be chosen, they were awarded the contract, and along with it a substantial budget to build a giant call center in the Dallas area.

The brothers were thrilled. They still had operations in California, where they lived, but they commuted every week to Dallas. All went well for two years. Then, in 1997, Columbia/HCA was hit with a major scandal over its billing practices, and the brothers' biggest supporter, CEO Rick Scott, was forced out. They feared their Texas adventure was coming to an end. Instead HCA allowed them not only to keep the contract but to purchase the facility at a small fraction of what it had cost to build. That changed everything. They suddenly owned a state-of-the-art call center that could serve as a platform for both improving and expanding the services they offered. In 1999, they decided it was time to consolidate operations in Dallas and to rename the company. They called it Beryl, after the gemstone known for the variety of colors it comes in.

Spiegelman readily admits that because they had no training and very limited experience, they had to figure out the business as they went along. There are advantages to building a company that way, not least of which is that you're unaware of the conventional wisdom in the industry or among business savants, and so you do things that you might otherwise not have tried. In the process, you sometimes innovate without realizing it. That's more or less how the Spiegelman brothers came up with a highly profitable business model, around which they built the nation's leading provider of outsourced patient communications services.

The centerpiece was Beryl's corporate culture—a term that they didn't learn until they were more than a decade into creating it. In their minds, they were simply trying to maintain a friendly, upbeat, family-oriented environment where employees could have a good time while working hard and providing a high level of service to customers. The physical space they occupied was a big help. Thanks to Columbia/HCA's munificence, Beryl had a facility that defied the stereotype of the dark, dreary call center with rows upon rows of operators huddled at workstations. Instead Beryl employees worked in open, expansive, well-lit rooms, with high ceilings and brightly colored walls. On any given day there would be bouquets of birthday balloons floating above some of the cubicles, and if you waited long enough you were apt to see a soccer-playing bear walking through, or a group of Michael Jackson impersonators, or the CEO in a matador outfit and on roller skates.

Although Paul Spiegelman was the CEO, it was his younger brother, Barry, who epitomized the fun-loving culture. (Mark had left to start another business in 2000.) The bonds he developed with customers and employees were strong and deep. So his death from brain cancer in 2005 shook the company to its core. People had known it was coming. After being in remission for seventeen years, the cancer had returned with a vengeance in 2003. During the final three months especially, the entire staff stepped up to keep Beryl running smoothly while Paul devoted his attention to his brother's care and his family's needs. Dozens of employees went out of their way to support the Spiegelmans and pay tribute to Barry, holding prayer vigils, sharing remembrances, and offering emotional testimonials.

Spiegelman was deeply moved by the outpouring of grief and love for his brother. As hard as he took the loss of his closest friend and confidant, he felt buoyed by the support he'd received from the Beryl staff. It reinforced his belief in the approach he and Barry had taken to the business: putting employees first. "Seeing how much people care about you because you care about them is priceless," he said. "They were like my extended family."

He was also acutely aware that since he was the sole remaining founder, decisions about Beryl's future were now his responsibility alone, and a lot of people were counting on him to make the right ones—not only those involved in the business, but Barry's widow and children and Mark's family, as well as his own. One important decision had to do with bringing in outside investors to provide growth capital and maybe some liquidity as well. The brothers had had plenty of suitors in the early 2000s, which they found disconcerting. Spiegelman said they felt outclassed and a little intimidated by the slick and aggressive investment bankers who kept calling on them. "It was sort of like

being the three little pigs up against a wolf with a whole lot of money,"
he later wrote. For his own education, he eventually agreed to sit down
with a couple of potential acquirers and their representatives. He came
away convinced that they had no idea why Beryl had been successful
and therefore were incapable of making an offer worth considering.

Early in 2009, however, the issue came back on the table. With
Congress gearing up to pass major health care legislation and hospitals
facing increasing pressure from regulators to improve the patient experience, Spiegelman could see a bright future opening up before Beryl,
but also some challenges. By then it had $30 million in annual sales
and three hundred employees who handled all types of telephonic patient contacts for hospitals across the country. If the company ramped
up its growth, maybe even did some acquisitions, it could vastly expand
its reach in the next five years, becoming a much larger and more significant player in the industry, five or six times its current size. Con-
versely, if the company didn't make substantial investments in technology
and product development, it ran the risk of having its position as
industry leader erode.

Beryl's senior managers were eager to take advantage of the opportunities they could see as clearly as Spiegelman did. He had upgraded
the team in the previous two years, choosing ambitious people with the
experience needed to run a larger business. He felt an obligation to give
them a chance to show what they could do.

He had personal reasons for bringing in outside investment as well.
For one thing, he felt that the kind of growth he envisioned required a
CEO with more experience than he had. It was going to cost a substantial amount of money to hire one, and he might need help to find the
right person. To make room, he was prepared to transition into a new
role as an active board chairman, which would free him up to pursue
some outside projects he was excited about (including the Small Giants
Community, which he had founded with my support). Since the publication of his book, he had come to believe more strongly than ever that

he had a message other entrepreneurs were ready to hear about the importance of creating great workplaces and people-centered cultures.

In the spring of 2009, Spiegelman began to search for an investment banker, interviewing a wide variety of firms and ultimately settling on a very small one, Nexus Health Capital, which he had known for years. The deal book took a few more months to prepare. In August the teaser letters went out and led to about twenty initial offers, all from private equity groups. Twelve of them came in for five-hour management presentations. "I'd never been through this process before," said Spiegelman. "So I was shocked when I found out I was supposed to choose one of them to become my business partner based on a five-hour meeting. I said, 'I can't do that. I have to know them better.'" Five of the twelve were selected to come back for further discussions. Spiegelman gave each suitor the same challenge: "What can you contribute to us besides money?"

One firm stood out from the rest: Flexpoint Ford, a Chicago-based private equity firm focused on the health care and financial services industries. Its partners seemed genuinely excited about getting involved with Beryl. They'd made it clear how much they admired Beryl's culture and appreciated the role it played in the company's financial success—specifically, its ability to charge 40 percent more than its competitors. But the investors' ace in the hole was a potential CEO with a solid résumé whom they'd met through their contacts in the industry. An experienced executive, Pam Pure had most recently been at McKesson, the giant health care company, where she'd served as president of McKesson Provider Technologies, growing the business from $900 million to $3 billion in seven years while increasing margins from 5.8 percent to 10.7 percent. Now Pure was looking for a good business in which she could apply her managerial skills, and Beryl seemed ideal. She loved the people, loved the culture, and loved what the company did. She could easily see it becoming a $200 million company in five years, and Spiegelman could easily see her as the new CEO leading the way.

Things moved forward. Flexpoint submitted a letter of intent with an initial offer that was a bit lower than what Spiegelman would have liked, but close enough. Beryl submitted its projections for the coming year. Due diligence began, and for the next two months Spiegelman was tossed around on the emotional waves of the sale process. Every day, it seemed, brought a new development and a new set of questions. Flexpoint was mainly concerned with Beryl's forecast for the coming years. Although the company had had steady double-digit growth in sales and profit every year for the past seven years, it lacked a sales organization, which raised questions about the reliability of its projections. The firm reduced its valuation accordingly. Spiegelman was annoyed but decided he could live with the lower price. He was much more troubled by what he perceived as Flexpoint's short-term focus.

Oddly enough, it was Pam Pure who drove the final nail into its coffin. She called him one evening in March 2010 and asked to meet. Over breakfast the next day, she said that after receiving Beryl's numbers for the first quarter of 2010, she couldn't sleep for two days. She could see that Beryl was unlikely to meet its financial projections for 2010, and on one level that didn't surprise her. The company simply wasn't set up for predictability. It didn't have the systems, the people, or the culture that could provide it. But private equity firms, as investors of other people's money, absolutely must have predictability. What's more, they demand it. There would be enormous pressure on Beryl to make its numbers in the first two years. Flexpoint was already suggesting that an important sales position not be filled and that the money be used instead to achieve the profit goals. "That's exactly what I'm talking about," she said. "What you've created here could be ruined because of their short-term need to see results." Aside from the potential damage to Beryl, she worried about winding up in a situation where she'd be forced to choose between the culture and the needs of the investors.

That did it. Spiegelman let Flexpoint know that Beryl was no longer for sale.

Over the next few months, he thought long and hard about the experience he'd just been through. What did it mean for his future? For Beryl's future? Sooner or later, the time would come for him to move on. How should he prepare for that day, given what he'd learned about the way private equity works? On March 3, 2011, while he was still in the midst of his deliberations, he sent me an e-mail message:

```
I've been thinking about whether it is realistic
to believe you can sell a Small Giant to a finan-
cial buyer and expect it to remain one. Having been
exposed to the world of private equity, I don't be-
lieve the financial buyers' business model would
ever support the way a company like ours is man-
aged. For them, the company is the product. They get
their profit when they sell it again, and they do
whatever they must to achieve the desired return on
their investment. I just can't see them valuing cul-
ture and employee and customer engagement the way
we do. That's why they generally change things once
they take over from founders. It seems like the best
option for companies like mine, if you want them
to go on, is either sale to an ESOP or generating
enough profit to keep the business going long-term.
I'm curious to know what you've found.
```

I told him what I reported in chapter 4: The only companies I've found that have stayed independent and private and have held on to the same high-performance culture for three generations or more are either employee-owned or family-owned.

The immediate question Spiegelman faced was: What now? His senior managers were eager to pursue the goals they'd decided on before Flexpoint entered the picture—the ones that the outside capital was supposed to help them achieve. That would require a big commitment from Spiegelman, both psychically and financially. Where would the capital come from? Ever since landing in a bank's "Special Assets" (that is, workout) department during the company's early years, he had had a strong aversion to debt. The alternative was for him to finance the growth partly by using more of the company's profit—and thus reducing its EBITDA—and partly by investing his own capital. That's what he decided to do.

The process of looking for an outside investor had taught him a tremendous amount about building value in a company like his. Perhaps the biggest lesson had to do with the need to build a sales organization that could reliably forecast where the future sales were coming from. He had also come to appreciate the importance of diversifying the product mix. Beryl could easily be seen as a one-trick pony, and therefore vulnerable, in that it did almost all of its business with hospital marketing departments. Finally, there was the technology factor. Spiegelman saw how the company could reap enormous benefits by upgrading its technology—for example, by moving its platform into the cloud.

As Beryl made these improvements, the bill kept rising. Annual expenses increased by $5 million for people alone, including six new senior managers whom Spiegelman brought on to upgrade his leadership team yet again. Sometime in the fall of 2011, Beryl's EBITDA bottomed out and began to increase again, but Spiegelman could see that the company still had a long way to go before it would start reaping the full benefits of the investment, and that gave him pause. "There were times when our CFO would tell me, 'Paul, I think you're going to have to put more money in,' and I was getting to the point where I really didn't want to do that anymore," he said.

Right about then, he received a phone call from a business development person at Stericycle, a $1.7 billion public company in the medical waste disposal business. The company, based in Lake Forest, Illinois, had recently launched a patient communications division and wanted to explore ways that Stericycle and Beryl might work together. Spiegelman said he'd be happy to talk, and two people flew in from Chicago to meet with him.

Thus began discussions that went on for nine months and included several visits to Beryl by Stericycle people, with more senior executives joining the parade as time went on. Stericycle was obviously interested in acquiring Beryl. Spiegelman said he didn't think the timing was right. It would take four years or more before his investments would begin to pay off and Beryl's profitability would rise above where it had been when he started. He suggested they talk again in a couple of years.

But Stericycle didn't want to wait. Its people asked to see some financials and then came back with a rough estimate of Beryl's value. Spiegelman put them off again, explaining that there would be a lot of other considerations if and when he ever did decide to sell, notably about preserving the culture. On the question of valuation, he estimated how profitable he expected Beryl to be once it was benefiting fully from the investments and came up with a price based on the estimate. He told Stericycle it would have to pay something in that range before he would consider selling.

Stericycle was unfazed. There were more visits and more discussions. Eventually the CEO and CFO of the parent company came to Beryl to look it over for themselves. "I knew that, just by them coming, our value was going to rise," Spiegelman said. He was particularly impressed that the CEO appeared to grasp immediately the importance of the culture. Indeed, he indicated that he would like Stericycle to develop something similar. Perhaps Spiegelman could help.

By then the negotiations were far enough along that a deal actually seemed possible. Spiegelman decided to fly to Chicago with four of his key managers and share the entire strategy going forward. According to Spiegelman's main contact, the Stericycle people were "blown away" by Beryl's management team, which appeared to be more sophisticated and experienced than the team they had in charge of the new division.

Subsequently the CEO paid another visit to Beryl with his CFO, and an agreement took shape. It was sealed in a follow-up telephone call. Stericycle's offer was 50 percent higher than Flexpoint's best offer. In effect, Spiegelman would be paid not only for the capital he'd invested, but also for his projections, which it was implicitly assumed the Beryl team would meet.

With the outline of a deal agreed to, Stericycle could proceed with due diligence. Spiegelman had been through the process once already, and it hadn't been pleasant. "I was stressed out the whole time," he said. "I gained weight. I stopped working out. It took me a year and a half to recover. This time was entirely different. I was so relaxed and calm through the entire process even my wife commented on the difference."

What exactly accounted for his equanimity? "In my experience, financial buyers go into due diligence looking for things that will give them grounds to argue the company isn't worth as much as they thought. With Flexpoint, I had to agree to a substantial reduction after due diligence, which caused some of the stress. Stericycle came in with even more people, but it was actually a pleasure. Everybody was easy to deal with. They weren't searching for anything wrong. They just wanted to validate the truth of what we'd given them. It was like night and day. I suspect that's because the private equity people have a four-to six-year time horizon, and the price they pay now can have a big impact on the return they get then. Strategic acquirers intend to keep you forever. So they just want to be sure you haven't misled them."

The deal finally closed on November 1, 2012. Stericycle offered stock options to all of Beryl's thirteen senior managers, and its CEO made it clear that he wanted Spiegelman to stick around as well. He agreed to stay for at least a year. In the following months, he said, all of his surprises were pleasant ones. Although he maintained an office at Beryl, he wasn't there often, and his senior managers did just fine without him. Several of them were asked to take on greater responsibilities in Stericycle.

As time went on, Spiegelman too found himself doing more and more for the company, which named him its chief culture officer. Much of the work had to do with promoting cultural initiatives in other parts of Stericycle. In that, he enjoyed the strong support of the CEO and other senior executives. The more Spiegelman did, the more he wanted to do. "I've become fascinated with this question of whether you can change a culture midstream," he said a year after the sale, "especially the culture of a large, publicly traded company. It really is an interesting situation I've found myself in, none of which I contemplated at the time I sold the company."

In addition, Spiegelman was increasingly being asked to help out by talking to and working with the owners of companies Stericycle was hoping to acquire, as well as the former owners of companies it had acquired. Given its pace of acquisitions—eight to ten per quarter—he had plenty of opportunity to observe other people at various stages of the exit process and to compare his emotions to theirs. "I can't believe the number of people who just freak out after the sale," he said. "It's like they flip a switch. But I understand it's because this is our life. This is what we've been doing for years and years. So I'm reminded how lucky I've been to wind up where I am."

And there lies the next important question, and the subject of the next chapter: What does it take to ease the transition to life after the sale?

9

—•●•—

Over the Rainbow

> **Your exit isn't over until you're fully engaged in whatever comes next.**

Entrepreneurs who've been through the whole exit process will often tell you it's much harder to leave a company than to start one. No one knows that better than Randy Byrnes, who was launched on his entrepreneurial journey in 1975, at the age of twenty-four, by the owner of an employment agency in York, Pennsylvania. He'd been working there for all of nine months as an "employment counselor," a job he'd taken in the mistaken belief that he could apply the knowledge he'd acquired while earning his master's degree in psychology. He soon discovered that he would actually be a salesman, not a counselor. But he needed the money, and so he stayed and was working the phones one day when the owner invited him to lunch. There his boss told him, "You're going to buy the company."

"With what?" Byrnes asked. "I'm on the draw. I already owe you money."

But the owner had it figured out. The business had been an investment for him—and a bad one at that—and he'd apparently decided that the only way he'd ever see a return was to have someone else buy it from him over time. He grabbed a napkin and wrote down the terms of the deal, according to which Byrnes would pay him $450 monthly for seven years, plus a bottle of Seagram's V.O. whenever they had a meeting. After work that day, Byrnes broke the news to his wife, Sue. "Hey, we're going to buy the agency," he said. She burst into tears.

And for good reason. At the time, she was earning $7,000 a year as an emergency room nurse at the local hospital. Her husband owed his employer $1,000. Their parents were adamantly opposed. And Byrnes had no relevant experience or training. "I'd never even taken a business course in college," he said. "You couldn't have known any less about business than I did."

Nevertheless, he and Sue ultimately decided to go ahead, figuring that there would be no better time for Byrnes to try his hand at entrepreneurship. He told the owner, who had him sign a two-page contract. Together they informed the other nine employees, seven of whom proceeded to quit. It wasn't personal, he realized: They were single mothers and they needed an income they could count on.

Despite his lack of qualifications, Byrnes turned out to be a good businessperson. As the company grew, it evolved from an employment agency (whose customers were people looking for a job) to a temporary help service (whose customers were companies looking for low-level employees) and a search business that recruited midlevel professionals, such as engineers or programmers, for corporate clients. One of his temporary-help salespeople then discovered a third service when a couple of customers told her that they also needed midlevel professionals on a temporary basis. She told Byrnes, who did some research and concluded there wasn't enough potential in that market to justify making a commitment to it. "I told her what I thought, and—God bless her—she put her hands down on my desk and said, 'Listen, you shithead, we need to be in this business.' I said, 'Okay, Holly. Then, damn it, if you think we should be in it, you figure out how.' Which she did. And that accelerated our growth over the next three years."

By the late 1980s, the company, now called The Byrnes Group, had three offices in southeastern Pennsylvania, forty employees, and annual revenues of $12 million and growing. Byrnes continued to implement a number of cutting-edge practices, including open-book management, that not only boosted performance but strengthened the culture, and the company's sales soared. In 1994 and 1995 The Byrnes Group had its two biggest years, reaching $32 million in annual revenues with forty-eight employees.

Right about then, Byrnes hit bottom. "I would find myself at two o'clock in the afternoon sitting in my office with a blank mind, not thinking about customers, not working, just sitting. I said to myself, 'This isn't right. These people are thinking I'm in here doing something for their welfare, and I'm not.' It was very uncomfortable. If I had someone working for me and not pulling their weight, there would be repercussions. I've seen other business owners ride their companies without contributing, and I have no respect for them."

He decided that he had to sell the company. Byrnes shared his decision with Linda Lohenitz, the most capable of his managers and, in effect, the second in command. Lohenitz, who had sensed his malaise, mentioned that she had a friend who was her counterpart at another staffing company, System One, in Tampa, Florida. Byrnes had met its founder and CEO, John West, who had made a good impression. So when she asked about telling West that Byrnes was looking for an exit, he encouraged her. She came back with the news that West was interested in discussing a possible merger.

Byrnes contacted West and then flew to Tampa, where he toured the System One facility and met with key managers. He was impressed with the organization's high energy level, the competence of its leaders, and West's efforts to form a board of outside advisers with expertise and experience that he lacked. Moreover, the two companies appeared to have similar values. He returned home optimistic about doing a deal.

The negotiations, however, turned out to be more difficult than he expected, mainly because he changed his mind about the value of his business midway through them. The sale was also more important to him than the acquisition was to West, which put Byrnes at a disadvantage. He wound up settling for what he considered to be a bad deal: an up-front payment of about $500,000 in cash, 22 percent of the stock in System One, and a seat on the board. His belief that he'd been outnegotiated and received less than his company was worth cast a pall over the closing on October 29, 1996.

And that was just the beginning. Byrnes soon discovered that the hardest part of an exit is what comes after the transaction—namely, the transition. It took him almost fifteen years to reach a point where he could say with confidence that he had moved on from the company he had owned.

. . . Until Your Well Runs Dry

I suspect most entrepreneurs don't really understand what they get out of running a business until they've left. After all, entrepreneurs are nothing if not action- and goal-oriented. They're naturally more inclined to focus on the immediate demands of the business than to reflect on the intangible rewards of owning and operating a company. But when you're no longer getting those rewards, you can't help but feel the loss. You may not know exactly what's missing. You may attribute your unhappiness to causes other than your recent exit. You may believe the problems are all in your head. And I suppose that's true: They *are* all in your head. But that doesn't make the loss any less real or the ensuing funk any easier to deal with. Until you do identify the causes, moreover, you're liable to have a difficult time treating the symptoms.

We've already seen several instances of owners who've been through this gauntlet after selling a business. Randy Byrnes's case is a little different because he later became a student of it—literally. He had been struggling for nine years to understand and overcome his own sense of loss when he decided, with the encouragement of his two daughters, to go back to school. "They asked me if I'd ever thought about teaching in college," he said. "I think they had a sense that, 'Gee, Dad doesn't seem to be doing too well.' I thought, 'Yeah, I can envision teaching in college.'"

To teach at the college level, however, he would need the customary ticket of admission, namely, a doctorate. He enrolled in a doctoral program run by Fielding Graduate University in Santa Barbara, California. It was a largely self-directed course of study, requiring a lot of self-discipline and a willingness to persevere. Persevere he did and in September 2009 Byrnes began work on his dissertation, which he titled "Transition at the Top: CEOs' Sense of Self When Separating from Their Company."

Over the next three months, he interviewed sixteen former owners of privately held companies ranging in size from fifteen to more than five hundred employees and from $1 million to $100 million in revenues. It proved to be just what he needed to explore his own feelings on his exit thirteen years earlier. Most of the people he interviewed had struggled as much as he had after exiting and for similar reasons. Struggling, he realized, was normal. He hadn't known that while going through it, and neither had they, which had made the experience even more difficult than it would otherwise have been.

The particular circumstances of Byrnes's sale had made it harder still. Three and a half years went by before the expanded System One was sold and Byrnes was finally able to cash out. During that time, he was in his own private purgatory. He had naïvely believed that The Byrnes Group and System One were joining in a marriage of equals. His miscalculation became apparent at the first board meeting, when he clashed with John West over the appointment of a chief operating officer of the combined companies. After the meeting West expressed his annoyance and let Byrnes know that his role was to be a supportive member of the team. Mainly that meant keeping his mouth shut as he watched the business he'd built being dismantled and almost half of the people he'd hired losing their jobs. "I felt deeply responsible," he said. "My frustration with the situation caused me to drift. I kept busy from day to day, but at the end of a month I would look back and couldn't identify anything I'd accomplished." Part of the problem, he acknowledges, was his failure to make any plans for what he would do after the sale. "I wish I had. Because I look back now and think about having unending days without a purpose."

Sue Byrnes described her husband's disposition during that period as "morose." His mood brightened somewhat when System One was sold in April 2000. The shareholders were paid in stock of the acquirer, TMP Worldwide Inc., the owner of the Monster.com Web site for job seekers. Byrnes distributed some of his shares among about twenty-five of his former employees and a couple of key advisers, none of whom had been expecting any payout at all. He said the gesture gave him deep satisfaction.

But the sale of System One did not solve Byrnes's existential problems. He had yet to find an occupation that could engage him the way his business once had. Meanwhile, he continued to drift for another five years, until he decided to go back to school. By the time he received his PhD, in June 2010, he at last had the clarity he'd been seeking, and it gave him a new perspective on both the business he'd spent twenty-one years building and his experiences after leaving it.

What he'd had and then lost, he realized, were four things: his identity, his purpose, his sense of achievement, and the network of personal connections he'd had with the people in his company, both individually and collectively.

By identity, he meant the ability to answer one of the simplest, most innocuous questions in the English language—namely, "What do you do?" Several erstwhile business owners have told me that it's a question they dread. When you run a business, the answer is obvious. When you used to run a business, the obvious answers are often anathema. Many ex-entrepreneurs have a visceral aversion to being seen as a former something-or-other or, worse yet, retired. Byrnes, for his part, was stumped by the what-do-you-do question. "People were really asking, 'Who are you and how do you contribute?'" he said. "Without an answer to that, I was lost. I think many people are lost."

Byrnes's purpose had been so deeply embedded in his company that he had taken it for granted until he lost it. The Byrnes Group, he wrote in his dissertation, had been "48 dedicated professionals who provided customized staffing solutions in the executive search, contract personnel, and temporary help sectors of the market." After the sale, "our joint commitment to one another to satisfy our customers' needs, enhance our associates' quality of life, and ensure the profitability and continuous growth of our company ceased. Never again would I lead these valued colleagues who trusted me to do the right thing and execute decisions with their best interests in mind."

The sense of achievement came from doing things that mattered, such as providing good jobs for single mothers. "We grew employees," Byrnes said. "We were a strong presence in the market. A lot of single moms were providing for their children independent of anyone else—a former spouse or whatever—because of what they could earn by being part of our company. That sense of achievement was profound."

As for his personal connections with employees, Byrnes may have underestimated their importance—Sue Byrnes thought so—because they had been such an integral part of his life from the age of twenty-three. After the sale, he found those connections impossible to replicate. "From 2000 to 2005, I got involved with some start-up companies as an investor, going on boards," he said. "I was probably trying to find another platform from which I could be deeply engaged with both the institution and the people, but it didn't work. The experience was not satisfying. At least in the first period, from 1996 to 2000, I still had a connection because I was on the System One board and had the sense of impacting the well-being of people I knew. With these other boards, there was no personal piece to it. So I realized that the personal connection was one of the great things I'd gotten out of my business, although I wasn't aware of it at the time. I had a need to be needed that I clearly didn't recognize."

Byrnes's discoveries were liberating. In identifying the essential needs that his former business had once filled for him, he learned a great deal about himself—that is, about who he is, what he wants, and why—which had two crucial benefits. His new insights allowed him to appreciate The Byrnes Group on a much deeper level than ever before, while simultaneously guiding him as he embarked on a new career as an executive coach.

So has Byrnes finally completed his transition, and thus his exit? "Yes, I can now look fondly and with deep gratitude on the opportunity I had with The Byrnes Group for twenty-one years, and the opportunity I have going forward. When I was doing the research for the dissertation, my question was always, 'What can I grow from this?' I wanted to use the knowledge to help other people. That's what I'm doing now."

Purpose, Tribe, and Structure

Byrnes may be unique in the lengths to which he has gone in analyzing how a CEO's sense of self is affected by the decision to exit a company he or she has built, but he is typical in another way. As proud as he is of the culture he nurtured at The Byrnes Group and as hard as he found it to lose the network of personal connections he had developed there, he does not want to repeat the experience. His new venture, Byrnes Associates, is a one-person business, and he plans to keep it that way. The personal connections he finds so important will be with clients, not employees.

That's a common pattern among former business owners. Most of those I've interviewed are clear that they don't intend to manage employees ever again. If they go back into business, as many do, they take on roles that do not require supervision of or have responsibility for more than two or three human beings. Even those ex-owners who've developed high-performance cultures in the past generally have no interest in doing it again with a new business. I suspect it's because they know how difficult and emotionally draining it can be to put together a team they'll enjoy working with—something they weren't aware of when they did it the first time.

There are some exceptions, of course, particularly among owners who exit at a relatively early age. Dave Hersh is a case in point. He was twenty-nine years old when he became founding CEO of a start-up called Jive Software, and thirty-seven when he stepped down eight and a half years later after a successful run. By then, Jive had established itself as a leader in so-called social business software and was on its way to an initial public offering. Hersh had no idea at the time what he was going to do next. Within a few years, however, he realized he needed to have another company to run. "But I had to go through a process to figure it out," he said.

He had become an entrepreneur the first time out of economic necessity. Two programmers he knew had developed some software that allowed people in a company to converse using online forums and instant messaging. The software was originally open source—that is, anyone could download and use it for free—but the developers had recently decided to incorporate with the goal of building a business around the concept. They invited Hersh to come in and lead the effort. Hersh had just moved from San Francisco to New Haven, Connecticut, so that his wife could attend graduate school. They'd arrived on September 10, 2001. The next day, 9/11, the economy ground to a halt. Lacking any other job prospects, Hersh accepted the offer.

And he did well. With no outside capital, Jive reached $15 million in annual sales and sixty-five employees in 2007. At that point, Hersh and his partners decided it was time to bring in private equity to make sure they didn't miss out on opportunities that had recently opened up thanks to a hot new product they'd developed. In August, Sequoia Capital invested $15 million, which Hersh used to build the sales and R&D teams, improve sales support, add services, and bring in new management. Despite a rocky start, followed by the Lehman Brothers bankruptcy and a large layoff, the company recovered and entered 2009 with a full head of steam. "We just kept winning deals and growing and making our numbers and doing everything we said we'd do," Hersh said.

But it came at a cost. "In order to get to that level of success, I put a lot of pressure on myself and was on the road a lot. I was so preoccupied with the company that my marriage started to crumble. We'd been married eight years and had two kids under six, and our communication completely broke down."

As it happened, Jive, which was based in Portland, Oregon, was opening an office in Palo Alto, California. Figuring that a change of scenery would be good for their marriage, Hersh and his wife decided to relocate to the San Francisco Bay Area, where they arrived with their two young daughters in October 2009. But the move didn't solve the underlying problem. "It became clear that it was going to be hard to play the role that the company needed of me while I was also playing the role I wanted to play at home," he said. The board, meanwhile, had begun to discuss taking Jive public. Hersh let the members know that he didn't want to be CEO of a public company. It was agreed that he would become chairman and be replaced as CEO by someone qualified to run the company up to and after an initial public offering.

Hersh changed jobs in February 2010 and began a slow and painful exit from the company he had helped launch. "It was incredibly hard," he said. "I'm a very loyal leader. By moving out of the CEO role, I felt I was letting people down. But I knew it was the right choice. It was more important for me to be a good father and husband."

His role as chairman didn't make the experience any easier. As often happens when a new CEO takes over, the culture changed quickly and dramatically. Employees began coming to Hersh and sending him e-mails saying Jive wasn't the same and expressing nostalgia for the way it had been. Most of them eventually left. Hersh himself lasted about a year. As the company approached its IPO, there was a need to reduce the number of insiders on the board. "I wanted to leave anyway," he said. "I was done. It wasn't my company anymore."

At thirty-nine, he had many productive years ahead of him, and after a couple of months off he started searching for what he would do next. He helped start a business and worked on a buyout. He joined a few boards, did a little angel investing, and advised not-for-profits. For the first couple of years he avoided institutional affiliations, but in 2012 he joined Andreessen Horowitz, a venture capital firm, as a board partner. "Independence was nice at first, after being a CEO, but it became a prison," he said. "I missed the camaraderie of the group. I felt disconnected. As an adviser or board member, you kind of swoop in periodically to pontificate, but you miss a lot of the data that forms the decisions. More important, you miss the camaraderie that comes with shared adversity and success. I really, really missed that. It's very important to me."

Hersh said he took the position at Andreessen Horowitz, which was part-time, to learn about venture capital but also to have "a place to hang my shingle while I figured out what I wanted to do." That proved to be more difficult than he'd imagined. What exactly was he looking for, anyway? Camaraderie, he knew, was one piece. Another, he realized somewhat belatedly, was creative control. "By that, I mean being able to dictate the structure, decisions, and outcome for the company based on your own value system as opposed to someone else's," he said. "It took me a long time to realize the level of creative control that I wanted in my next business. I probably could have saved myself a lot of time and energy had I realized that earlier on."

Through his reading—notably Viktor Frankl's *Man's Search for Meaning*—and his conversations with other ex-entrepreneurs in situations similar to his, Hersh became acutely aware of having lost the sense of purpose he'd had as CEO of Jive Software. "The scary part is being out in the ether, not being tethered to the world," he said. "You can read about it somewhere, but you really don't know it until you feel it."

He also felt the loss of structure in his life, which is one of the subtler benefits of being involved full-time in a business. The needs of the business force you to set up routines that keep you on course toward your goals. When you don't have that structure anymore, you find yourself with what Hersh calls "white spaces" in your day. "And you don't always fill them in with good things. I'm somebody who does really well if I know that there's an order and a structure to my days. When everything is haphazard, it requires a lot of willpower to force the good things on yourself. With structure, you can build in the things that are good for you, and you don't have to think about them. They don't require willpower, which is a finite resource."

By the time I met him, Hersh had figured out what it all added up to. There were things he needed, and he'd concluded that he could only get them by building another business from scratch. "Three things in particular," he said. "Purpose: I need one unified purpose behind what I do. Tribe: I need a community of people around me who I can be a part of and help organize and make their lives better. And three is structure: just having structure to my life and something that I can commit to on a daily basis. I've seen what happens when you have a vacuum of all three of those, and it's not a pretty thing. I'm definitely due for a project that I can sink my teeth into again."

Different Strokes

As I noted in chapter 1, an entrepreneur's exit isn't complete until he or she has found whatever comes next and becomes fully engaged in it. To get there, both Randy Byrnes and Dave Hersh have had to go through a process of figuring out exactly what they lost when they left the companies they'd built. Although they are hardly alone in that regard, it would be a mistake to overgeneralize about the experiences of former business owners. While there are some frequently recurring patterns, it's easy to find exceptions to each of them. For that matter, it's easy to find examples of people—sometimes within the same company—whose experiences are vastly different.

Consider Attila Safari and his partner Bill Flagg, the former owners of RegOnline, based in Boulder, Colorado. Safari had founded the company in the late 1990s to produce and market software he had developed for managing small to medium-size events via the Web. Recognizing that sales and marketing were not his strong suits, he had approached Flagg about becoming a partner in 2002. At the time, RegOnline had four employees and was doing about $1 million a year in sales. Flagg, a Detroit native, was a serial entrepreneur whose previous businesses had sold advertising for commemorative posters, year-at-a-glance calendars, and mouse pads. He and Safari decided to do a three-month trial to see whether they liked working with each other. Their thirteen-year age difference notwithstanding—Safari was forty-six, Flagg was thirty-three—they got along splendidly. So they went ahead and signed a partnership agreement, and Flagg bought 20 percent of the stock. With Safari as CEO and Flagg as president, RegOnline flourished. In the next four years the workforce expanded to seventy people, and annual sales grew to about $10 million, with net pretax margins of 45 percent. As the company blew past revenue and profit targets, Safari awarded Flagg another 10 percent of the stock.

Everything was going so well that Flagg wished it could just continue indefinitely—but that, he realized, would depend on his partner. He asked Safari whether he intended to sell the business someday. "Hell, yes," Safari said. Flagg responded that he would help fund Safari's retirement by raising the capital to buy his share of the business. "My preference was always to build the company and not sell it," Flagg said. "But it was a little bit of a dilemma for me because I liked being partners with Attila and didn't want to end the partnership. I was just afraid that if I didn't figure something out, a crazy offer might come in one day, and Attila would take it."

And that's more or less how RegOnline got sold, although the process didn't play out exactly as Flagg had imagined. It began in early 2007 with a phone call to a competitor, Thriva, that he and Safari were interested in acquiring. "I called Matt Erlichman, the founder, who said, 'Oh, that's funny, because we're about to announce next week that we're getting acquired by Active,'" said Flagg. "Then he turned the tables and asked if we'd be interested in talking to Active. I said, 'Not unless it's a really high multiple.' I think I told him twenty times earnings. He said, 'I think that's in range of what they're willing to pay, but let me make an intro.'"

Like Thriva, the Active Network, based in San Diego, was a competitor with a different niche from RegOnline's. Backed by more than $170 million in VC funding, it had been on an acquisition binge and was very interested in buying RegOnline, but its first offer—in the $30 million range—was much too low. Safari and Flagg quickly rejected it. A couple of months went by, and then an e-mail arrived from Active's president asking the partners to meet him and Active's CEO for lunch in Boulder. After spending most of the meal on the requisite small talk, the president finally popped the question. "Okay," he said. "What's your number?"

Flagg and Safari had discussed that very question on the way over and agreed that $40 million was about right. To Flagg's surprise, however, his partner said, "Fifty million dollars." The president, who was the dealmaker, had no reaction, but both Safari and Flagg noticed that the CEO smiled. As they headed back to their office after lunch, Safari said, "Shit! I was too low. They would have gone higher." Shortly thereafter, Active came back with an offer in the $50 million range.

The negotiations grew serious at that point, although Flagg tried to restrain Safari's enthusiasm. "I'd had people make offers on companies I owned in the past," Flagg said, "and I knew how you can get overly excited and attached to the idea of selling and making millions of dollars. I also knew that we would only have negotiating leverage if we were willing to walk away." They needed the leverage, because they were determined to make Active increase its offer. From a footnote in an audit report Active had sent them, they had learned that it had paid more for Thriva than it was offering for RegOnline, even though their company was more profitable. That was unacceptable. "I said, 'Attila, if this is our valuation now, and we're growing 30 percent a year, in another two years the valuation will be $100 million. We can use that. We don't need to sell.' I was secretly hoping he'd call off the sale."

But Safari was caught up in the process. "That's the part that's kind of strange," he said. "Once you're on that locomotive and you've started talking, it's very hard to stop and step back and go, 'Okay, do I really want to do this?' I fell into that mode of negotiating, and it was just back and forth, back and forth."

The numbers under discussion were far beyond any amount that Flagg could hope to raise, and so that possibility was off the table. The main question remaining concerned the percentages to be paid in cash and stock. In September 2007, Safari and Flagg flew to San Diego to check out Active's operation and continue the negotiations. In the course of the visit, it became clear that their hosts were eager to get a deal done before the end of the year. "You know, why don't we put the deal off for a year," Flagg said. "I think we've really got more growth and we're having a lot of fun here. We're not in a hurry to sell." Active raised its offer by $10 million.

The locomotive picked up steam from there. Due diligence took barely two weeks and consisted of little more than a review of the financials. The negotiations over details in the contract took a bit longer. The deal closed on October 31, 2007. Safari and Flagg received the bulk of the cash then. Although they didn't have an earnout, they did agree to receive the rest of their money over the next two years. Exactly how much Active paid overall is open to debate because a substantial portion of the proceeds was in the stock of a privately owned company. Active valued the deal at $65 million, but, as Safari ruefully noted, its estimate assumed a share price that the company never achieved after it went public in May 2011.

"I really have two regrets," he said. "One is I definitely felt like I was fooled into believing things that weren't true. Their timeline for going public and their estimates of the stock's worth were hot air. The other regret, again in hindsight, is what I lost. I'd built a really nice company I was very proud of. I had my own little kingdom, seventy employees, and was busy. I had a fulfilling, productive life. To go from that to staying at home and not having a lot to do, that didn't feel good."

Initially, however, neither he nor Flagg had the option of staying at home. They both had agreements with Active that kept them on the job after the sale. In return, they received stock options that vested over two years. It wasn't a happy experience for either of them. Safari couldn't handle the move from CEO to middle manager. "The first six months, you're so busy getting things restructured that you don't really feel it," he said, "but you gradually see the meddling creeping in and less reliance on me and just not wanting me to be involved in decision making."

Flagg stayed at RegOnline for six months after the sale and then agreed to help apply its management practices to other businesses

Active owned. "We did unconventional things like having a noncommissioned sales team and no MBAs or high-paid managers recruited from other companies," he said. "On those two points alone, Active was probably half as profitable as RegOnline." As usual, however, the changes he recommended were never made. In addition, Active began to implement policies at RegOnline that violated both his and Safari's core principles about dealing with employees and customers. "After a while, I just couldn't stomach it anymore," Flagg said. "Their systems prevented me from being able to make a real difference." He left in April 2010. Safari, who was still working there part-time, left completely a few months later.

From that point, their paths diverged sharply. While Flagg had regrets about selling RegOnline, Safari's were much deeper and longer-lasting. It didn't help that he lost a substantial amount of his cash proceeds from the sale in the stock market crash of 2008. Worse, spending time at home proved to be bad for his marriage: He got divorced in 2010. Through it all, he couldn't stop kicking himself for what he had come to regard as a boneheaded decision to sell. "You ask yourself, 'What was I thinking?'" he said. "You built this great company, and it's continued doing well after you sold it despite the total mismanagement of it, and it would have been worth a lot more today. In hindsight, you go, 'I could have stepped back, maybe gone to work two, three days a week rather than six, seven, and had more personal time with my kids and family. It would have been a more fulfilling life.'

"I think ego gets in the way," Safari continued. "You tell yourself, 'I can always start another company and be just as successful.' Maybe it's true with some people, but not in my case. I just didn't have the energy to start again." At one point he did team up with a friend to buy residential properties, fix them up, and sell them. It went well for a couple of years, until his friend—who handled the renovation work—had a massive stroke. Safari didn't feel he could go forward with the business on his own. So what would he do next? "I have no idea."

Flagg's experience could hardly have been more different. Whether by luck, instinct, or innate caution, he had chosen not to invest his cash from the sale, unlike Safari, who signed on with a professional money manager, and thus he had been unscathed by the stock market crash. As for his home life, it had improved considerably. He had gotten married in 2008, and his wife had given birth to their first child in 2009. Meanwhile, he had been inundated with business opportunities. "Lots of stuff came flying at me after the sale, and I was starting to get involved in different stuff while still at RegOnline and Active," he said. "So I had a lot of really interesting opportunities coming up."

Perhaps because he had started and sold companies before, or perhaps because RegOnline had been his partner's business more than his, Flagg's identity and sense of purpose weren't as tied up in the company as Safari's had been. Accordingly, his transition period was much shorter. Even before he left, he had begun doing some angel investing and working with entrepreneurs to grow their businesses. Inspired by Zingerman's Community of Businesses in Ann Arbor (where he'd attended the University of Michigan), he had started The Felix Fun, "a Boulder-based community of great, bootstrapped, built-for-life companies . . . the kind that customers love to shout from the rooftops about, employees thrive in, and owners want to grow old with." Flagg does not actually run any of the companies in the community. "I'm not managing," he said. "I have partners who are the owner-operators. I am a backseat driver to them, which is nice because I get to see lots of cool sights and I get to help advise them about turning left or right. That's fun. I have gotten a lot of enjoyment out of it.

"It's much different, though, than me driving a bus full of people who are excited about where we're going and I'm choosing exactly where it is. I do miss that level of intensity of engagement that we had at RegOnline. But it's hard to create when you start out. Before you get the team, you have to go through having the wrong people, hiring and firing, and all that. It's painful. I'd be willing to put up with it again to have a team that I grew myself. Because at a certain point you really get into a humming place with your core team. I bet if you could just snap your fingers and have a great team in a successful, growing company, most people would be up for doing it again. But building a new team from the ground up again is too painful for them."

Common Wisdom

To be sure, there are many factors that account for the divergent paths of Safari and Flagg following the sale of RegOnline, including age, personality, background, and general outlook on life, to name just four. The point is that you can't necessarily tell what one person's experience will be from looking at someone else's. That said, I will take the risk of offering a few general rules for the transition stage of the exit process, based on the research I've done. I'll leave it to you to decide whether or not they apply in your case.

1. Everybody needs to be going somewhere.
For most business owners, the exit marks the start of a transition to something else. The fortunate ones know what the something else is before they exit. The less fortunate have to figure it out when they get there—and most will tell you how much they wish they had done it before they left rather than afterward. It is simply much easier to go *to* something rather than just *from* something.

Jack Stack of SRC Holdings received some advice on that score that strikes me as applicable to almost any owner thinking about exiting a business. As I recounted in chapter 4, Stack has spent more than thirty years building a company that he could leave "with a clean conscience," as he put it. By that, he means a company with a strong balance sheet, an educated workforce, leaders capable of carrying on without him, and a proven management system. By the summer of 2013, he had achieved all four and was confronted with the decision to stay, leave, or drastically cut back. He sought the advice of a legendary Springfield businessman, eighty-two-year-old Edwin "Cookie" Rice, who has worked for more than sixty years at his family-owned bottling company. "He asked me a great question," Stack said. "'Do you have something better to do?' I thought about it, and honestly, I don't." So he remains at SRC for the time being. Other owners might want to ask themselves the same question before deciding whether or not to leave their businesses, and, if the answer is yes, force themselves to spell out what the "something better" is.

2. Most transitions take time.

There are few entrepreneurs—even experienced and sophisticated entrepreneurs—who know what to expect the first time they exit a business. The longer they've been working in and on the business, the greater the shock is likely to be and the more time they'll need to get over it. Norm Brodsky (chapters 2 and 4) founded his first company, Perfect Courier, in 1979, and although he subsequently started several other companies—including the most valuable one to date, CitiStorage—he never actually exited until he sold them in 2007, almost three decades after he started.

He thought he was ready to move on. He wasn't.

"I can see now that I was very lucky I didn't have to leave immediately," he said. "I was still involved in running it for a few years. If I wasn't, I would have been devastated. Because your business becomes your identity, which I didn't realize while it was happening. So when you sell your business, you're giving up a part of your soul, but nobody tells you about it. The only thing people talk about is the money. They don't talk about preparing yourself for the mental suffering or the need to change. Today my wife, Elaine, and I have our own identity in the community that has nothing to do with the business. But I needed at least three years to adjust."

Based on my conversations with former owners, I'd say that a three-year transition is about average. As we've seen, many entrepreneurs require much more time, and some need much less. Not surprisingly, those who need the least time are serial entrepreneurs who have experienced more than one exit. If you're used to moving from one business to the next, it's far less likely that you'll rely on any one company to define your identity or provide you with a sense of purpose and feelings of achievement, and far more likely that you'll find structure and camaraderie somewhere else.

3. Managing money is a whole new business.

Whatever emotional challenges you may have after selling your business, there's nothing quite as exhilarating as checking your bank account after the cash is transferred and seeing all those numbers separated by commas. While an owner of a private company may have high worth on paper, it's mostly theoretical until that moment. Realizing what you've done, you will probably feel a surge of pride, as well you should. You did build that business, after all. You couldn't have done it without help from a lot of other people, but you were the quarterback, and the business wouldn't have succeeded without you.

By the same token, nothing can take the fun out of selling a business faster than losing a large portion of that money on ill-conceived investments, as Jeff Huenink, the former owner of Sun Services of America (chapter 8), found out the hard way. "When we sell, we don't realize that we're entering another business—managing your assets—and what made us successful at our previous business is not necessarily going to make us successful at the new one," he said. "I got greedy after I took my money out. I thought I was smarter than I was and lost a good part of it in the market, and by investing in pre-public companies without understanding all the rules. Then I bought a home building company in Orlando that we took from zero to $40 million in sales and won a J.D. Power award for quality and did other great things. But we ultimately shut it down when the housing market collapsed. I lost about $3 million on that one."

Unfortunately, it's not enough to have a well-vetted money manager. Huenink had one. So did Attila Safari, another victim of the stock market plunge. "I think you need a board of advisers," said Huenink. "You'd measure your investment results and have the board review them. Maybe it would be a group of entrepreneurs who've sold their companies—like a Vistage group, people who will give you honest input and advice." That's the idea behind Evolve USA (chapter 6). In any case, it's a good idea to proceed with caution and to develop a plan that sets firm limits on the amount of money you put at risk.

4. Once an entrepreneur, always an entrepreneur.

Forgive me for stating the obvious, but not everyone becomes an entrepreneur. Why one person does and another doesn't is a subject best left to people who have more knowledge of the human psyche than I have. But whatever led you to become an entrepreneur in the first place probably won't go away just because you no longer own a business. You'll have an itch that you will feel a need to scratch—exactly how, only you can determine. In the meantime, you're likely to be unhappy in certain situations. Hence the following corollaries:

Corollary #1: You probably won't do well in retirement.

For many business owners, as I've noted, retirement is a dirty word—which is not to say that they don't think about what they would do if they had more leisure time. Building a company calls for a considerable amount of self-sacrifice, and what you're sacrificing is mainly the time you could spend with your family or pursuing other interests. Maybe you squeeze in some golf or fishing or gardening or cooking. Maybe you dream about a life in which that's all you do. Don't count on that bringing you happiness. "After the sale, I was playing a lot of golf and doing a lot of other things I thought I would really enjoy," said Jeff Huenink.

"But I realized that for me, golf is a great game when you can play it for relaxation and a change of pace. But when you play it three or four times a week, it becomes like a job, and you expect to do better at it. That got to be very frustrating for me."

Tony Hartl (chapter 7) experienced something similar after he sold Planet Tan. You may recall that he had set a goal of earning his fortune by the age of forty, at which point he would do the things he'd postponed while building his company. Shortly after the sale, he took off to see the world. "I traveled for three months and was having so much fun, but then my mom got sick and I came home. After she passed away, I left to go traveling again, but it just wasn't the same. It was like having the most magnificent meal every day, but not being able to appreciate it. I needed to be home and to feel grounded. I felt like I had lost my sense of purpose. I missed my mother and my company. I missed the meaningful work. I missed the engagement. I missed the camaraderie. I just needed to get home."

Then, of course, there's Barry Carlson (chapters 1 and 6), who had no problem with the concept of retiring. It's what he planned to do after selling his company, Parasun. He managed to stay retired for all of about eighteen months. Within two and a half years, he was back working full-time.

Ray Pagano (chapter 1) is something of an outlier, in that he was still in retirement, and professed to enjoy it, five years after the sale of Videolarm. Even he, however, had succumbed to the urge to start a couple of new businesses—first, the yachting ornaments business with his wife and later a healthy snack vending machine business with his son.

Corollary #2: You'll probably make a lousy employee.

Most entrepreneurs know intuitively that once you've been the boss, it's very hard to go back to being someone else's employee. Unless you're working for a very special company—and there are a few—you're bound to miss the independence you had while you were running the show.

More to the point, you may well have forgotten how to be a good employee and a constructive member of someone else's team. You'll probably become a pain in the neck to the person you're working for, much as Randy Byrnes became a pain in the neck to System One's CEO, John West. You'll criticize decisions you don't agree with, and you'll do it at the wrong time and in front of the wrong people. Then you'll sulk when you feel you're not being listened to or treated with the deference you've grown used to.

Nevertheless, I can't say that going from boss to employee never works. Things turned out reasonably well for Ashton Harrison (chapter 4) after she sold her company, Shades of Light, and stayed on to work for the new owners. Paul Spiegelman (chapter 8) found his work as chief culture officer of Stericycle, which had bought his company, Beryl Health, both stimulating and rewarding. So did Gary Hirshberg (chapters 7 and 8), who helped start two new businesses for Danone while he continued to serve as CEO and later chairman of Stonyfield Farm.

It's worth noting, however, that, of those three, only Harrison had an earnout. Exiting entrepreneurs typically become employees of the acquirer when they have to stay on as a condition of the sale and are being paid a substantial portion of the sale price over time, with the amount dependent on the performance of the company. The problem is that as soon as the deal is signed, the seller assumes all the responsibility, and risk, for reaching the targets, and the buyer loses all financial incentive to help. Meanwhile, the operations of the two companies are being merged, which deprives the seller of the freedom he or she is used to having and requires to succeed. "The entrepreneur thrives on creativity and innovation, and the acquiring company thrives on process," notes John Warrillow (chapters 2 and 3) of The Sellability Score, who has heard plenty of horror stories. "The entrepreneur needs autonomy to operate, and the buyer needs people to fit in and follow the rules. The result is that most earnouts end early, with the entrepreneur leaving voluntarily or getting fired." He advises sellers to walk away from any deal in which the cash they'll receive at closing doesn't meet the minimum they're willing to accept for the business.

5. Too early is a lot better than too late.
As Attila Safari learned to his deep regret, the transition stage is the worst time to discover that you didn't consider all of the possible options before you sold your business. It's the one stage of the exit process that almost never allows for do-overs.

There are some rare exceptions. In December 2004, Rob Dube and Joel Pearlman sold their thirteen-year-old office products company, Image One, to Danka Business Systems PLC for a lump sum cash payment up front plus a three-year earnout. Under the terms of the deal, Image One would retain its name and use Danka's enormous resources—including a five-hundred-person sales force—to expand around the country. Hardly was the ink on the contract dry than Dube and Pearlman began regretting their decision, as they quickly ran into the corporate politics and sluggish bureaucracies endemic to giant corporations. "We had all kinds of incentives to do great, and we wanted to," says Dube. "But we were prevented from doing our best work, which was incredibly frustrating."

It turned out, however, that Danka had even more serious problems than they realized, and a new CEO was hired in March 2006 to turn the company around. Image One didn't fit into his plans. That June—barely eighteen months after the initial sale—Danka gave the company back to Dube and Pearlman in exchange for their agreement to forgo the money still owed on their earnout.

By then, their business goals had changed dramatically. Whereas before the sale they had been focused on growing Image One as much and as fast as possible, they now decided that they didn't necessarily care how big the company became or how rapidly it expanded. Yes, they wanted to keep growing the business, but they were equally intent on enhancing their culture, making a difference in people's lives, and giving back to the community. They also developed the habit of sitting down annually to review their visions of where they and the company would be ten to twenty years hence.

So it is possible to get a second chance with the same company. What you need is incredibly good luck. Fortunately, there are other, more predictable ways to secure a happy outcome. They all involve taking the time to go through the first two stages of the exit process—exploratory and strategic—long before anything happens that might force you (or tempt you) to choose a particular path. That means considering the various options you'd like to have, exploring each of them, and—like Dube and Pearlman—revisiting your vision of the future on a regular basis.

Starting early is especially important, I should reiterate, if you aspire to create a great company that (to use Jim Collins's definition) outperforms its industry, makes a distinctive impact on the world, and keeps doing it generation after generation. It is difficult enough to produce consistently extraordinary financial results in one generation. It takes years and years to develop the people, the culture, and the management mechanisms that can give your successors a decent chance to build on what you've done.

Finishing Big

Norm Brodsky was sitting in his office on the third floor of the four-story building that he'd built in 2000, when New York's zoning laws still permitted such construction on the Brooklyn side of the East River. From his desk, he had a panoramic view of the Manhattan skyline, interrupted only by the occasional tugboat, barge, or sightseeing craft. Under the terms of the agreement he'd signed when he sold CitiStorage and his other companies, he had unfettered access to and use of both this floor and the one above it. The latter was where he and his wife,

Elaine, lived when they were not traveling or at another of their homes—in Florida, in Colorado, and on the Long Island shore.

Even though his transition after the sale had turned out to be more difficult and to take more time than he'd anticipated, Brodsky had no regrets about selling. "People ask me all the time, 'Don't you miss it?' I say, 'No, I'm glad I'm away from it.' The funny part for me is that I look back now and say, 'What a fool!' I mean, I loved what I did, but there are so many ways to own a business and not be tethered to a desk or to a specific location, but still be in control in the background. It is a great, great thing that I have going in two of my businesses."

He was referring to the hotels in North Dakota and the fast-casual restaurants in New York City that he had cofounded and financed in the years following his exit from CitiStorage. Another business he'd financed had failed and he was likely to lose his investment in a fourth, but the hotel and the restaurant chains had been very successful, making up many times over for his losses on the others. Thanks to his partners and the wonders of modern technology, moreover, he doesn't have to spend much time physically at either one of them, although he was more or less constantly monitoring them. He couldn't be happier about the whole arrangement. "I'd never go back into a business again where I had to sit there and be tethered to a desk," he said.

The change has affected not just how Brodsky spends his time, but how he thinks. "It's completely different," he said. "I was going to say 'smarter,' but I'm not sure that's it. Age plays a role because it makes you realize how valuable time is. Normally, as a business owner, you're working, you love what you do, you get old, and you don't realize there are other ways to do things. I had an opportunity to see it because I sold the business. The result is that I value my time differently. I guess that if I hadn't sold, I might be just as happy doing what I did before, but I would have missed out on this great opportunity."

So why hadn't he always operated this way? "You can't start here," he said. "Maybe somebody smarter than me can, but I wouldn't know how." Without the wealth he'd amassed by building and then selling CitiStorage, as well as the knowledge he'd acquired during a lifetime of entrepreneurship, he would have had neither the financial resources to launch the new companies nor the business savvy to stay involved from afar. "Selling the business wasn't the end for me. It was the beginning of a new career. I mean, think about it. I'm still on the cutting edge—in the Bakken shale oil fields, in the fast-casual restaurant trend, with the people I advise. I get an opportunity to see lots and lots of things. Because I sold the business, I had an opportunity to realize, 'Hey, this is pretty neat. I can do a lot more than I did before.'"

Making money plays a curious role for Brodsky these days. If his ventures weren't making money, he would certainly consider them failures, but he didn't get involved with them to increase his wealth. He readily acknowledges that he has already made more money than he will ever spend or will leave to the next generation. Most of his fortune—including whatever he adds to it in the coming years—will eventually go to charity. What motivates him is the joy of discovering and thriving in a new career that suits him perfectly. Along with it comes the satisfaction of knowing that he is contributing to society even more of what he and other entrepreneurs have always contributed: jobs, economic growth, and "the wealth of nations."

Basil Peters, too, finished big, although he needed a few years to find his true calling. After selling his company Nexus Engineering to Scientific Atlanta and serving out his year-long commitment there, he took some time off to think and travel before accepting an offer in 1995 to become CEO of a Silicon Valley start-up called ICTV. "I have the classic Canadian inferiority complex," he said. "All over the world people see Silicon Valley as being bigger and brighter. I just wanted to experience it." After two and a half years, he decided that the Valley was no better than his hometown as a place to start and build companies. He found a replacement, stepped down as CEO, and returned to Vancouver to do what he loved: growing and selling technology companies.

What he didn't love was managing other people. So he became an investor, initially of his own money, later as the head of a hedge fund, and eventually as CEO of a venture capital fund he'd taken the lead in organizing. There he had success arranging some early exits. He left after five years, however, because he believed the fund was hurting start-ups by insisting they take more money than they could handle. (His partners felt that the $50 million fund couldn't afford to make any investment of less than $2 million.) He proceeded to launch his own angel fund and continued to orchestrate early exits of companies he'd invested in. He also began helping other people design and execute successful early exits, which became his passion. In 2009, he published his book, *Early Exits*, in which he laid out his thesis that the current era will someday be looked upon as a golden age for technology entrepreneurs. "So far, in my career, I've never seen a time when it's so easy for technology entrepreneurs to start companies on very little capital, to grow them very quickly, and to exit them just a few years from start-up," he said. "Lots of entrepreneurs can make incredible fortunes in just two or three years." His book and blog generated numerous speaking requests, which began eating up almost all of his time.

He wasn't complaining. "I'm happy to say that I'm having just the time of my life right now doing what I am doing," he said. "And I think it's something I can do for another couple of decades or so. Between investing in a few companies and helping them and other companies exit and helping others learn how to do it, I'm having as much fun as I'm allowed to have. I don't have any plans to do anything else."

Martin Babinec (chapter 3) finished big as well. Unlike many others, he experienced few, if any, withdrawal symptoms when he stepped down as CEO of TriNet in 2008 or when he relinquished his post as chairman of the board in 2009. He attributed the relative ease of his transition in part to the realization he had had early in his journey: He was an employee working for the shareholders, of whom he was just one. He was working for the angel investors to whom he owed the survival of TriNet in 1990—two years into his journey—when the company was days away from being forced into liquidation. He was also working for the managers and employees who had put money into the company at crucial points and who had stuck with him through hard times while earning far less than they could have made elsewhere.

But it was the sale of a majority stake to Select Appointments in 1995 that drove the point home. "Once that threshold is crossed, that's when the reality really hits that the work you're doing is for the benefit of all the shareholders," he said. "You also realize that your future is not your own. When you give control to a single party, that party has the ability to say whether or not you're the right guy to run the company." Had that reality been difficult to accept? "No, not for me. Because I believed in what we were doing, and it was the right thing to do for our team, as well as our investors."

He did acknowledge, however, that—after resigning as CEO in 2008—he'd had some trouble acclimating himself to the idea that someone else was now in charge. "When you've been running a company that you founded for twenty years, no one is going to be able to step in and look at it the same way you do, and that's sometimes tough to accept," Babinec said. It was particularly hard when some of his most loyal and longtime employees decided they didn't have a future under the new regime and moved on. But he'd gotten over it and had nothing but praise for the job his successor, Burton Goldfield, had done in shepherding TriNet to its initial public offering on the New York Stock Exchange on March 27, 2014.

It no doubt helped his equanimity that he remained a major shareholder and member of the board throughout. It also helped that, after turning his CEO duties over to Goldfield, he continued to work full-time as chairman for almost two years. But I suspect the most critical factor was his decision to use that time to think seriously and deeply about what he would do next. As a result, when he finally stopped working fulltime for TriNet, he had no issues about his identity or his sense of purpose. He had already begun to lay the groundwork for his next project: a not-for-profit called Upstate Venture Connect (UVC), whose goal was to spark an entrepreneurial renaissance that could revitalize upstate New York.

Nor was UVC his only passion. He also helped launch StartFast, a "mentorship-driven start-up accelerator" that every year brings five to ten technology start-ups to Syracuse, New York, for three months of intensive coaching. He became an active angel investor. He was involved in setting up four different seed capital funds for upstate New York start-ups. He served as a limited partner and adviser to several venture capital funds. After a family vacation in Jamaica got him thinking about how to make a difference in an underdeveloped country, he began building a network that connects first-time entrepreneurs there with experienced entrepreneurs in the U.S. And, finally, he cofounded a for-profit software business, IntroNet, to streamline the process of making and tracking introductions and referrals to others in a user's professional and personal networks—a platform that he expects will help all of his ventures.

Was he having fun? "I'm having a blast," he said. "I'm like a kid in a candy shop. I couldn't think of anything I'd rather be doing. I have the luxury of not having to worry about things financially, and that gives me the freedom to pursue what I want to be doing, not what I have to be doing. But I couldn't have done any of this without first building TriNet. It has allowed me to have the life I have now."

We began this chapter by looking at owners who'd left their companies and found themselves longing for intangibles that they hadn't realized the company had given them—things like purpose, identity, a sense of achievement, creative control, tribe, and structure. Brodsky, Peters, and Babinec represent the opposite end of the spectrum. All three have managed to reacquire, or retain, those intangibles in their new lives, though with a difference: They are happier and having more fun than ever. It's worth examining how and why.

Obviously money is one ingredient. Wealth in itself may not be the magic cure-all that most people imagine it to be, but the lives of owners do change when they cash out for a significant amount of money, partly because it provides the freedom to do other things and partly because it removes the fear of financial disaster. Even entrepreneurs with a high net worth on paper and a substantial income from the business are constantly at risk of losing it all. Once you turn your illiquid, privately owned stock into liquid assets of one sort or another that risk is greatly diminished, if not eliminated, with the result that you can pretty much stop worrying about money—provided you don't do foolish things with it.

But happiness is more than the absence of worry. For the majority of entrepreneurs, the aforementioned intangibles appear to play a much larger role. So what have Brodsky, Peters, and Babinec done that has allowed them to succeed where many others have struggled?

The answer, I believe, has to do with service. They've each found their bliss—or at least a substantial part of it—in helping others to succeed in business. Almost all of the former owners I've interviewed for this book have looked for ways to be of service following their exits, and building businesses is what successful entrepreneurs know how to do. It's only logical for many of them to conclude that they can be of greatest service by sharing with less experienced entrepreneurs the expertise they've acquired over the course of their careers.

When you think about it, service is a factor—perhaps the primary factor—in creating the sense of purpose that successful entrepreneurs derive from their businesses. At the very least, they serve their customers; it's unlikely that they'd succeed if they didn't. Many of them consciously serve their employees and their communities as well. When owners who've exited say they've lost their purpose and identity, what they've really lost is their sense of being in service to something apart from and greater than themselves as well as the chance to do it with kindred spirits (tribe) in a format that forces them to set priorities (creative control and structure) and provides a continual measure of their progress (sense of achievement).

Of all the lessons that can be drawn from the experiences of the people in this book, I believe this is the most important one. The stories remind us that a business is not only an economic organization, but also a social one, giving purpose and meaning to our lives and providing the camaraderie, direction, and fulfillment most of us feel a compelling need for.

That said, it's easy to understand why when entrepreneurs exit the companies they have created we tend to focus on the economic side of the equation—that is, the amount of money the business has sold for and the amount of wealth the owner has walked away with. Given the almost universal craving for financial independence, it is certainly noteworthy when someone achieves it.

But if you're an owner preparing to exit your business, you would be making a mistake to think only about how much you can get for it. The bigger challenge is to figure out, in advance if possible, what will take the place of those other important needs that your company has filled, as Brodsky, Peters, and Babinec have done. If you can manage, as they have, to use your new wealth as a stepping stone to an even higher calling, you can truly be said to have finished big.

ACKNOWLEDGMENTS

I could not have written this book without the help of scores of people—so many, in fact, that my principal fear in writing these acknowledgments is the likelihood of leaving someone out. (Please forgive me if I have failed to note your contribution. If you let me know, I will try to make amends.)

Let's begin where I began—with the series of columns entitled "The Offer" that Norm Brodsky and I wrote for *Inc.* magazine from 2006 to 2008. The idea to chronicle Norm's experience of deciding whether to sell his companies came from our editor at the time, Loren Feldman, now the small business editor of the *New York Times*. We received great support from the entire team at the magazine, led by then editor in chief Jane Berentson, and from *Inc.*'s readers, and we were both very grateful to them all.

The overwhelming response to the series got me thinking about doing a book on business exits. I talked it over with the two people I rely on most for advice about such matters—my incomparable agent, Jill Kneerim, and my peerless publisher, Adrian Zackheim. They encouraged me, and so I started to do some preliminary research. It took me just two or three conversations to discover how little I actually knew about the subject. Thus began a long process of education, which continues. Along the way, I've had many, many teachers, advisers, mentors, cheerleaders, and confidants.

Starting out, of course, my teachers were Norm and his partners at CitiStorage—Elaine Brodsky, Sam Kaplan, and Louis Weiner—and to them I owe an immense debt of gratitude. As always, I relied heavily on my frequent coauthor, mentor, and friend, Jack Stack, cofounder and CEO of SRC Holdings, to think through the implications of what I was learning. My former *Inc.* colleagues George Gendron and John Case were also great sounding boards, as they have been throughout my career. So were my good friends Martin Babinec, Chip Conley, Ping Fu, Paul Saginaw, Paul Spiegelman, Tom Walter, Ari Weinzweig, and Steven Wilkinson. Doug Tatum, the founder of Tatum and author of *No Man's Land*, was incredibly generous with his help and advice from the start and introduced me to Bob Tormey, who later became my chief guide to the more technical aspects of selling a business. Steve Kimball, Basil Peters, Sam Kaplan, Brendan Anderson, Jeff Kadlic, John Warrillow, and Jerry F. Mills were very helpful on that score as well. Corey Rosen, the founder of the National Center for Employee Ownership, provided deep insight into employee-owned companies that had dealt with succession issues. Then there were my various *Inc.* editors—Loren Feldman, Eric Schine, Larry Kanter, and Jane Berentson—who helped with the articles I wrote for the magazine on subjects related to exiting, some of which I've incorporated into *Finish Big.* I also want to thank *Inc.*'s owner, Joe Mansueto; its president and editior in chief, Eric Schurenberg; and editor Jim Ledbetter for their continuing support even though it must have seemed at times that this book would never see the light of day.

Most of the raw material for the book came from in-depth interviews I did with more than seventy-five current and former business owners. Some of them I already knew, but most I met through friends and colleagues. Vistage chair Sterling Lanier was particularly helpful in that regard. He offered to let his fellow chairs in the Vistage network know about my project; and Tim Fulton, Gil Herman, and the late Gary Anderson came through with key introductions to former owners who had great stories and insights.

I can't stress strongly enough my appreciation to the current and former owners who trusted me with the intimate and often painful details of their stories. Almost all of them agreed to speak on the record, which took considerable courage in many instances. They had nothing to gain personally from opening up to me. They did it for one reason: their desire to help their fellow entrepreneurs. I wish only that I'd had the space to tell all of their stories. Even those whose stories I wasn't able to include provided me with important insights that are reflected in the pages of this book. So let me offer my thanks (in alphabetical order) to:

John Abrams (South Mountain Company); Joel Altschul (United Learning); Jack Altschuler (Maram Corp.); Jim Ansara (Shawmut Design & Construction); Michael Ansara (The Share Group); Robin Azevedo (McRoskey Mattress Co.); Martin and Krista Babinec (TriNet); Jim Ball (Fast Cash); Mitch Bernet (Integra Logistics); Bill Butler (W. L. Butler Construction); Randy and Sue Byrnes (The Byrnes Group); Barry Carlson (Parasun); Bob Carlson (Reell Precision Manufacturing); Loren Carlson (CEO Roundtable); Amy Castronova (Novatek Communications); Yvon Chouinard (Patagonia); Chip Conley (Joie de Vivre Hospitality); Kit Crawford (Clif Bar & Company); Steve Dehmlow (Composites One); Rob Dube (Image One); Charlotte Eckley (O&S Trucking); Gary Erickson (Clif Bar & Company); Bill Flagg (RegOnline); Richard Fried (Sea Change Systems); Ping Fu (Geomagic); Kevin Grauman (The Outsource Group); Clint Greenleaf (Greenleaf Book Group); David Hale (Scale-Tronix); Peter Harris (Cadence); Ashton and Dave Harrison (Shades of Light); Tony Hartl (Planet Tan); Edie Heilman (Mariposa Leadership); Al Herback

(Calumet Photographic); Dave Hersh (Jive Software); Gary and Meg Hirshberg (Stonyfield Farm); Kathy Houde (Calumet Photographic); Jeff Huenink (Sun Services); Rob Hurlbut (Niman Ranch); Dave Jackson (First Choice Health Care); Jeff Johnson (Arcemus); Jean Jodoin (Facilitec); Ed Kaiser (Polyline Corp.); Phil Kaplan (Adbrite); Steve Kimball (Tuscan Advisors); Kenny Kramm (FlavorX); Bruce Leech (CrossCom National); Michael LeMonier (MedPro Staffing); Martin and Linda Lightsey (Cadence); Steve MacDonald (Parasun); Bobby Martin (First Research); Ted Matthews (Promonad); Ron Maurer (Zingerman's Community of Businesses); Fritz Maytag (Anchor Brewing); Mike McConnell (Niman Ranch); Jean Moran (LMI Packaging Solutions); John Morris (NetLearning); Gary Nelson (Nelson Corp.); Bill Niman (Niman Ranch); Nicolette Hahn Niman (BN Ranch); Jim O'Neal (O&S Trucking); Ray Pagano (Videolarm); Bill Palmer (Commercial Casework); Aaron Patzer (Mint.com); Basil Peters (Nexus Communications); John Ratliff (Appletree Answers); Adeo Ressi (The Founder Institute); Paul Rimington (Diemasters Manufacturing); Attila Safari (RegOnline); Paul Saginaw (Zingerman's Community of Businesses); Nancy Sharp (Food-for-Thought Catering); Kyle Smith (Reell Precision Manufacturing); Bruce D. Snider (*Custom Home* magazine); Janet Spaulding (Videolarm); Paul Spiegelman (Beryl Health); Jeff Swain (Niman Ranch); Todd Taskey (Solutions Planning Group); Bob Wahlstedt (Reell Precision Manufacturing); Tom, Larry, and Kevin Walter (Tasty Catering); John Warrillow (Warrillow & Co.); Ari Weinzweig (Zingerman's Community of Businesses); Bob Woosley (iLumen); and Ed Zimmer (ECCO).

I recorded most of the interviews digitally and soon realized that I would never finish the book if I attempted to transcribe them all myself. Luckily, I was able to team up with some conscientious transcribers who did it for me, including Margaret Gompertz, Jane Shahi, Jenniffer May, Tricia Otto, and Steven Terada. I thank you all.

Even with their help, this book took me much longer to write than

I anticipated when I started out. My publisher, Adrian Zackheim, stuck with me, for which I am very grateful. I can't say enough good things about him and his terrific team at Portfolio, including Will Weisser, Jacquelynn Burke, Brittany Wienke, Jesse Maeshiro, Noirin Lucas, Jeannette Williams, Roland Ottewell, Alissa Theodor, and cover designer Pete Garceau, not to mention Adrian's amazing staff of editors. I had the pleasure of working with three of them: Courtney Young, Brooke Carey, and Natalie Horbachevsky. They were all great, but I have to give special recognition and thanks to Natalie, who shepherded me through the final stages to publication and improved the book immensely with her spot-on editing.

Throughout I enjoyed the unflagging support and encouragement of the world's greatest literary agent, Jill Kneerim of Kneerim, Williams & Bloom, ably assisted by Hope Denekamp. I would be lost without them. I also want to extend my thanks to Bart Nagel, who made me look good in the cover photo, and to Jay Goltz, the founder and CEO of The Goltz Group in Chicago. Not only did he come up with the title for my previous book, *Small Giants*, but he also suggested *Finish Big*. If only the Cubs could compile a similar record of success.

I know that no one is happier to see this book published than my wife of forty-four years, the former Lisa Meisel, who has had to carry the lioness's share of grandparenting duties while I have been working on it. Fortunately we've been blessed with a wonderful grandson, Owen, and two fabulous granddaughters, Kiki and Fiona. They have brought us no end of joy as have Owen and Kiki's parents—our son, Jake, and his wife, Maria—and Fiona's parents—our daughter, Kate, and her husband, Matt. And now we welcome a new grandson, Jack Arthur Knightly, to the family. As I've noted before, they make it both possible and meaningful for me to do what I do.

INDEX